REA's Test Prep Books Are The Best!

(a sample of the <u>hundreds of letters</u> REA receives each year)

" This [REA] book was much better than reading a college textbook. Get it, it's worth it! By the way, I passed [the CLEP test] with flying colors!!! "

Student, Poughkeepsie, NY

" Very good guide for the CLEP exam. "

Student, Omaha, NE

" Compared to the other books that my fellow students had, your book was the most useful in helping me get a great score. "

Student, North Hollywood, CA

" Your book was responsible for my success on the exam, which helped me get into the college of my choice... I will look for REA the next time I need help. "

Student, Chesterfield, MO

" Your book was such a better value and was so much more complete than anything your competition has produced — and I have them all! "

Teacher, Virginia Beach, VA

" Just a short note to say thanks for the great support your book gave me in helping me pass the test... I'm on my way to a B.S. degree because of you! "

Student, Orlando, FL

(more on next page)

(continued from front page)

" I just wanted to thank you for helping me get a great score on the AP U.S. History exam... Thank you for making great test preps! "

Student, Los Angeles, CA

" Your *Fundamentals of Engineering Exam* book was the absolute best preparation I could have had for the exam, and it is one of the major reasons I did so well and passed the FE on my first try. "

Student, Sweetwater, TN

" I used your book to prepare for the test and found that the advice and the sample tests were highly relevant... Without using any other material, I earned very high scores and will be going to the graduate school of my choice. "

Student, New Orleans, LA

" What I found in your book was a wealth of information sufficient to shore up my basic skills in math and verbal... The practice tests were challenging and the answer explanations most helpful. It certainly is the *Best Test Prep for the GRE*! "

Student, Pullman, WA

" I really appreciate the help from your excellent book. Please keep up the great work. "

Student, Albuquerque, NM

" I am writing to thank you for your test preparation... your book helped me immeasurably and I have nothing but praise for your *GRE* preparation. "

Student, Benton Harbor, MI

(more on back page)

THE BEST TEST PREPARATION FOR THE

CLEP

COLLEGE-LEVEL EXAMINATION PROGRAM

HUMAN GROWTH & DEVELOPMENT

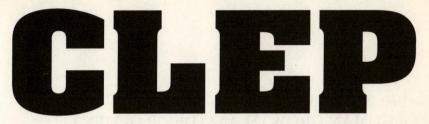

With CD-ROM for Windows™
REA's TEST*ware*® for the
CLEP Human Growth & Development

Staff of Research & Education Association

Research & Education Association
61 Ethel Road West
Piscataway, New Jersey 08854

The Best Test Preparation for the
CLEP HUMAN GROWTH AND DEVELOPMENT
With CD-ROM for Windows
REA's TEST*ware®* for the CLEP Human Growth and Development

Year 2005 Printing
Copyright © 2004, 2003, 2001, 2000, 1998, 1996 by
Research & Education Association, Inc. All rights
reserved. No part of this book may be reproduced in
any form without permission of the publisher.

Printed in the United States of America

Library of Congress Control Number 2003108720

International Standard Book Number 0-87891-342-4

Windows™ is a trademark of Microsoft Corporation.

REA® and TEST*ware®* is a registered trademark of
Research & Education Association, Inc., Piscataway, NJ 08854.

D05-0102

CONTENTS

ABOUT RESEARCH & EDUCATION ASSOCIATION

Founded in 1959, Research & Education Association is dedicated to publishing the finest and most effective educational materials—including software, study guides, and test preps—for students in middle school, high school, college, graduate school, and beyond.

REA's test preparation series includes books and software for all academic levels in almost all disciplines. Research & Education Association publishes test preps for students who have not yet completed high school, as well as high school students preparing to enter college. Students from countries around the world seeking to attend college in the United States will find the assistance they need in REA's publications. For college students seeking advanced degrees, REA publishes test preps for many major graduate school admission examinations in a wide variety of disciplines, including engineering, law, and medicine. Students at every level, in every field, with every ambition can find what they are looking for among REA's publications.

REA's practice tests are always based upon the format of the most recently administered exams, and include every type of question that can be expected on the actual exams.

REA's publications and educational materials are highly regarded and continually receive an unprecedented amount of praise from professionals, instructors, librarians, parents, and students. Our authors are as diverse as the subject matter represented in the books we publish. They are well-known in their respective disciplines and serve on the faculties of prestigious high schools, colleges, and universities throughout the United States and Canada.

Today, REA's wide-ranging catalog is a leading resource for teachers, students, and professionals. We invite you to visit us at *www.rea.com* to find out how "REA is making the world smarter."

ACKNOWLEDGMENTS

We would like to thank Pam Weston, VP, Publishing, for setting the quality standards for production integrity and managing the publication to completion; John Paul Cording, VP, Technology, for coordinating the design, development and testing of the software; Larry B. Kling, VP, Editorial, for supervising revisions; Jeanne Audino, Senior Editor, for preflight editorial quality control; Robert Coover for coordinating revision of the book; Omar J. Musni, Project Editor, and Jennifer Kovacs for their editorial contributions; Christine Saul, Senior Graphic Designer, for cover design; and Wende Solano for typesetting the manuscript.

INDEPENDENT STUDY SCHEDULE

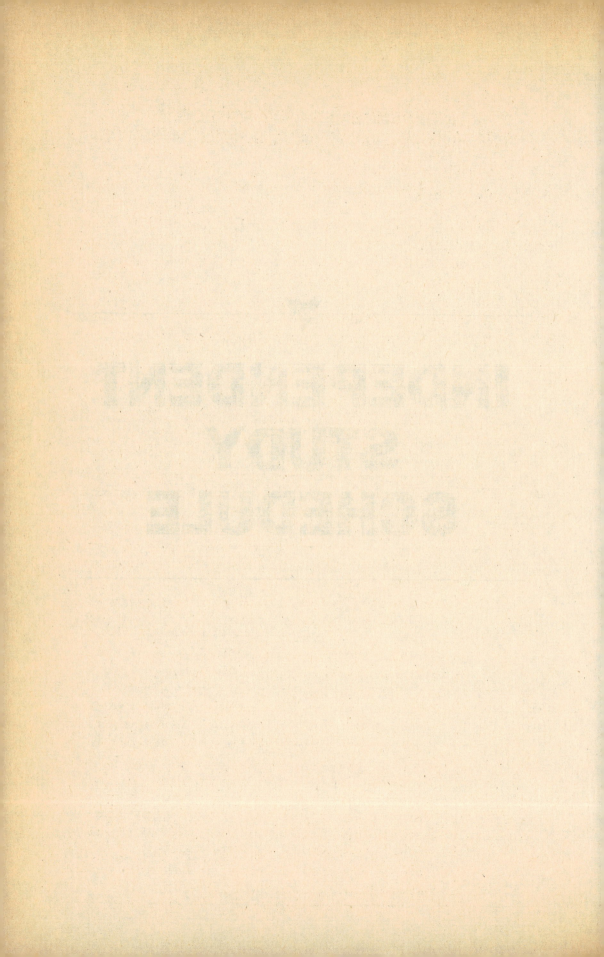

INDEPENDENT STUDY SCHEDULE:
CLEP HUMAN GROWTH AND DEVELOPMENT CBT

This study schedule is a "road map" to help you prepare thoroughly for the CLEP Human Growth and Development CBT. You may want to expand or condense it (the best way to do the latter is to collapse each two-week period into one) depending on how soon you'll be taking the CLEP. Be sure to set aside enough time—at least two hours a day—to study. No matter which schedule works best for you, the more time you spend studying, the more prepared and relaxed you will be on the day of the exam. Keep at your side a blank sheet of paper and a textbook whose content parallels the exam's topical coverage. Jot down any notes or questions that come to mind as you read our review or after you score each of your practice tests.

Week	Activity
1	Read and study Chapter 1, which introduces you to the CLEP Human Growth and Development exam.
2	Take Practice Test 1 on TEST*ware*; determine your basic strengths and weaknesses by looking at the different sections on the score report. You'll now have the basis for determining the areas you need to work on.
3	Begin carefully reading the Human Growth and Development course review included in this book. Stop at the end of Section 6, "Language Development." (You should cover one section per day; give yourself the seventh day off or, if necessary, use it to troubleshoot your weak areas.)
4	Finish reading the Human Growth and Development course review, which ends with Section 12, "Atypical Development."
5	Take Practice Test 2 on TEST*ware*. Carefully review all incorrect answer explanations. If there are any types of questions or particular subjects that seem difficult to you, review those subjects by studying again the appropriate section of the Human Growth and Development course review along with your textbook.
6	Take Practice Test 3 on TEST*ware*. Carefully review all incorrect answer explanations. If there are any types of questions or particular subjects that seem difficult to you, review those subjects by studying again the appropriate section of the Human Growth and Development course review along with your textbook.

▼

CHAPTER 1
PASSING THE CLEP
HUMAN GROWTH &
DEVELOPMENT CBT

Chapter 1

PASSING THE CLEP HUMAN GROWTH AND DEVELOPMENT CBT

ABOUT THIS BOOK & TEST*ware*®

This book provides you with comprehensive preparation for the CLEP Human Growth and Development (Infancy, Childhood, Adolescence, Adulthood, and Aging) Computer-Based Test, or CBT. Inside you will find a concise review of introductory human development, as well as tips and strategies for test-taking. We give you three full-length REA practice tests, all based on the official CLEP subject exam. Our practice tests contain every type of question that you can expect to encounter on the CLEP CBT. Following each practice test you will find an answer key with detailed explanations designed to help you more completely absorb the test material.

All 34 CLEP exams are computer-based. As you can see, the practice tests in our book are presented as paper-and-pencil exams. The content and format of the actual CLEP subject exam are faithfully mirrored. We detail the format and content of the CLEP Human Growth and Development exam on pages 4–6.

The practice tests in this book and software package are included in two formats: in printed form in this book, and in TEST*ware*® format on the enclosed CD. **We recommend that you begin your preparation by first taking the practice exams on your computer.** The software provides timed conditions, automatic scoring, and scoring information that makes it easier to target your strengths and weaknesses.

ABOUT THE EXAM

Who takes CLEP exams and what are they used for?

CLEP (College-Level Examination Program) examinations are usually taken by adults who have acquired knowledge outside the classroom and wish to bypass certain college courses and earn college credit. The CLEP Program is designed to reward students for learning—no matter where or how that knowledge was acquired. CLEP is the most widely accepted credit-by-examination program in the country, with more than 2,900 colleges and universities granting credit for satisfactory scores on CLEP exams.

Although most CLEP examinees are adults returning to college, many graduating high school seniors, enrolled college students, and international students also take the exams to earn college credit or to demonstrate their ability to perform at the college level. There are no prerequisites, such as age or educational status, for taking CLEP examinations. However, because policies on granting credits vary among colleges, you should contact the particular institution from which you wish to receive CLEP credit.

Most CLEP examinations include material usually covered in an undergraduate course with a similar title to that of the exam (e.g., Human Growth and Development). However, five of the exams do not deal with subject matter covered in any particular course but rather with material taken as general requirements during the first two years of college. These general exams are English Composition (with or without essay), Humanities, College Mathematics, Natural Sciences, and Social Sciences and History.

Who develops and administers the CLEP CBT exams?

The CLEP CBTs are developed by the College Entrance Examination Board, administered by Educational Testing Service, and involve the assistance of educators throughout the country. The test development process is designed and carried out to ensure that the content and difficulty of the test are appropriate to the college level.

When and where is this exam given?

The CLEP Human Growth and Development exam is administered each month throughout the year at more than 1,400 test centers in the U.S. Candidates abroad will be accommodated on request. To find the test center nearest you and to register for the exam, you should obtain a copy of the free booklets *CLEP Colleges* and *CLEP Information for Candidates and Registration Form*. These booklets are available at most colleges where CLEP credit is granted, or by contacting the CLEP Program at:

CLEP Services
P.O. Box 6600
Princeton, NJ 08541-6600
Phone: (609) 771-7865
Fax: (609) 771-7088
Website: www.collegeboard.com/clep
E-mail: clep@info.collegeboard.org

Military personnel and CLEP

CLEP Exams are available free-of-charge to eligible military personnel and eligible civilian employees. The College Board has developed a paper-based version of 14 high volume/high pass rate CLEP tests for DANTES Test Centers. Contact the Educational Services Officer or Navy College Education Specialist for more information. Visit the College Board website for details about CLEP opportunities for military personnel.

HOW TO USE THIS BOOK

What do I study first?

Read over our test-format outline, test-taking tips, and course review. Then use the first practice test as a diagnostic to determine your area(s) of weakness. Once you find out where you need to spend more time, focus your efforts on those specific problem areas. To reinforce your facility with the subject matter, we advise keeping at your side a college-level textbook that covers the appropriate material.

To get the most out of your study time, follow our Independent Study Schedule located in the front of this book. The schedule is based on a four-week program but can be condensed to two weeks, if necessary, by collapsing each two-week period into one.

When should I start studying?

It's never too early to start studying for the CLEP Human Growth and Development exam. The earlier you begin, the more time you will have to sharpen your skills. Don't leave it to the last minute; cramming is not an effective way to study, since it doesn't allow you the time needed to learn the test material.

FORMAT AND CONTENT OF THE CLEP CBT

The CLEP Human Growth and Development exam covers the kind of material that is typically part of a one-semester introductory course in developmental psychology or human development. Test-takers should be conversant with the major theories and research connected with physical, cognitive, and social development. The exam will present you with *approximately* 90 questions to be answered in 90 minutes.

The *approximate* breakdown of topics on the CLEP Human Growth and Development CBT is as follows:

10%	***Theories of development***
	Cognitive-developmental
	Learning
	Psychoanalytic
5%	***Research strategies and methodologies***
	Case study
	Correlational
	Cross-sectional
	Experimental
	Longitudinal
	Observational
10%	***Biological development throughout the lifespan***
	Development of brain and nervous system
	Heredity, genetics, genetic testing
	Influences of drugs
	Motor development
	Nutritional influences
	Perinatal influences
	Physical growth and maturation, aging
	Prenatal influences
	Sexual maturation
7%	***Perceptual development throughout the lifespan***
	Critical periods
	Hearing
	Sensorimotor activities
	Sensory deprivation
	Vision
12%	***Cognitive development throughout the lifespan***
	Environmental influences
	Information processing
	Memory
	Piaget, Jean
	Play

Problem solving
Vygotsky, Lev

8% ***Language development***
Development of syntax
Environmental, cultural, and genetic influences
Language and thought
Pragmatics
Semantic development
Vocalization and sounds

4% ***Intelligence throughout the lifespan***
Concepts of intelligence and creativity
Developmental stability and change
Heredity and environment

10% ***Social development throughout the lifespan***
Aggression
Attachment
Gender
Moral development
Peer relationships
Prosocial behavior
Social/class influences
Social cognition

8% ***Family and society throughout the lifespan***
Abuse and neglect
Cross-cultural and ethnic variation
Family relationships
Family structure
Mass media influences
Social/class influences

8% ***Personality and emotions***
Achievement motivation
Development of emotions
Erikson, Erik
Freud, Sigmund
Locus of control
Self-control and self-regulation
Temperament

8% ***Learning***
Classical conditioning
Discrimination and generalization
Habituation
Observational learning and imitation
Operant conditioning

5%   *Schooling and intervention*
      Applications of developmental principles within the school
      Facilitating role transactions in adulthood
      Intervention programs and services
      Preschool, day care, elder care
      Training in parenting skills

5%   *Atypical development*
      Alzheimer's, dementia, Parkinson's
      Antisocial behavior, delinquency
      Asocial behavior, fears, phobias, obsessions
      Attention-deficit/hyperactivity disorder
      Autism
      Consequences of hereditary diseases
      Giftedness
      Learning disabilities
      Mental retardation

ABOUT OUR COURSE REVIEW

Our topical review is divided into 13 sections that correspond to the subject matter you can expect to encounter on the CLEP exam.

SCORING YOUR PRACTICE TESTS

How do I score my practice test?

The CLEP Human Growth and Development CBT is scored on a rights-only basis, meaning that only correct answers are scored. The conversion table on page 8 provides an estimate of your scaled score. Since scaled scores vary from one form of a test to another, your score on the actual exam may be higher or lower than what our table indicates. Again, you will suffer *no penalty* for incorrect guesses on the CLEP CBT.

When will I receive my score report?

The test administrator will print out a full Candidate Score Report for you immediately upon your completion of the CBT (except for CLEP English Composition with Essay). Your scores are reported only to you, unless you ask to have them sent elsewhere. If you want your scores reported to a college or other institution, you must say so when you take the examination. Since your scores are kept on file for 20 years, you can also request transcripts from Educational Testing Service at a later date.

PRACTICE-TEST RAW SCORE CONVERSION TABLE*

Raw Score	Scaled Score	Course Grade	Raw Score	Scaled Score	Course Grade
90	80	A	43	42	
89	80		42	41	
88	79		41	41	
87	78		40	40	
86	78		39	39	
85	77		38	38	
84	77		37	37	
83	76		36	37	
82	75		35	36	
81	75		34	35	
80	74		33	34	
79	73		32	33	
78	72		31	32	
77	72		30	31	
76	71		29	30	
75	70		28	29	
74	70		27	28	
73	69		26	27	
72	68		25	26	
71	67		24	25	
70	66		23	24	
69	65		22	23	
68	64		21	23	
67	63		20	22	
66	62		19	22	
65	61		18	21	
64	60		17	21	
63	59		16	20	
62	59	B	15	20	
61	58		14	20	
60	57		13	20	
59	56		12	20	
58	56		11	20	
57	55		10	20	
56	54		9	20	
55	53		8	20	
54	52		7	20	
53	52		6	20	
52	51		5	20	
51	50	C	4	20	
50	49		3	20	
49	48		2	20	
48	47		1	20	
47	46		0	20	
46	45				
45	44				
44	43				

* This table is provided for scoring REA practice tests only. With the advent of computer-based testing, the College-Level Examination Program uses a single across-the-board credit-granting score of 50 for all 34 CLEP computer-based exams. Nonetheless, on account of the different skills being measured and the unique content requirements of each test, the actual number of correct answers needed to reach 50 will vary. A "50" is calibrated to equate with performance that would warrant the grade C in the corresponding introductory college course.

STUDYING FOR THE EXAM

It is crucial for you to choose the time and place for studying that works best for you. Some students set aside a certain number of hours every morning, while others choose to study at night before going to sleep. Only you can determine when and where your study time will be most effective. But be consistent and use your time wisely. Work out a study routine and stick to it!

When you take our practice tests, try to make your testing conditions as much like the actual test as possible. Turn off the television or radio, and sit down at a quiet table or desk free from distraction. Use a timer to ensure that each section is accurately clocked.

As you complete each practice test, score it and thoroughly review the explanations for the questions you answered incorrectly; but don't review too much at one sitting. Concentrate on one problem area at a time by reviewing the question and explanation, and by studying our review until you are confident that you completely understand the material.

Keep track of your scores and mark them on scratch paper. By doing so, you will be able to gauge your progress and discover general weaknesses in particular sections. You should carefully study the review sections that cover your areas of difficulty, as this will build your skills in those areas.

TEST-TAKING TIPS

You may never have taken a standardized computer-based test like the CLEP Human Growth and Development exam, but it's not hard to learn the things you need to know to be comfortable on test day.

Know the format of the CBT. CLEP CBTs are *not adaptive* but rather fixed-length tests. In a sense, this makes them kin to the familiar paper-and-pencil exam in that you have the same flexibility to go back and review your work in each section. Moreover, the format hasn't changed a great deal from the paper-and-pencil CLEP. For this exam, you can expect to encounter approximately 90 questions that need to be answered within 90 minutes. You are likely to see some so-called pretest questions as well, but you won't know which they are and they won't be scored.

Use the process of elimination. If you don't immediately see the correct answer among the choices, go down the list and eliminate as many as you can. Confidently casting aside choices will help you isolate the correct response, or at least knock your choices down to just a few strong contenders. This approach has the added benefit of keeping you from getting sidetracked and distracted by what in fact may be just an occasional tricky question. Importantly, your score is based only on the number of questions you answer *correctly*.

Work quickly and steadily. You will have just 90 minutes to work on the roughly 90 questions on the exam, so work quickly and steadily to avoid spending an inordinate amount of time on any one question. Taking our practice tests will help you learn to budget your time.

Learn the directions and format for each section of the test. This will put extra time on your side that you can use to review your work.

Acquaint yourself with the CBT screen. Familiarize yourself with the CLEP CBT screen beforehand by logging on to the College Board Website. Waiting until test day to see what it looks like in the pretest tutorial risks injecting needless anxiety into your testing experience.

Be sure that your answer registers before you go to the next item. Look at the screen to see that your mouse-click causes the pointer to darken the proper oval. This takes far less effort than darkening an oval on paper, but don't lull yourself into taking less care!

THE DAY OF THE EXAM

Preparing for the CLEP CBT

On the day of the test, you should wake up early (after a decent night's rest, one would hope) and have a good breakfast. Dress comfortably so that you are not distracted by being too hot or too cold while taking the test. Plan to arrive at the test center early. This will allow you to collect your thoughts and relax before the test, and will also spare you the anxiety that comes with being late. *No one* will be allowed into the test session after the test has begun.

Before you set out for the test center, make sure that you have your admission form, Social Security number, and a photo ID with your signature (e.g., driver's license, student identification card, or current alien registration card). You need proper ID to get into the test center.

You may wear a watch to the test center, but it cannot make any noise, which could disturb your fellow test-takers. No calculators, computers, dictionaries, textbooks, notebooks, scrap paper, briefcases, or packages will be permitted; drinking, smoking, and eating are prohibited.

Good luck on the CLEP Human Growth and Development CBT!

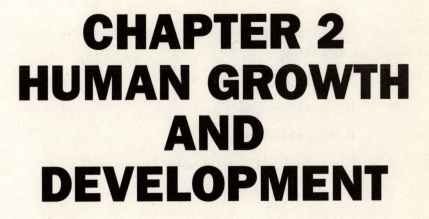

CHAPTER 2
HUMAN GROWTH
AND
DEVELOPMENT

Chapter 2

HUMAN GROWTH AND DEVELOPMENT REVIEW

The following Human Growth and Development review is divided into twelve sections, as follows:

1: **Theories of Development**

2: **Research Methods**

3: **Biological Development**

4: **Perceptual and Sensorimotor Development**

5: **Cognitive Development**

6: **Language Development**

7: **Intelligence**

8: **Social Development**

9: **Family and Society**

10: **Personality and Emotion**

11: **Learning**

12: **Schooling and Intervention**

13: **Atypical Development**

By thoroughly studying this course review, you will be well-prepared for the material on the CLEP Human Growth and Development exam.

1 THEORIES OF DEVELOPMENT

HISTORICAL APPROACHES TO THE STUDY OF PSYCHOLOGY

Wilhelm Wundt (1832–1920) began the first experimental psychology laboratory in 1879 at the University of Leipzig, Germany. This occurred as a result of the merger of **philosophy** (questioning truth) and **physiology** (scientific analysis of living organisms). Wundt studied **introspection**, the careful analysis of one's own conscious experiences. Since 1879 there have been several historical approaches to the study of psychology:

Historical Approach (Associated names)	Description
Structuralism Edward Titchener (English, 1867–1927)	Examined the structure of the mind, analyzed structure and content of mental states by introspection, and was concerned with reducing experience to its basic parts.
Functionalism William James (American, 1842–1910)	Proposed the study of how the mind adapts us to our environment. Influenced by Charles Darwin's theories of evolution and natural selection. Felt conscious experience is adaptive and always changing.
Behaviorism Ivan Pavlov (Russian, 1849–1936) John B. Watson (American, 1878–1958) B. F. Skinner (American, 1904–1990)	Stressed the study of observable behavior, not unobservable consciousness.
Psychoanalysis Sigmund Freud (Austrian, 1856–1939)	Emphasized the study of unconscious mental processes; argued that people are driven by sexual urges and that most emotional conflicts date back to early childhood experiences.

Gestalt Max Wertheimer (German, 1880–1943)	Emphasized perception and that stimuli are perceived as whole entities rather than parts put together ("The whole may be greater than the sum of its parts.")
Humanistic Carl Rogers (American, 1902–1987) Abraham Maslow (American, 1908–1970)	Stressed that humans have enormous potential for personal growth. Emphasized importance of free will, the human ability to make choices, and the uniqueness of the individual.
Cognitive Jean Piaget (Swiss, 1896–1980)	Studied internal, mental representations that are used in perceiving, remembering, thinking, and understanding.

BEHAVIORAL PERSPECTIVE

The **behaviorist perspective** is that personality is a collection of learned behavior patterns. Personality, like any other learned behavior, is acquired through classical and operant conditioning, social learning, discrimination, and generalization.

Skinner's Ideas

B. F. Skinner (1904–1990) and other traditional behaviorists believed that everything a person does is ultimately based on past and present rewards and punishments and other aspects of operant conditioning. He rejected the idea that personality is made up of consistent traits and denied that a personality or self initiates or directs behavior.

Skinner did not use the term personality. For Skinner, what other theorists call personality is nothing more than a collection of learned behaviors that have been reinforced in the past. He believes that personality is a person's observed behaviors and does not contain internal traits or thoughts. Consistency in behavior occurs because of consistency in environmental experiences. Also, according to behaviorists, because personality is learned, it can be changed by rearranging experiences and situations.

Social Learning

The group of psychologists who emphasize behavior, environment, and cognition as important in determining personality are known as **social learning theorists** (sometimes referred to as **cognitive-behavioral** or **so-**

cial-cognitive approach). Social learning theorists differ from the behavioral view of Skinner by emphasizing that people can regulate and control their own behavior despite changes in their environment. **Albert Bandura**, **Walter Mischel**, and **Julian Rotter** are three social learning theorists.

Bandura believes that learning occurs by observing what others do and that these observations form an important part of personality. Bandura suggested that the way that people behave in a variety of situations is determined by **self-efficacy**, or their expectations of success. Those high in self-efficacy will approach new situations confidently and persist in their efforts because they believe success is likely. People low in self-efficacy expect to do poorly and avoid challenges. According to Bandura, **reciprocal determinism** (sometimes called **reciprocal influences**) influences individual differences in personality. This means that personality, behavior, and environment constantly influence one another and shape each other in a reciprocal fashion.

According to **Mischel**, personality and situational variables are important in explaining behavior. Mischel believes that behavior is characterized more by **situational specificity** than by consistency. That is, we often behave differently in different situations.

Rotter believed personality is determined by a person's **generalized expectations** about future outcomes and reinforcements. Rotter proposed that **locus of control** influences how we behave. Those with an **internal locus of control** see themselves primarily in control of their behavior and its consequences. Persons with an **external locus of control** see their behavior as controlled by fate, chance, or luck and are less likely to change their behavior as a result of reinforcement because they do not understand the relationship between the reinforcement and their behavior.

Evaluating the Behavioral Perspective

The main strengths of the behavioral perspective are its strong research base and its testability.

Criticisms of proponents of the behavioral perspective of personality include:

- They do not consider possible unconscious motives or internal dispositions or traits that might be consistent from situation to situation.

- There has been little effort to integrate possible biological factors or genetic influences into their theories of personality.

- Historically, they have relied too much on animal research.

- They have not paid attention to possible enduring qualities of personality.

- They tend to be **reductionistic**, meaning they try to explain the complex concept of personality in terms of one or two factors.

- They have focused more on environment and less on cognition.

COGNITIVE THEORY

Until his death in 1980, Jean Piaget was a predominant figure in the field of cognitive psychology. It is safe to postulate that perhaps no other single individual has had greater influence on educational practices than Piaget. Basically, his theory of cognitive development is based on the notion that cognitive abilities (or one's ability to think) are developed as individuals mature physiologically and have opportunities to interact with their environment. Piaget described these interactions as the *equilibration* of *accommodation* and *assimilation* cycles or processes. In other words, when individuals (who, according to Piaget, are innately endowed with certain cognitive predispositions and capabilities) encounter a new or novel stimulus, they are brought into a state of *disequilibrium.*

That is a way of saying that they are thrown off balance; they do not know or understand what is new or unfamiliar. However, through the complementary processes of **accommodation** (or adjusting prior knowledge gained through former experiences and interactions) and **assimilation** (fitting together the new information with what has been previously known or understood), individuals come to know or understand that which is new. Once again, individuals are returned to a state of *equilibrium* where they remain until the next encounter with an unfamiliar something. For Piaget, this is how learners learn.

Piaget also predicted that certain behaviors and ways of thinking characterize individuals at different ages. For this reason, his theory is considered a **stage theory**. Stage theories share the common tenet that certain characteristics will occur in predictable sequences and at certain times in the life of the individual.

According to Piaget, there are four stages of cognitive development, beginning with the **sensorimotor** stage describing individuals from birth to around the age of two. The second stage, **preoperational** (describing cognitive behavior between the ages of two and seven), is characterized by egocentrism, rigidity of thought, semilogical reasoning, and limited social cognition. Some cognitive psychologists have observed that this stage seems to describe how individuals think more in terms of what they can't do than what they can do. This stage describes the way that children in preschool and kindergarten go about problem-solving; also, many children in the primary grades may be at this stage in their cognitive development.

The next two stages, however, may be most important for elementary and secondary school teachers since they describe cognitive development during the times that most students are in school. The third stage, **concrete operations**, is the beginning of operational thinking and describes the thinking of children between the ages of seven and eleven. Learners at this age begin to decenter. They are able to take into consideration viewpoints other than their own. They can perform transformations, meaning that they can understand reversibility, inversion, reciprocity, and conservation. They can group items into categories. They can make inferences about reality and engage in inductive reasoning; they increase their quantitative skills, and they can manipulate symbols if they are given concrete examples with which to work. This stage of cognitive development is the threshold to higher-level learning for students.

Finally, **formal operations** is the last stage of cognitive development and opens wide the door for higher-ordered, critical thinking. This stage describes the way of thinking for learners between the ages of eleven and fifteen, and for Piaget, constitutes the ultimate stage of cognitive development (thus, also describing adult thinking). Learners at this stage of cognitive development can engage in logical, abstract, and hypothetical thought; they can use the scientific method, meaning they can formulate hypotheses, isolate influences, and identify cause-and-effect relationships. They can plan and anticipate verbal cues. They can engage in both deductive and inductive reasoning, and they can operate on verbal statements exclusive of concrete experiences or examples. These cognitive abilities characterize the highest levels of thought.

SOCIAL THEORY

Another theoretical approach to understanding human development is offered by Erik Erikson, another important stage theorist, who described pyschosocial development. For each of eight stages, he identified a developmental task explained in terms of two polarities. For the purposes of this review, only those stages describing school-age individuals will be included.

According to Erikson, preschoolers and primary-school-aged children must be able to function in the outside world independently of parents.

When children are able to do this, they achieve a sense of **initiative**; when children are not able to move away from total parental attachment and control, they experience a sense of **guilt**. Thus, this stage of psychosocial development is the stage of initiative versus guilt. The child's first venture away from home and into the world of school has considerable significance when viewed in light of this theory; it is imperative that teachers assist students in their first experiences on their own, away from parental control.

Erikson's next stage of development is one involving a tension between **industry** and **inferiority**. For example, if the child who enters school (thus achieving initiative) acquires the skills (including academic skills such as reading, writing, and computation, as well as social skills in playing with others, communicating with others, forming friendships, and so forth) that enable him or her to be successful in school, then the child achieves a sense of industry; failure to achieve these skills leads to a sense of inferiority.

PERSONALITY THEORY

Psychodynamic theories (also called **psychoanalytic theories**) of personality descended from Sigmund Freud and his theory of personality.

For most psychodynamic theorists, personality is mainly **unconscious**. That is, it is beyond our awareness. In order to understand someone's personality, the **symbolic** meanings of behavior and deep inner workings of the mind must be investigated. Early experiences with parents shape personalities, according to psychodynamic theorists.

Freud's Theory

Sigmund Freud (1856–1939) was a medical doctor from Vienna, Austria, who specialized in neurology. His psychodynamic approach to personality developed as a result of his work with adult patients who had psychiatric and emotional problems.

Freud's theory emphasized three main points:

(1) Childhood experiences determine adult personality.

(2) Unconscious mental processes influence everyday behavior.

(3) Conflict causes most human behavior.

According to Freud, each adult personality consists of an **id**, **ego**, and **superego**.

Personality component	When it develops	How it functions
Id	at birth	pleasure principle; unconscious instincts; irrational; seeks instant gratification; contains the libido
Ego	around six months	reality principle; mediates id and reality; executive branch
Superego	around six years	morality principle; personal conscience; personal ideals

According to Freud, the **id** is unconscious and has no contact with reality. It works according to the **pleasure principle**—the id always seeks pleasure and avoids pain. The id contains the **libido** or sexual energy.

The **ego** evolves from the id and deals with the demands of reality. It is called the **executive branch** of personality because it makes rational decisions. The **reality principle** describes how the ego tries to bring individual id demands within the norms of society. The ego, however, cannot determine if something is right or wrong.

The **superego** is capable of determining if something is right or wrong because it is our conscience. The superego does not consider reality, only rules about moral behavior.

According to Freud, behavior is the outcome of an ongoing series of conflicts among the id, ego, and superego. Conflicts dealing with sexual and aggressive impulses are likely to have far-reaching consequences because social norms dictate that these impulses be routinely frustrated.

Freud considered personality to be like an iceberg—most of our personality exists below the level of awareness just as most of an iceberg is hidden beneath the surface of the water. Freud referred to the hidden part of our personality as the **unconscious**. Even though Freud felt that many thoughts, memories, and desires were unconscious, they nonetheless influence our behavior.

The **conscious** part of our personality consists of whatever we are aware of at any particular point in time.

The **preconscious**, according to Freud, contains material that is just below the surface of awareness but can be easily retrieved. An example of preconscious awareness would be your mother's birthdate. You were not thinking of your mother's birthdate but can if you need or want to.

Defense mechanisms are unconscious methods used by the ego to distort reality and thereby protect us from anxiety. Anxiety can result from the irrational pleasure demands of the id or from the superego causing guilty feelings about a real or imagined transgression.

Common defense mechanisms are:

Rationalization	Creating false but plausible excuses to justify unacceptable behavior. Example: Reducing guilt for cheating on your taxes by rationalizing "everyone does it."
Repression	Pushing unacceptable id impulses out of awareness and back into the unconscious. Sometimes called "motivated forgetting." Example: Having no memory of an unpleasant experience.
Reaction Formation	Behaving in exactly the opposite of one's true feelings. Example: A mother who feels resentment toward a child may be overly cautious and protective.
Regression	Reversion to immature patterns of behavior. Example: Temper tantrums.
Projection	Attributing one's own thoughts, feelings, motives, or shortcomings to others. Example: A wife who constantly suspects her husband of having an affair because unconsciously she has thought of having an affair.
Displacement	Shifting unacceptable feelings from their original source to a safer, substitute target. Example: You are mad at your boss, but you do not yell at your boss; instead you become angry with a family member when you return home.
Sublimation	A useful, socially acceptable course of behavior replaces a socially unacceptable or distasteful impulse.

	Example: A person who feels aggression due to a lack of control plays an aggressive game of basketball with friends every other day.
Intellectualization	By dealing with a stressful situation in an intellectual and unemotional manner, a person detaches himself from the stress. Example: A person who has lost a family member due to illness will willingly speak of the medical terminology of the illness but will not discuss the emotional aspects of the illness.
Denial	Denying that a very unpleasant thing has happened. Example: A person with severe stomach pains, possibly an ulcer, refuses to see a doctor because he feels it is only indigestion.

Stages of Psychosexual Development

Freud believed that we go through five stages of psychosexual development in forming our personalities. Each stage represents a different **erogenous zone** or part of the body where pleasure originates.

Freud's Psychosexual Stages

Stage	Age	Erogenous Zone	Description
Oral	0–18 months	Mouth	Stimulation of mouth produces pleasure; enjoys sucking, biting, chewing. Weaning is major task or conflict.
Anal	18–36 months	Anus	Toilet training is major task. Expelling and retaining feces produces pleasure.
Phallic	3–6 years	Genitals	Self-stimulation of genitals produces pleasure. **Oedipal** (for boys) and **Electra** (for girls) conflicts occur—children have erotic desires for opposite-sex parent as well as feelings of fear and hostility for same-sex parent. Successful

			resolution of this conflict results in identification with same-sex parent.
Latency	6–12 years	None	Sexual feelings are repressed. Social contacts beyond immediate family are expanded.
Genital	Puberty onward	Genitals	Establishing intimate, sexual relations with others is main focus.

According to Freud, children experience conflicts between urges in their erogenous zones and societal rules. **Fixation** can result when these urges are either frustrated or overindulged in any one erogenous zone. Fixation results in one's personality becoming permanently locked in the conflict surrounding that erogenous zone.

Freud felt that the first three psychosexual stages were the most important for personality development. Examples of possible personality traits resulting from fixations in the first three psychosexual stages are presented here.

Stage	**Examples of traits related to fixation**
Oral	Obsessive eating Smoking Drinking Sarcasm Overly demanding Aggressiveness
Anal	Extreme messiness Overly orderly Overly concerned about punctuality Fear of dirt Love of bathroom humor Anxiety about sexual activities Overly giving Rebelliousness
Phallic	Excessive masturbation Flirts frequently Excessive modesty Excessively timid Overly proud Promiscuity

2 RESEARCH METHODS

Psychological research is based on the scientific method. The **scientific method** consists of

(1) defining a research problem;

(2) proposing a hypothesis and making predictions;

(3) designing and conducting a research study;

(4) analyzing the data; and

(5) communicating the results and building theories of behavior.

A **sample** is a subset of a population selected to participate in the study. All of the participants in a research study make up the sample. A **population** includes all members of a class or set from which a smaller sample may be drawn and about whom the researcher wants to draw conclusions. A **random sample** is one in which every member of the population being studied has an equal chance of being picked for inclusion in the study. A **biased sample** occurs when every member of a population does not have an equal chance of being chosen. A **stratified sample** is one in which every relevant subgroup of the population is randomly selected in proportion to its size. A **subject** is an individual who is actually participating in the research study. **Replications** refer to research studies that are repeated, often under different conditions, in order to ensure the reliability of the results.

THE EXPERIMENT

Psychologists use experiments to determine **cause-and-effect relationships.** An **experiment** requires that the researcher systematically manipulate or control one or more variables and then observe how the research subjects or participants respond to this manipulation. The variable that is manipulated is called the **independent variable.** The response that is measured after the manipulation of the independent variable is known as the **dependent variable.**

An experiment consists of at least two groups of subjects. The **experimental group** is the group that is exposed to the manipulation of the independent variable. Some experiments have more than one experimental group, meaning there are several manipulations of the independent variable. The **control group** of an experiment is not exposed to manipulation of the independent variable. The responses of subjects in the control group are compared to the responses of subjects in the experimental group(s) in order to determine if the independent variable(s) had any effect on the dependent variable.

Subjects usually are assigned to groups in an experiment based on **random assignment**, which ensures that each participant had an equal chance of being assigned to any one of the groups. Random assignment helps guarantee that the groups were similar to one another with respect to important characteristics before the manipulation of the independent variable. When subjects are not randomly assigned to groups, it is referred to as a **quasi-experiment**.

Subject bias occurs when research participants' behavior changes because they know they are being studied or because of their expectations. A **placebo** is an inactive substance given in the place of a drug in psychological research. A **placebo effect** occurs when a participant believes they are experiencing a change due to an administered drug that is really a placebo. **Observer** or **researcher bias** occurs when the expectations of the researcher influence what is recorded or measured. **Double-blind technique** is used to control both subject and observer biases. In the double-blind technique, neither the subjects nor the researcher who is measuring the dependent variable know who is assigned to which group in an experiment. A **single-subject experiment** involves the participation of only one subject. The independent variable is systematically changed over time, and the subject's behavior at one time is compared with the same subject's behavior at another time. In this case, time is used as the control.

NONEXPERIMENTAL METHODS

Nonexperimental methods of research do not include the systematic manipulation of variables by the researcher and thus cannot be used to discuss cause-and-effect relationships.

Correlational research involves measuring two (or more) variables in order to determine if they are related. If the value of one variable increases in value as the other also increases in value, this is known as a **positive correlation**. A **negative correlation** occurs when there is an inverse relationship between the variables measured; as the value of one increases, the value of the other decreases. A **correlation coefficient** is a number that represents the strength of the relationship between the variables measured. A correlation coefficient can range in value from 0 to 1. A correlation coefficient of 0 indicates no relationship between the variables measured. A correlation coefficient of 1 indicates a perfect relationship between the two variables: You can predict one variable perfectly by knowing the value of the other. Therefore, the closer a correlation coefficient is to 1, the stronger the relationship between the variables measured, and the closer a correlation coefficient is to 0, the weaker the relationship. Even if a strong correlational relationship is found, however, cause-and-effect conclusions *cannot* be made because there was no systematic manipulation by the researcher.

Naturalistic observation is a research method that occurs in a natural setting that has not been manipulated by the researcher. The researcher systematically observes and records what occurs in an unobstrusive manner. This is done so that the behavior of the subjects being tested is not altered. **Interobserver reliability** is the amount of agreement between two (or more) observers who simultaneously observe the same event.

A **case study** is an in-depth study of a single subject. It can include interviews, observations, and test results.

The **survey method** of collecting data requires the researcher to ask a group of people about behaviors, thoughts, or opinions. Data is collected through questionnaires or interviews.

COMPARING RESEARCH METHODS

Method	Strengths	Weaknesses
Experiment	Can make cause-and-effect relationships. Researcher has control.	Sampling errors. Often hard to generalize to real world.
Correlation	Can study real-world behavior. Can determine relationships.	Cannot determine cause-and-effect.
Naturalistic Observation	Can gather information in its usual setting as it naturally occurs.	Cannot determine cause-and-effect. Observer bias possible.

Method	Strengths	Weaknesses
Case Study	Intensive information can be gathered about individuals.	Cannot determine cause-and-effect. Expensive and time consuming. May not be able to generalize information gathered to others. Biased sample possible.
Survey	Large amounts of information can be gathered from many people in a relatively short period of time.	Cannot determine cause-and-effect. Biased sample possible. Response bias possible. Survey questions might not be reliable or valid.

ETHICAL GUIDELINES

The **American Psychiatric Association (APA)** has published ethical guidelines to follow when conducting psychological research with human subjects. Some important points from these guidelines include:

- Psychologists are responsible for the ethical conduct of research conducted by them or by others under their supervision.

- Psychologists conduct research with due concern for the dignity and welfare of the participants.

- Psychologists inform participants that they are free to participate, to decline to participate, or to withdraw from the research at any time.

- Psychologists inform participants of significant factors that may be expected to influence their willingness to participate.

- Psychologists must obtain informed consent from research participants prior to filming or recording them.

- Participants should be fully debriefed following any deception.

- Psychologists inform research participants of their anticipated sharing or further use of personally identifiable research data.

- Psychologists provide a prompt opportunity for participants to obtain appropriate information about the nature, results, and conclusions of the research.

- Psychologists must honor all commitments made to research participants.

- The APA also presents additional guidelines for the use and care of animals in research.

A **psychological test** is an objective, standardized measure of a sample of behavior. Both intelligence and personality tests are considered psychological tests. Any good psychological test must meet three criteria—it must be standardized, reliable, and valid.

STANDARDIZATION

Standardization involves developing uniform procedures for administering and scoring a test and developing norms for the test.

Uniform procedures require that the testing environment, test directions, test items, and amount of time allowed be as similar as possible for all individuals who take the test.

Norms are established standards of performance for a test. Norms inform us about which scores are considered high, average, or low. Norms are determined by giving the test to a large group of people representative of the population for whom the test is intended. Future test-takers' scores are determined by comparing their scores with those from the **standardization sample**, or group that determined the norms.

A **percentile score** indicates the percentage of people who scored below a score that one has attained. If you attain a percentile score of 75, for example, that means that you scored higher than 75 percent of the sample of people who provided the test norms.

RELIABILITY

Reliability is a measure of the consistency of a person's test scores. A test's reliability can be measured in several ways:

Test-retest reliability	Giving the same individuals the same test on two different occasions. If the results are similar, then the test is considered to have good test-retest reliability.

Split-half reliability	Individuals take only one test, but the test items are divided into two halves and performance on each half is compared. If individuals performed about equally well on each half of the test, the test has good split-half reliability.
Alternate-form reliability	Two alternate forms of the test are administered on two different occasions. Test items on the two forms are similar but not identical. If each person's score is similar on the two tests, alternate-form reliability is high.

Correlation coefficients are usually used to represent reliability. A **correlation coefficient** is a numerical index that represents the degree of relationship between two variables.

VALIDITY

A **valid test** is one that measures what it purports to measure. Methods to measure validity include:

Content validity	The test's ability to cover the complete range of material (or content) that it is supposed to measure.
Criterion validity	Compares test scores to actual performance on another direct and independent measure of what the test is supposed to measure.
Predictive validity	A form of criterion validity. How well a test score predicts an individual's performance at some time in the future.
Face validity	How well the test and test items appear to be relevant.
Construct validity	How well a test appears to represent a **theoretical** or **hypothetical construct** (abstract qualities). It is the extent to which scores on a test behave in accordance with a theory about the construct of interest.

3 BIOLOGICAL DEVELOPMENT

THE NERVOUS SYSTEM

Functions of the nervous system:

(1) processes incoming information

(2) integrates incoming information

(3) influences and directs reactions to incoming information

Divisions of the Nervous System

The nervous system is divided into the **central nervous system** and the **peripheral nervous system**.

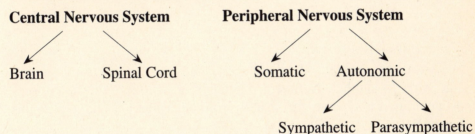

All nerves encased in bone make up the **central nervous system.** The central nervous system is responsible for processing information and directing actions.

The **peripheral nervous system** is made up of all nerves that are not encased in bone. Its main function is to carry messages to and from the central nervous system.

The **somatic division** of the peripheral nervous system carries messages inward to the central nervous system from the sensory organs (by means of **afferent** or **sensory neurons**) and outward from the central nervous system (by means of **efferent** or **motor neurons**) to the muscles for action. A **reflex arc** occurs when an afferent message travels to the spinal cord and an efferent message for action immediately returns to the muscle, bypassing the brain.

The **autonomic division** of the peripheral nervous system is responsible for involuntary functions of the body. This autonomic nervous system is divided into the **sympathetic** (known as the "fight or flight" branch; activates the body for emergencies) and **parasympathetic** (quiets the body and conserves energy) **branches**.

Sympathetic Branch	Parasympathetic Branch
Dilates pupils	Constricts pupils
Inhibits tears	Stimulates tears
Inhibits salivation	Increases salivation
Activates sweat glands	Decreases heart rate
Increases heart rate	Constricts blood vessels
Increases respiration	Decreases respiration
Inhibits digestion	Stimulates digestion
Releases adrenaline	Contracts bladder
Stimulates glucose release	Stimulates elimination
Relaxes bladder	Stimulates sexual arousal
Inhibits elimination	
Inhibits genitals	

Neurons

Neurons are specialized cells that transmit information from one part of the body to another. **Nerves** are bundles of neurons. The function of most neurons is to receive information from other neurons and to pass this information on.

Structural features of neurons:

Soma — The cell body of the neuron.

Dendrites — The branching projections of neurons that receive information from other neurons and conduct information toward the cell body.

Axon — The long, thin fiber that transmits information away from the cell body of a neuron toward other neurons.

Myelin Sheath — An insulating material that encases some axons and permits faster transmission of information. Prevents neurons from communicating randomly.

Synapse — The small space between neurons where communication takes place.

Terminal Buttons — Small knobs at the end of axons that secrete chemicals.

Synaptic Cleft — A microscopic gap between the terminal button of one neuron and the cell membrane of another. The place where chemicals are released.

Communication within the Nervous System

The nervous system is considered an **electrochemical system**. Communication within a neuron is *electrical*; communication between neurons is *chemical*.

Neurons are filled with and surrounded by electrically charged molecules called **ions.** A neuron at rest has an ion distribution that makes the axon more negatively charged than the outside of the nerve cell. **Resting potential** is the stable, negative charge of an inactive neuron and is the term used to describe the difference in electrical potential between the outside and the inside of a resting nerve cell. Under these conditions the soma and axon are said to be **polarized**. The brief change in electrical charge that is caused by a dendrite being stimulated, or **depolarized**, and by the resultant inflow of positively charged sodium ions is called an **action potential**. A **spike** is a nerve impulse generated by the neuron reaching action potential. After the firing of an action potential comes the **refractory period** when no further action potentials can fire.

The firing of a neuron or action potential is an **all or none proposition**. This means that the neuron will fire an action potential of a high magnitude independent of the size of the original stimulus. In other words, if there is no stimulus, there will be no action potential. If there is a stimulus, weak or strong, there will be an action potential.

A neuron passes its message on to another neuron by releasing chemical **neurotransmitters** into the synapse. A **presynaptic neuron** sends the neural message and a **postsynaptic neuron** receives the message. A neurotransmitter can stimulate a postsynaptic neuron only at specific **receptor sites** on its dendrites and soma. Receptor sites respond to only one type of neurotransmitter. This **lock and key model** means that specific neurotransmitters work only at specific kinds of synapses. Neurons that respond to the same neurotransmitter form a **neurotransmitter system**.

Neurotransmitters may excite or inhibit the next neuron. Stimulation of an **excitatory synapse** makes the neuron more likely to respond; stimulation of an **inhibitory synapse** makes production of an action potential less likely.

Examples of neurotransmitters include:

Neuro-transmitter (Abbreviation)	Function	Associated Disorders
Acetylcholine (ACh)	Excitatory neurotransmitter related to movement of all muscles, as well as arousal, attention, anger, aggression, sexuality, and thirst.	Memory loss in Alzheimer's disease
Dopamine (DA)	Inhibitory neurotransmitter that controls posture and movement.	Parkinson's disease; Schizophrenia
Gama-aminobutyric acid (GABA)	Inhibits central nervous system and regulates anxiety and movement.	Anxiety disorders; Huntington's disease
Glutamate (Glu)	Major excitatory neurons in central nervous system; important for learning and memory.	Memory loss; Alzheimer's disease
Norepinephrine (NE)	Important for psychological arousal, mood changes, sleep, and learning.	Bipolar mood disorder
Serotonin (5-HT)	Regulates sleep, mood, appetite, and pain.	Depression

Antagonists are drugs that inhibit neurotransmission. **Agonists** are drugs that stimulate neurotransmission.

Endorphins and **neuromodulators** are chemicals that act at the synapse of neurons. Endorphins are **neuropeptides** (made from **amino acids**) and occur naturally in the brain. They decrease a person's sensitivity to pain. **Neuromodulators** do not carry neural messages directly, instead they can either increase or decrease the activity of specific neurotransmitters.

THE BRAIN

Gray matter refers to the neurons in the brain **without myelin**. **White matter** in the brain consists of **myelinated neurons**. The **cerebral cortex** is the outer surface of the brain. It contains fissures called **sulci** and convolutions called **gyri**. The cerebral cortex processes all perceptions and complex thoughts. In evolutionary terms, it is the most recently developed brain structure.

The brain can be monitored using certain devices.

PET scanning (positron emission tomography) creates a visual image of functioning in various parts of the brain by tracing chemical activity.

MRI (magnetic-resonance imaging) scanner is another imaging technique that provides clear pictures of the structural anatomy and chemistry of the brain by passing a strong magnetic field through the person's head.

CAT scan (computerized axial tomography) presents a picture of the human brain by passing X-ray beams through the head at various angles.

EEG (electroencephalograph) records the electrical activity of the brain.

The brain can be divided into the **hindbrain,** the **midbrain,** and the **forebrain.**

The Hindbrain

The **hindbrain** is located in the bottom portion of the brain and is an extension of the spinal cord. In evolutionary terms, it is the oldest portion of the brain. The major components of the hindbrain are:

Medulla — The oblong structure at the top of the spinal cord that controls many vital life-support functions such as breathing, heart rate, and blood pressure.

Pons — Located above the medulla. Connects the lower brain regions with higher brain regions. Also helps regulate sensory information and facial expressions.

Cerebellum — Located at the rear of the brain. Controls movement, coordination, balance, muscle tone, and learning motor skills.

Reticular Activating System (lower) — Monitors the general level of activity in the hindbrain and maintains a state of arousal. Essential for the regulation of sleep and wakefulness. Sometimes referred to as the **reticular formation**.

The Midbrain

The **midbrain** continues upward from the pons portion of the hindbrain and lies between the hindbrain and the forebrain. The midbrain relays sensory information from the spinal cord to the forebrain. The upper portion of the reticular activating system is located in the midbrain.

The Forebrain

Not only does the **forebrain** make up the largest part of the brain, it is also the most highly developed portion of the brain. The major components of the forebrain are:

Cerebrum — The largest part of the forebrain. Responsible for complex mental activities. Its outer surface is the **cerebral cortex** and is divided into two **cerebral hemispheres**. Contains four major lobes: the **frontal lobe** that controls voluntary movement and includes the **motor cortex**; the **parietal lobe** that contains the primary **somatosensory area**, which manages skin senses; the **occipital lobe** is located in the back of the head and contains the **visual cortex**; and the **temporal lobe** contains the **auditory cortex** and is located on each side of the head above the temples.

Limbic System — Related structures that control emotion, motivation, and memory. Contain **amygdala** and **hippocampus**.

Corpus Callosum — Enormous communication network that connects the right and left cerebral hemispheres.

Thalamus — Relays and translates information from all of the senses, except smell, to higher levels in the brain.

Hypothalamus — Plays a major role in the regulation of basic biological drives and controls autonomic functions such as hunger, thirst, and body temperature. Regulates the **pituitary gland**.

Hemispheres of the Brain

The cerebrum is divided into two hemispheres known as the **right** and **left cerebral hemispheres**. The main interconnection between the two hemispheres of the brain is a large set of axons called the **corpus callosum**. Severe **epilepsy** may be treated by cutting the corpus callosum, which results in a split brain.

The left hemisphere controls the right side of the body and the right hemisphere controls the left side of the body. Although both hemispheres are capable of carrying out most tasks, the left hemisphere is often more active in verbal and logical tasks and the right hemisphere usually specializes in spatial, artistic, and musical tasks.

HORMONES AND THE ENDOCRINE SYSTEM

The **endocrine system** is a system of glands that release chemical messengers called **hormones**, which are carried by the bloodstream to target organs.

Major glands of the endocrine system:

Gland	Hormones Secreted	Description
Adrenal Cortex	Steroids	regulates salt and carbohydrate metabolism
Adrenal Medulla	Adrenaline Noradrenaline	prepares body for action
Gonads	Estrogen Progesterone Testosterone	affects reproductive organs, sexual behavior, and physical development
Hypothalamus	Neurosecretions	controls the pituitary gland
Pancreas	Insulin Glucagon	regulates sugar metabolism
Pituitary Gland	Thyrotropin Oxytocin Corticotrophin Prolactin	master gland; controls growth and other glands
Thyroid Gland	Thyroxine Calcitonin	regulates metabolism

DRUGS

Drugs are also used in deliberate attempts to alter one's state of consciousness. The drugs that people use recreationally are psychoactive.

Psychoactive drugs are chemical substances that influence the brain, alter consciousness, and produce psychological changes. **Drug abuse** or **recreational drug use** is the self-administration of drugs in ways that deviate from either the medical or social norms of a society. **Addiction** is a physical dependence in which continued use of a psychoactive drug is necessary to prevent withdrawal symptoms. **Withdrawal symptoms** vary with different drugs, but may include nausea, headache, chills, and craving for the drug. Avoiding these withdrawal symptoms motivates a person who is addicted to continue using the drug. Tolerance refers to a progressive decrease in a person's responsiveness to a drug; as a result, increasing amounts of the drug are required to produce the same effect. Most drugs produce tolerance effects, but they vary in how rapidly they occur.

Psychological dependence can occur without addiction and exists when one must continue to take a drug in order to satisfy mental and emotional cravings for the drug. The psychological pleasure received from using the drug is what motivates a person who is psychologically dependent.

Several major categories of psychoactive drugs, including depressants, stimulants, hallucinogens, and narcotics, are discussed in the next sections.

Depressants

Depressants, or **sedatives**, are drugs that depress the functioning of the central nervous system.

Examples:
alcohol, barbiturates (e.g., Seconal, Nembutal), and tranquilizers (e.g., Valium, Librium, Xanax).

Methods of administration:
Oral or injected.

Main effects:
Alcohol at first produces mild euphoria, relaxation, and lowered inhibitions. As dose increases, more of the brain's activity is impaired, resulting eventually in sleep, or with increased consumption, even death.

Barbiturates or "downers" have a calming, sedative effect; they can reduce inhibitions and promote sleep.

Tranquilizers lower anxiety and also have a calming, sedative effect. They promote relaxation and work with the neurotransmitter GABA, which is associated with inhibitory synapses.

Medical uses:
Alcohol can be used as an antiseptic.

Barbiturates are used as sleeping pills or as anticonvulsants.

Tranquilizers are prescribed to lower anxiety.

Side effects:

Impaired coordination, increased urination, emotional swings, depression, impaired judgment, quarrelsomeness, and hangover are some potential side effects of the consumption of alcohol.

For barbiturates, side effects include impaired coordination and reflexes, and drowsiness.

Side effects of tranquilizers are lethargy, sleepiness, and decreased muscular tension.

Potential for addiction/psychological dependence:

Alcohol: High/High

Barbiturates: High/High

Tranquilizers: Moderate to High/High

Withdrawal symptoms:

For alcohol, withdrawal symptoms include tremors, nausea, sweating, depression, irritability, and hallucinations.

Withdrawal symptoms for barbituates are trouble sleeping, anxiety, seizures, cardiovascular collapse, and even death.

For tranquilizers, restlessness, anxiety, irritability, muscle tension, and trouble sleeping are possible withdrawal symptoms.

Stimulants

Stimulants increase central nervous system activity.

Examples:

nicotine, caffeine, amphetamines (e.g., Benzedrine, Dexedrine, Methadrine), and Cocaine.

Methods of administration:

Oral, sniffed, injected, smoked, and freebased.

Main effects:

Nicotine increases metabolic processes (e.g., pulse rate), lowers carbohydrate appetite, and can produce alertness or calmness.

Caffeine promotes wakefulness and increases metabolism but slows reaction times.

Amphetamines (e.g., "speed," "uppers") stimulate neurotransmission at the synapse. Both the central nervous system and the sympathetic branch in the autonomic nervous system are affected. They can increase energy and excitement and reduce fatigue and appetite.

Cocaine increases feelings of excitement and a euphoric mood, boosts energy, and acts as an appetite suppressant.

Medical uses:

Stimulants are used in the treatment of hyperactivity and narcolepsy. Cocaine has been used as a local anesthetic.

Side effects:

The main side effects of stimulants include increased pulse and blood pressure, restlessness, reduced appetite, increased sweating and urination, insomnia, and increased aggressiveness.

Potential for addiction/psychological dependence:

Nicotine: High/Moderate to High
Caffeine: Moderate/Moderate
Amphetamines: Moderate/High
Cocaine: Moderate to High/High

Withdrawal symptoms:

Nicotine: Anxiety, increased appetite, and irritability.
Caffeine: Headache and depression.
Amphetamines: Increased appetite, depression, sleeping for long periods, fatigue, and irritability.
Cocaine: Sleeping for long periods, fatigue, irritability, increased appetite, and depression.

Hallucinogens

Hallucinogens ("psychedelic drugs") are chemical substances that alter perceptions of reality and may cause hallucinations and other distortions in sensory and perceptual experiences.

Examples:

Several synthetic drugs, such as LSD (lysergic acid di-ethylamide) and PCP (phencyclidine), as well as substances extracted from plants, such as marijuana.

Methods of administration:

Smoked, snorted, or swallowed.

Main effects:

LSD is derived from a fungus (ergot) that grows on rye. Even small doses (i.e., 10 micrograms) can produce effects that last for hours, including mild euphoria, hallucinations, body image alterations, loss of control of one's attention, and insightful experiences or "mind expansion."

PCP is an anesthetic often called "angel dust." It works by binding to the potassium channels in the brain and muscle-activating neurons. It may cause loss of contact with reality, aggressive behavior, hallucinations, and insensitivity to pain.

Marijuana is a mixture of leaves, flowers, and stems from the hemp plant. Its active ingredient is tetrahydrocannabinol or THC. When smoked, THC enters the bloodstream through the lungs and reaches peak concentrations in 10 to 30 minutes; its effects may last for several hours. It generally produces euphoria and relaxation and, in sufficient doses, can produce hallucinations. In addition to being a hallucinogen, marijuana is also a stimulant at higher doses and a depressant at lower doses.

Medical uses:

Most hallucinogens have no medical uses; marijuana, however, has been used in the treatment of glaucoma. Its use in the treatment of HIV and nausea from chemotherapy is under study.

Side effects:

LSD: Possible panic reactions, anxiety, dilated pupils, paranoia, and jumbled thought processes.

PCP: Violent and bizarre behaviors.

Marijuana: Dry mouth, bloodshot eyes, poor motor coordination, memory problems, and anxiety.

Potential for addiction/psychological dependence:

LSD: Low/Low
PCP: Unknown/High
Marijuana: Low/Moderate

Withdrawal symptoms:

Possible withdrawal symptoms for the hallucinogens include anxiety, difficulty sleeping, hyperactivity, and decreased appetite.

Narcotics

Narcotics, also referred to as opiates or analgesics, are used to relieve pain and induce sleep.

Examples:

opium, morphine (e.g., Percodan, Demoral), and heroin.

Methods of administration:

Oral, injected, or smoked.

Main effects:

Opium is an unrefined extract of the poppy-seed pod.

Morphine is a refined extract of opium and is stronger in its effects.

Heroin is derived from morphine and is even more potent in its pure form.

Because these narcotic drugs are all derived from opium, they reduce pain by blocking neurotransmission. Narcotics appear to reduce pain because they are chemically similar to the body's own natural opiates. They fit into the body's own opiate receptors and mimic their effects, thereby stopping pain from reaching the cortex. Immediately after injection, opiates produce a pronounced feeling of intoxication and euphoria and physical pain is relieved.

Medical uses:
Relief of pain.

Side effects:
The opiates seem to block so many afferent impulses in the brain that not only is pain blocked but also hunger, anxiety, and motivation. Constipation, nausea, and impaired coordination are other possible side effects.

Potential for addiction/psychological dependence:
Opium: High/High
Morphine: High/High
Heroin: High/High

Withdrawal symptoms:
Symptoms of withdrawal from narcotic addiction include diarrhea, chills, sweating, runny nose, muscle spasms, restlessness, and anxiety.

PRENATAL DEVELOPMENT

Prenatal development refers to the period of development from conception to birth. The average pregnancy lasts 270 days or 40 weeks.

At conception, the **female egg** or **ovum** is fertilized by the **male sperm**, usually in the **Fallopian tube**. This results in a **fertilized egg**, which is called a **zygote**. The zygote repeatedly divides as it travels down the Fallopian tube to the **uterus**, where it becomes attached to the uterine wall. The three stages of prenatal development are outlined below.

Ovum or **Germinal**	The first two weeks after conception. Is a microscopic mass of multiplying cells. Zygote travels down Fallopian tube and implants itself on the wall of the uterus. **Placenta** (provides nourishment and allows wastes to pass out to the mother) begins to

form. **Umbilical cord** carries nourishment from and waste to the placenta. Thin membranes keep fetal and maternal bloodstreams separate.

Embryo   Second to eighth week after conception. Only about one inch long by end of this stage. Most vital organs and bodily systems begin to form. Major birth defects are often due to problems that occur during this stage. **Amniotic sac**, or fluid-filled sac, surrounds embryo to serve as protection and provide a constant temperature.

Fetus   From two months after conception until birth. Muscles and bones form. Vital organs continue to grow and begin to function. During last three months, brain develops rapidly.

An outline of *what* develops *when* during the prenatal period is as follows:

Approximate prenatal week	**Development**
2nd week	Implantation on uterine wall.
3rd–4th week	Heart begins to pump.
4th week	Digestive system begins to form. Eyes begin to form.
5th week	Ears begin to form.
6th week	Arms and legs first begin to appear.
7th–8th week	Male sex organs form. Fingers form.
8th week	Bones begin to form. Legs and arms move. Toes form.
10th–11th week	Female sex organs form.
12th week	Fetus weighs about one ounce. Fetal movement can occur. Fingerprints form.
20th week	Mother feels movement. Reflexes—sucking, swallowing, and hiccuping appear.

	Nails, sweat glands, and soft hair developing.
27th week	Fetus weighs about two pounds.
38th week	Fetus weighs about seven pounds.
40th week	Full-term baby born.

Teratogens are any agents that may cross the placental barrier from mother to embryo/fetus, causing abnormalities. What abnormalities occur depends on what is developing prenatally as well as what the harmful agent is. Possible teratogens include maternal diseases, diet, drug use (including alcohol and nicotine), exposure to X-rays, and other environmental influences. For instance, **fetal alcohol syndrome** (resulting in short nose, thin upper lip, widely spaced eyes, small head, mental retardation) can occur as a result of alcohol consumption during pregnancy.

Because so many vital organs and body parts are developing during the **embryo stage**, harmful agents are especially dangerous during this prenatal period. This is often referred to as a **critical period** in development. A critical period is any time during development that some developmental process must occur or it never will. For example, if something interferes with legs developing or forming prenatally, they will not develop or be formed later.

Perceptual Development

The five senses, although not fully developed, are functional at birth. For instance, infants can hear prior to birth. Shortly after birth, newborn infants, or **neonates**, appear capable of discriminating between sounds of different duration, loudness, and pitch. Newborns also appear to prefer the sound of a human voice. By six months of age, infants can discriminate between any two basic sounds used in language. In fact, they can make distinctions between sounds that older children and adults can no longer make because these sounds are not heard in their spoken language.

The sense of **smell** is also well-developed in the newborn. By six weeks of age, infants can smell the difference between their mothers and strangers.

Infants respond to the four basic **tastes** (sweet, sour, salty, and bitter), but they usually prefer sweet.

Infants are also responsive to **touch**. Some research has shown that female infants may be more sensitive to touch than males. One area of study related to touch in young infants is the study of reflexes. A number of **reflexes** (involuntary responses to stimuli) can be elicited in newborn infants. All healthy newborns exhibit them and many of these reflexes will disappear with age. For example, healthy newborn infants will blink when a light shines in their eyes. This reflex does not disappear with time. But other reflexes, such as the **moro** (extension of arms when infant feels a loss of support), **palmar** (hand grasp), and **rooting** (turns toward object brushing cheek and attempts to suck) will disappear over the course of the first year of life.

At birth, neonates can see although their **visual acuity** is very poor (about 20/400 to 20/800 compared to average adult visual acuity of 20/20). Newborn infants can focus best on objects that are about nine inches away. They can also follow a moving object. Young infants also prefer to see the human face and other visual stimuli that have contour, contrast, complexity, and movement. By the time infants can crawl, they indicate that they have **depth perception** by refusing to crawl across the deep side of a **visual cliff**.

Motor Development

Maturation is a term used to describe a genetically programmed biological plan of development that is relatively independent of experience.

The **proximodistal principle** of development describes the center-outward direction of motor development. For instance, children gain control of their torso before their extremities (e.g., they can sit independently before they can stand).

The **cephalocaudal principle** describes the head-to-foot direction of motor development. That is, children tend to gain control over the upper portions of their bodies before the lower part (e.g., they can reach and grasp before they can walk).

Developmental norms describe the average age at which children display various abilities. The developmental norms for motor development are as follows:

Age	Behavior
1 month	While prone (on stomach), can lift head.
2 months	While prone, can hold chest up. Can roll from side to back.

3 months	Can roll over. Will reach for objects.
6–7 months	Sits without support. Stands holding on to objects.
8–10 months	Crawls.
8–12 months	Pulls self up to stand.
11–12 months	"Cruises"—walks by holding on to objects.
12–18 months	Walks alone.

4 PERCEPTUAL AND SENSORIMOTOR DEVELOPMENT

PSYCHOPHYSICS

Psychologists study the senses because we come to know our world primarily through them and what we sense often affects our behavior. Our senses inform us of the presence of stimuli or of any change in a stimulus. The first experimental psychological techniques were developed for the study of sensation. These techniques were called **psychophysical methods**.

Psychophysics is an area of psychology that examines the relationship between sensory stimuli and individual psychological reactions to these stimuli. Psychophysics has been traditionally concerned with detecting thresholds. The smallest amount of a stimulus that can be detected or noticed at least 50 percent of the time is called the **absolute threshold**. **Difference threshold** or **just noticeable difference (jnd)** measures how much a stimulus must change before it becomes noticeably different.

The study of just noticeable difference thresholds led to **Weber's Law**, which states that the amount of change needed to produce a jnd is a **constant proportion** of the original stimulus intensity. Weber's Law indicated that the more intense the stimulus, the more the stimulus intensity has to be increased before a change is noticed. For example, if music was being played softly, a small increase in sound would be noticeable. If the music was being played loudly, it would require a much greater increase in sound to perceive a difference in volume. Stated mathematically, Weber's Law asserts:

$$\frac{\Delta I}{I} = C$$

where

ΔI = jnd

I = stimulus of intensity I

C = a constant

Fechner generalized Weber's finding to a broader relationship between sensory and physical intensity. **Fechner's Law** states that constant increases in a sensation produce smaller increases in perceived magnitude:

$$S = k \log I$$

This equation asserts that the magnitude of sensation, **S**, increases in proportion to the logarithm (log) of stimulus intensity, **I**.

Signal detection theory is a mathematical model that states that individual expectations, prior knowledge, and response bias influence the probability that a stimulus will be recognized. Signal detection theory does not deal with the concept of thresholds but deals only with varying probabilities that a stimulus will be detected. It takes into account the willingness of people to guess by determining the probability of a person guessing that there is a stimulus, or signal, present when there actually is one and the probability of a person guessing that there is a signal when there is not one. The person's response will depend on the criterion she or he sets for how certain she/he must feel before responding "yes, I detect it."

VISION

The sense of vision is sometimes referred to as our most essential, or our **dominant, sense.**

Light

Light is the physical stimulus for vision. The **visual spectrum** (light that is visible to the human eye) is made up of various wavelengths of light, measured in nanometers (nm). A nanometer is one-billionth of a meter, and the visual spectrum varies from 400 nm to about 700 nm. Wavelength determines color, and the amplitude, or height of the wave, determines brightness.

Structure of the Eye

When light enters the eye, it travels the following path:

Cornea

The transparent outer bulge in front of the eye.

↓

Pupil

The dark circle in the center of the iris of the eye. The **iris** is the colored muscle that surrounds the pupil and controls the amount of light that enters the eye.

↓

Lens

Focuses light onto the retina. **Accommodation** occurs when the curvature of the lens adjusts to alter visual focus — the lens flattens for distant objects and fattens for close objects.

↓

Retina

Converts light into impulses that can be transmitted by neurons to the brain.

After light passes through the cornea, pupil, and lens of the eye, it goes through the **vitreous humor** until it reaches the retina. The retina consists of several layers of cells, including:

Cones — Photoreceptors that are responsible for color vision and visual acuity. They are concentrated in the central region of the retina, the **fovea**.

Rods — Photoreceptors that are responsible for vision in dim light, peripheral vision, and black-and-white vision. Their density is greatest just outside the fovea and then gradually decreases toward the periphery of the retina.

Bipolar Cells — Cells through which a visual stimulus passes after going through the rods/cones and before going to the ganglion cells.

Ganglion Cells — The axons of the ganglion cells form the **optic nerve**. The optic nerve carries the visual message to the occipital lobe of the brain for interpretation.

Other features of the retina include:

Fovea — Tiny spot in the center of the retina that contains only cones. Visual acuity is greatest at this spot.

Blindspot — Location where optic nerve leaves retina; contains no rods or cones. You cannot see anything that reaches this part of your retina.

Horizontal Cells — Retinal cells that connect rods with other rods and cones with other cones. Appear responsible for **Opponent-Process Theory** of color vision.

Amacrine Cells — Large retinal neurons that connect ganglion cells laterally. The functions of most amacrine cells are unknown.

Eye to Brain Pathways

Visual information from the right side of the visual field for each eye exits from the left optic nerve of each eye and meets at the **optic chiasma**, where it is combined and sent to the left side of the brain. Visual information from the left side of the visual field exits from the right optic nerves of both eyes, which also meet at the optic chiasma where they are combined and sent to the right side of the brain. In the brain, the visual information is further processed in the thalamus and then sent to the visual cortex located in the occipital lobe of each hemisphere. The occipital cortex contains cells known as **feature detectors**, including **simple cells**, or **edge detectors**, which respond to lines or edges; **complex cells**, which respond to the motion and color of objects; and **hypercomplex cells**, which respond to an object's orientation, movement, shape, corners, width, color, and length.

Light and Dark Adaptation

When entering a darkened room, full dark adaptation of the eyes takes place in about 30 to 40 minutes due to a chemical reaction in the rods and cones. The cones adapt first, but they are absolutely less sensitive than the rods, so that the absolute threshold for the cones stops decreasing after 10 minutes or so in the dark while the rods continue adapting for 20 or more minutes. The rods cannot discriminate colors, however, and this is why you cannot make out colors in very dim light. When reentering a bright area, the rods quickly lose their dark adaptation and the eyes become light adapted as the cones quickly take over.

Color Vision

The three attributes used to describe color are **hue** (determined by wavelength of light; it is the color of visible light), **brightness** (which is a function of the overall intensity of all the wavelengths), and **saturation** (purity or richness of color).

Longer wavelengths of light appear red (around 700 nm), middle wavelengths appear green (500 nm), and shorter wavelengths appear blue (470 nm). Achromatic colors cannot be distinguished on the basis of hue. Only chromatic colors differ in saturation.

Mixing paints and pigments is **subtractive color mixing** because the two paints being mixed absorb or subtract more wavelengths of light than either one does alone. In subtractive color mixing, yellow mixed with blue results in a green color.

Additive color mixing occurs when beams of light combine. Colored lights add their dominant wavelengths to the mixture, stimulating more cones. Both the human eye and color television work according to additive color mixing. Mixing lights produces a color lighter than the darker of the two starting colors. This is why white is produced in an additive mixture by mixing all colors together. The **primary colors** of additive mixtures are **red, green, and blue**. These primary colors may be combined in various proportions to match almost all colors. No one primary color can be matched by a mixture of the other two.

For every color, there is another color that is its complement. **Complementary colors** are colors that appear directly opposite one another on the **color circle** and when mixed together in the proper portion, produce a mixture that appears neutral gray. In additive color mixing, yellow and blue are complementary colors and when mixed together, produce gray.

If you stare at a highly saturated patch of color for 20 seconds or so and then look at a white piece of paper, you will see the complementary of the color you were just looking at. When this occurs, it is called a **negative afterimage**.

The **Young-Helmholtz Theory** or **Trichromatic Theory** of color vision proposes that there are three kinds of color receptors in the cones of the eye, one for each of the three primary colors. Physiological data has supported this hypothesis. Three different kinds of cones have been discovered, one sensitive to red light, one sensitive to green light, and one that responds to blue light. According to the Young-Helmholtz Theory, when you look at a red object, the red cones are stimulated to send a message to the brain so that you sense redness. All other colors are perceived as a result of the mixture of red, green, or blue cones being stimulated. A **yellow** object, for example, stimulates green and red cones to respond. The color **white** occurs when red, blue, and green cones are stimulated equally, and **black** results from no cone stimulation.

Ewald Hering noted that certain kinds of color blindness were not well explained by the Young-Helmholtz Theory. The most common form of color blindness is red-green blindness. Individuals with red-green blindness find it difficult to sense red or green but have no trouble seeing yellow. This does not agree with the Young-Helmholtz Theory, which implies that yellow is a mixture of red and green. Hering argued that yellow was just as much a primary color as red or green or blue and developed the Opponent-Process Theory of color vision.

The **Opponent-Process Theory** states that there is a red-green receptor, a yellow-blue receptor, and a dark-light (or black-white) receptor.

Only one member of a pair can respond, either red *or* green, yellow *or* blue, dark *or* light, but *not* red *and* green or yellow *and* blue. If one member of a receptor pair is stimulated more than its opponent, the corresponding color will be seen. For example, if red is stimulated more than green, the color red will be seen, and vice versa. If both members of a pair are stimulated equally, they cancel each other out and this leaves only gray. (Members from non-opponent pairs may interact and be stimulated at the same time, resulting in colors such as yellow-red or blue-green.)

The Young-Helmholtz Theory seems to be a good description of visual processing in the retina because cones have been found to be sensitive to red, green, and blue (and not to red-green and blue-yellow). The Opponent-Process Theory seems to be a better explanation of color vision at higher levels within the brain—at the optic nerve and beyond.

HEARING

The ear functions to convert sound waves from the external environment into nerve impulses that reach the brain and are then transformed into the sensation we know as sound.

Measuring Sound

Sound travels as a series of invisible waves in the air. Frequency is one physical dimension of sound. The **frequency** of sound is the number of complete waves that pass a given point in space every second and is measured in units called **hertz (Hz)**. One cycle per second is 1 Hz. The longer the wavelength, the lower the frequency. The human ear can hear between 20 to 20,000 Hz. A **pure tone** is made up of only one frequency. Frequency determines the **pitch** of a sound (how high or low a tone sounds). Pitch is a psychological dimension of sound. It varies with frequency but may also be changed by intensity.

Amplitude is another physical dimension of sound and refers to the height of the sound waves. It determines the loudness of a sound, which is a psychological dimension. The loudness of sound is measured in **decibels (dB)**. The threshold of hearing is 0 dB. A whisper is about 25 dB, and a normal conversation is 60 dB. A person could experience hearing loss if exposed to sound over 90 dB for a period of time. Sound over about 130 dB can produce pain. The decibel scale is a logarithmic one. Thus, a sound that is 100 dB more intense than another sound is 10 million times more powerful.

Structure of the Ear

As sound waves travel through the air in the environment, they funnel into the ear where they collide with the **eardrum**, or **tympanic membrane**, which is like a tight drumhead within the ear canal. Sound waves set the eardrum in motion, which causes three small bones, the **auditory ossicles**, to vibrate by means of a chain reaction. First the eardrum causes the **hammer**, or **malleus**, to vibrate, which in turn sets the **anvil**, or **incus**, to vibrate, causing the **stirrup**, or **stapes**, to vibrate. The stirrup is attached to the **oval window**. As the oval window moves back and forth, it sets up waves in the fluid of the **cochlea**, which is a snail-shaped structure that contains the nerve endings essential for hearing. By the time the sound has reached the oval window, it is many times stronger then when it first struck the eardrum. Within the cochlea is the **organ of Corti**, which contains about 16,000 hair cells, or **cilia**. The movement of the fluid within the cochlea causes the cilia to bend and, as they bend, nerve impulses are sent via the auditory nerve to the brain. The neural pathway from the cochlea to the auditory cortex has been described as the most complicated of all sensory pathways.

The ear can be divided into three sections, the outer ear, the middle ear, and the inner ear. In order to hear, the sound wave must enter the outer ear and pass through the middle ear into the inner ear. The structure of the ear is as follows:

Outer Ear

Gathers the sound. Sound travels by means of air conduction. Consists of pinna (external ear) and tympanic membrane (eardrum).

↓

Middle Ear

Transmits the sound by means of bone conduction. Consists of malleus (hammer), incus (anvil), and stapes (stirrup).

↓

Inner Ear

Transforms sound into **neural energy** by means of fluid conduction. Consists of oval window, cochlea, cilia, basilar membrane, organ of Corti, and semi-circular canals (determine balance).

Theories of Hearing

Several theories have been developed to explain how hearing works. The main question these theories are attempting to answer is how neural impulses are coded within the inner ear to give the brain different kinds of auditory information.

Place theory is based on the idea that different sound frequencies actually trigger different neurons. The **basilar membrane** is a membrane inside the cochlea that is sensitive to frequency differences in sound vibrations. The middle frequencies distort the basilar membrane at the apex of the cochlea and high frequencies distort the basilar membrane at the base of the cochlea, near the oval window. Place theory, therefore, attempts to explain the reception of sound waves between 5,000 and 20,000 Hz by stating that different frequencies stimulate cilia at different places within the cochlea. Place theory has difficulty explaining tones below 5,000 Hz, however. These low tones tend to stimulate cilia throughout the entire organ of Corti.

Frequency theory accounts for sounds between 20 and 300 Hz, the lowest tones heard by the human ear. Frequency theory asserts that neural activity is coded in terms of the rate, rather than the place, at which neurons are triggered. Frequency theory is based on the notion that auditory neurons fire at rates well correlated with the frequency of the sound. Frequency theory cannot, however, account for high-frequency sounds because it is impossible for a single neuron to fire, recover, and fire again as fast as would be necessary to follow a high frequency tone.

Volley theory accounts for tones from 300 to 5,000 Hz (mid-range frequencies), in which several neurons fire out of sequence in volleys to sum 300 to 5,000 cycles per second. According to this theory, auditory neurons fire in volleys that are correlated with the frequency of the sound.

DEPTH PERCEPTION

Sensation and perception are related because perception involves the interpretation of sensory information.

Nativists and the **direct perception theory** assert that perception is an innate mechanism and a function of biological organization. **Empiricists** and the **image and cue theory** assert that perceptions are **learned** based on past experience. The **ecological view** of perception argues that perception is an automatic process that is a function of information provided by the environment. The **constructionist view** of perception holds that we construct reality by putting together the bits of information provided by our senses. **Perceptual set** is a readiness to perceive a stimulus in a particular way.

Depth perception involves the interpretation of visual cues in order to determine how far away objects are. There is currently a debate as to whether depth perception is an inborn ability or a learned response as a result of experience (nature vs. nurture).

Gibson and Walk (1960) developed an apparatus they called the **visual cliff** that is used to measure depth perception in infants and toddlers. The visual cliff consists of an elevated glass platform divided into two sections. One section has a surface that is textured with a checkerboard pattern of tile, while the other has a clear glass surface with a checkerboard pattern several feet below it so it looks like the floor drops off. Gibson and Walk hypothesized that if infants can perceive depth, they should remain on the "shallow" side of the platform and avoid the "cliff" side, even if coaxed to come across by parents. When they tested infants from 6 to 14 months of age, Gibson and Walk found that infants would crawl or walk to their mothers when the mothers were on the "shallow" side of the platform, but would refuse to cross the "deep" side, even with their mothers' encouragements to cross. The results of this and other visual cliff studies still do not prove that depth perception is innate because, before infants can be tested, they must be able to crawl and may have already learned to avoid drop-offs.

Two types of visual cues, binocular cues and monocular cues, allow us to perceive depth.

Binocular Cues

Binocular cues for depth require the use of both eyes. The two binocular cues are convergence and retinal disparity.

Convergence involves the interpretation of muscular movements related to how close or how far away an object is. For an object closer than approximately 25 feet, our eyes must converge (move inward) in order to perceive it as a single object clearly in focus. Our perceptual system uses this muscular movement as a cue for closeness. For an object farther than 25 feet, our eyes tend to focus on infinity (little to no muscular movement required), and again, our perceptual system uses this as a cue that the object must be far away.

Retinal disparity is the difference in locations, on the retinas, of the stimulation by a single object. This means that an object viewed by both eyes will stimulate one spot on the right retina and a different spot on the left retina. This is due to the fact that the object is at a different distance from each eye. Retinal disparity is also used as a cue for depth because the eyes are set a certain distance apart in the head, and objects closer than 25 feet are sensed on significantly different locations on each eye's retina. Viewing objects that are close causes considerable retinal disparity (very different portions of each retina are stimulated) and viewing objects at a distance creates little retinal disparity (similar portions of each retina are stimulated).

Monocular Cues

Monocular cues for depth require the use of only one eye. Two-dimensional presentations (e.g., photographs, television) also rely on monocular cues to indicate depth. Monocular cues for depth include:

Linear Perspective — Parallel lines appear to converge on the horizon (e.g., railroad tracks).

Relative Size — Closer objects appear larger; the larger of two figures will always appear closer because the two objects will project retinal images of different sizes.

Overlap or Interposition — Objects that are overlapped or partially concealed by other objects will appear farther away.

Gradient of Texture — Objects that are closer have greater detail or texture than those far away.

Aerial Perspective — Close objects are bright and sharp; distant objects are pastel and hazy.

Relative Motion or Motion Parallax — When moving our head from side to side, nearby objects appear to move more than distant objects; far objects appear to move slower than nearby objects.

Height on a Plane or Height in a Field — Objects that are closer appear to be lower in the field than objects that are farther away.

Looming Effect or Optical Expansion — When we approach objects, objects close to us appear to be moving toward us faster than those farther away.

Accommodation — Lens of eye must bend or adjust to bring to focus objects that are relatively close.

PERCEPTUAL ORGANIZATION

We tend to organize our sensations into meaningful perceptions. Perceptual organization is the basis of **Gestalt Psychology**. Gestalt psychologists assert that we tend to organize our perceptions immediately into wholes, and emphasize that the whole is greater than the sum of its parts. Gestaltists have presented a number of descriptive principles of perceptual organization:

Figure-ground — We group some sensations into an object, or "figure," that stands out on a plain background. The figure is the distinct shape with clearly defined edges and the ground has no defined edges. Reversible or ambiguous figures have no clearly defined figures and backgrounds (the figure and background can be reversed).

Similarity — Stimuli that are similar in size, shape, color, or form tend to be grouped together.

Nearness or Proximity — Stimuli that are near each other tend to be grouped together.

Continuity — Perceptions tend toward simplicity or continuity; lines tend to be seen as following the smoothest path. Lines interrupted by an overlapping object are seen as belonging together if they result in straight or gently curving lines when connected.

Closure — Figures that have gaps in them are seen as completed and are perceived as recognizable figures.

Common Fate — Objects that move together tend to be grouped together.

Simplicity — Every stimulus pattern is perceived in such a way that the resulting structure is as simple as possible.

Orientation — Objects with the same orientation are seen as part of a group.

Apparent Motion or Phi Phenomenon — Perceived motion when the object is, in fact, stationary. (For example, when two lights are placed side by side in a darkened room and flashed alternately, one light moving back and forth is perceived.)

PERCEPTUAL CONSTANCIES

Another important characteristic of visual perception is the **perceptual constancy**, or **stability**, of the shape, size, brightness, and color of objects in our visual fields. We are able to recognize the same objects at a variety of angles, at various distances, and even under different colored lighting because of perceptual constancies.

Size Constancy — Objects we are familiar with seem to appear the same size despite changes in the distance between us and the objects.

Shape Constancy — Objects appear to be the same shape despite changes in their orientation toward the viewer.

Brightness or Lightness Constancy — Objects appear to stay the same brightness despite changes in the amount of light falling on them.

Color Constancy — The hue of an object appears to stay the same despite changes in background lighting.

5 COGNITIVE DEVELOPMENT

ELEMENTS OF THOUGHT

Thinking is defined as the manipulation of mental representations. **Cognition** includes the mental activities involved in the acquisition, storage, retrieval, and use of knowledge.

John Watson proposed that thinking is merely subvocal speech and is not a mental activity. He felt that we talk to ourselves *so quietly* that it is not apparent that we are doing so. Other researchers have confirmed that thinking is *not* subvocal speech. For instance, individuals who cannot speak can think.

Concepts

A basic element of thought is the notion of concepts. A **concept** is a label that represents a class or group of objects, people, or events that share common characteristics or qualities. We organize our thinking by using concepts, and concepts allow us to think about something new by relating it to a concept we already know.

Some concepts are well-defined, and each member of the concept has all of the defining properties; no nonmember does. These are sometimes referred to as artificial concepts. An example of an artificial concept would be registered voters — you either are or are not registered to vote.

Other concepts are not so clearly defined but are encountered in our everyday life. These natural concepts have no set of defining features but instead have characteristic features — members of this concept must have at least some of these characteristics. Bird is a natural concept. Birds range from chickens to sparrows to ostriches. Prototypes are objects or events that best represent a natural concept. A sparrow or robin would be considered a prototypical bird by many individuals. New concepts are easier to learn if they are organized around a prototype.

Mental Imagery

Mental imagery refers to mental representations of things that are not physically present. Research has shown that imagery can play an important role in thinking. Some psychologists believe that thinking with mental images differs from thinking with words, just as pictures differ from sentences. Some psychologists feel that we store mental images based on an **analog code**, or a representation that closely resembles the physical object. Others argue that mental images are stored based on **propositions**, or in terms of abstract descriptions, and these descriptions are used to create an image.

Roger Shepard and Jacqueline Metzler reported evidence that supports the analog view of mental imagery. They found that it took subjects longer to rotate an object 180 degrees than to rotate it 20 degrees, just as it takes longer to rotate physical objects a greater distance. Stephen Kosslyn found that subjects make judgments about mental images in the same way that they make judgments about an actual picture. That is, it took them longer to make judgments about small mental images than about large ones. Forming large mental images took longer than forming small ones. These results also support the analog view.

Cognitive maps contain our mental images of what is where. They are mental representations of particular spatial arrangements. For instance, you probably have a cognitive or mental map of the United States, as well as one for your state, your town, your campus, your house, etc. Cognitive maps are not accurate copies of the environment but instead represent each individual's perspective. Researcher E. C. Tolman reported that even laboratory rats appear to form cognitive maps. As a result of experience in a maze, they seemed to develop a mental awareness of not only the physical space in the maze, but also the elements within the space. The rats used their cognitive maps to locate food even when the usual path to the food was blocked.

Reasoning

Reasoning involves transforming information to reach a conclusion. It includes evaluating and generating arguments to reach a conclusion. **Inductive reasoning** involves reasoning from the specific to the general. For example, drawing conclusions about all members of a category or concept based on only some of the members is inductive reasoning. **Deductive reasoning** is reasoning from the general to the specific. Making a prediction based on a theory involves deductive reasoning. **Logical reasoning** includes mental procedures that yield valid conclusions. Formal tasks have been developed that measure logical reasoning. Two such tasks are syllogisms and analogies.

Syllogisms are arguments made up of two propositions, called premises, and a conclusion based on these premises. They require deductive reasoning.

For example, is the following reasoning valid?

"All cats are animals."

"All cats have four legs."

"Therefore, all animals have four legs."

No, the reasoning is not valid. There are some animals that do not have four legs.

An **analogy** is a type of reasoning task that is always made up of four parts. The relationship between the first two parts is the same as the relationship between the last two. Analogies require inductive reasoning. For example:

"Light is to dark as summer is to _____."

Light is the opposite of dark, therefore, summer is the opposite of winter.

PROBLEM SOLVING

Problem solving is the mental activity used when we want to reach a certain goal that is not readily available. Problem solving includes: *understanding* the problem; *planning* a solution; *carrying out* the solution; and *evaluating* the results.

Problem representation or the way you think about a problem can make it easier or harder to solve. We can represent problems visually, verbally, with symbols (e.g., mathematically), or concretely with objects. A chart, or matrix, that represents all possible combinations of solutions could also be used to keep track of what solution has been and has not been tried.

Some problem-solving strategies include:

Algorithms — Every possible solution is explored. Guarantees problem will be solved eventually, although can be time consuming.

Heuristics — "Rules of thumb" or shortcuts that help solve problems. They seem to offer the most reasonable approach to reaching the goal. However, there is no guarantee that a solution will be reached.

Subgoals or Means-Ends Analysis — Intermediate steps for solving a problem. Part of the problem is solved with each subgoal. Often not obvious how to divide problem into subgoals.

Analogy — Solution to an earlier problem is used to help solve current problem. Often difficult to recognize similarity between problems, however.

Working Backwards — For a problem with a well-specified goal, you begin at the goal and work backwards. Worth considering when working forward has not been successful.

Expert Systems or Artificial Intelligence — Computer programs that solve specific problems. Most use algorithms.

Incubation — Putting the problem aside for a while and engaging in some other activity before returning to the problem.

Trial and Error — One solution after another is tried in no particular order until a solution is found. Can be very time consuming.

Some problem solving problems include:

Functional Fixedness — The inability to solve a problem because the function we assign to objects tends to remain fixed or stable. We tend to see objects only in terms of their customary functions.

Mental Set — Tendency to persist with old patterns for problem solving even when they are not successful.

Confirmation Bias — Tendency to confirm rather than refute a problem's hypothesis even when there is strong evidence that the hypothesis is wrong. Often tend to ignore information that is inconsistent with the hypothesis.

Creative problem solving involves coming up with a solution that is both unusual and useful. Creative thinking usually involves **divergent thinking**, or thinking that produces many different correct answers to the same problem or question. Creating a sentence with the word "Springfield" would involve divergent thinking—there is no one specific correct response. A response to the question "What is the capital of Illinois?" would require **convergent thinking**—one correct answer is expected. Convergent thinking does not appear to be related to creativity. Although all creative thought is divergent, not all divergent thought is creative. Tests (e.g., Remote Associates Test) have been developed that measure creativity. Almost all of these tests require divergent thinking. In general, these tests of creativity have not been good at predicting who will be creative in real-life problem-solving situations. There is a modest correlation between creativity and intelligence. Highly creative people tend to have above average intelligence, but not always. Furthermore, having a high IQ does not necessarily mean that someone is creative.

DECISION MAKING

Decision making requires you to make a choice about the likelihood of uncertain events. Although most of us try to be systematic and rational in making decisions, we do not always live up to these goals. We often lack clear rules about how to make the best decision. Similar to other cognitive tasks, decision making requires us to combine, manipulate, and transform our stored knowledge. When we have no procedures to use in decision making, we tend to rely on heuristics that include availability, representativeness, additive model, and anchoring.

The **availability heuristic** involves judging the probability of an event by how easily examples of the event come to mind. This can lead to bad decision making when the probability of the mentally available events do not equal the actual probability of their occurrence. For instance, in deciding whether one should drive after consuming alcohol, one could decide that this would be a safe thing to do because nothing bad happened the two previous times driving occurred after alcohol consumption.

The **representativeness heuristic** occurs when you decide whether the sample you are judging matches the appropriate prototype. This is probably the most important decision making heuristic, and it usually leads to the correct choice. Decisions concerning diagnosing an illness are often based on the representativeness heuristic—that is, judging how similar the symptoms are to those of the specific disease.

An **anchoring heuristic** occurs when you estimate an event's probability of occurrence and then make adjustments to that estimate based on additional information. We tend, however, to make adjustments that are too small. For instance, you ran out of drinks at your last party. In deciding how many drinks to buy for this year's party, your estimate will probably be based on how many drinks you bought last time and how early into the party these drinks ran out.

The **additive model** is another method for decision making. It occurs when we rate the attributes of each alternative and then select the alternative that has the highest sum of ratings. Additive strategies for decision making are examples of compensatory models. Compensatory models allow attractive attributes to compensate for unattractive attributes. Noncompensatory decision models do not allow some attributes to compensate for others. One bad rating results in eliminating that alternative.

Decisions can also be made by elimination of negative aspects, whereby less attractive alternatives are gradually eliminated. Alternatives are eliminated until there is only one that satisfies all the necessary criteria.

PIAGET'S THEORY

The most rapid cognitive development takes place during the first few years of life when the brain is growing rapidly. As the following sections on Piaget's theory and memory development indicate, however, cognitive development is best described as a life-long process.

The Swiss researcher and writer **Jean Piaget** (1896–1980) spent most of his adult life describing the cognitive development of children. Although Piaget was never trained as a psychologist (his formal schooling was in biology and zoology), his theory of cognitive development has had a dramatic impact on how we view the abilities of children.

Piaget felt that cognitive development proceeded through four stages: the **sensorimotor stage**, which lasts from birth to approximately 18 months of age; the **preoperational stage**, which lasts from two to seven years of age; the stage of **concrete operations**, which covers the years seven to twelve, and finally, **formal operations**, which extends from twelve years on.

According to Piaget, the order in which children pass through these stages is invariant, or does not vary. The rate at which children pass through these stages does vary from child to child.

Piaget wrote that each stage of cognitive development represents a qualitatively different way of thinking. That is, children in each stage think differently from children in the other stages. Therefore, it is not just that children acquire more information as they grow older, but *how* they think actually changes with age.

Children pass from one stage to another as a result of biological maturity and experiences in their environment.

The major characteristics of each of these four stages follow.

Sensorimotor Stage

Children "think" during this stage as a result of coordination of sensory input and motor responses. Because the child has not developed language, intelligence is nonverbal or nonsymbolic (the child cannot mentally represent objects or events). This stage is divided into six substages that outline how cognitive development proceeds during this stage. These six substages also represent the development of **object permanence**. Piaget was the first to suggest that infants lack object permanence—that is, they cannot mentally represent or think about objects that they are not directly interacting with (or, put another way, "out of sight, out of mind").

Preoperational Stage

Preoperational thinkers can now symbolize, or mentally represent, their world. They can now think about objects that they are not interacting with at the present time. This period is dominated by a rapid development of language, which is a form of symbolic thinking. Children do have several limitations during this stage, however. These include **irreversibility**, or the inability to mentally reverse a physical action to return an object to its original stage, **centration** (tendency to focus on one detail in a situation to the neglect of other important features), and **egocentrism** (inability to consider another's viewpoint). These three limitations are used to describe why preoperational children cannot solve conservation tasks (i.e., they do not understand that quantity cannot be judged by appearance alone). A preoperational child might believe that when you pour water from a tall, thin glass into a wide-mouthed, shorter glass, you have less water. The child centrates attention on the appearance of more water and cannot mentally reverse the operation and think about pouring the water back into the tall, thin glass.

Concrete Operations

During concrete operations, children understand conservation. They understand, for example, that when water is poured from a tall, thin glass into a wide-mouthed, shorter glass, there is the same amount of water. Concrete operational children, therefore, can decenter their attention and understand reversibility. Concrete thinkers can also arrange objects according to size or weight and can divide something into its parts. Mathematical operations develop during this stage. Children are limited in this stage because thinking can only be applied to concrete objects and events, and they will have difficulty dealing with hypothetical problems.

Formal Operations

Formal operational thinkers can handle hypothetical problems. They are, for instance, able to project themselves into the future and think about long-term goals. Scientific reasoning is also possible. That is, the ability to isolate a problem, review it systematically, and figure out all possible solutions is evident. The formal thinker is capable of understanding and appreciating the symbolic abstractions of algebra and literary criticism, as well as the use of metaphor in literature. Formal operations, therefore, involve the development of logical and systematic thinking.

Other key terms from Piaget's theory include:

Scheme or **Schema**	Basic thought structures about what the world, objects, events, etc. are like.
Organization	Combining and integrating simple schemes.
Adaptation	Modifying existing schemes to fit new experiences. Consists of assimilation and accommodation.
Assimilation	Interpreting an event or experience based on our current scheme or thought structure. (For example, a child who calls all four-legged animals—even cats—"doggie." This child's current scheme seems to be that if you have fur and four legs, you are a dog.)
Accommodation	Changing or adjusting a scheme based on experience, understanding, etc. (e.g., the above mentioned child's dog scheme accommodates or adjusts to the notion that at least some four-legged animals are "cats").

Criticisms of Piaget's theory include his underestimation of children's cognitive abilities. Studies have shown that children are capable of performing many tasks (e.g., conservation) at earlier ages than Piaget predicted. Piaget also paid little attention to individual differences. Some aspects of his theory (e.g., formal operations) may be culturally specific.

MEMORY DEVELOPMENT

Over the course of development, children use more and more sophisticated methods to remember, and their memory performance improves as a result. Although young infants (before three months of age) demonstrate memory capability when they recognize and remember familiar people, smells, objects, etc., in their environment, the use of intentional strategies for remembering have not been documented until around two years of age. These early strategies for remembering include looking, pointing, and naming.

By early elementary school, children are using rehearsal as a method for remembering. Rehearsal is a generic term for a variety of memory strategies that involve repetition as a method for remembering (e.g., repeating the phone number over and over until you dial it or, writing your spelling words ten times each).

Organization, or **clustering**, strategies develop by late elementary school and involve the semantic grouping of materials into meaningful units (e.g., grouping spelling words by their prefix).

Elaborative strategies involve creating verbal or visual connections that add meaning to material and do not develop until adolescence or later. An example would be creating the phrase "Every good boy does fine" to remember that "e," "g," "b," "d," and "f" are the lines of the treble clef in music.

Metamemory is one's knowledge about memory, and it has been divided into person (everything we know about the memory abilities of ourselves and others), task (everything we know about memory tasks), and strategy (everything we know about techniques of learning and remembering) factors. As with strategy use, metamemory improves with age during childhood. At first, young children are unrealistic and make overly optimistic predictions about their memories (i.e., they believe they can remember everything!) and with age they become more realistic in their expectations. They also know more about possible strategies for remembering with age.

ENCODING

Memory is the storing of information over time. **Encoding** is the process of placing information into memory. **Storage** is the process of retaining information in memory. Getting information out of memory is called **retrieval**. You must pay attention to the information that you want to place, or encode, in your memory.

Fergus Craik and Robert Lockhart proposed three levels for encoding incoming information. They suggested that whether we remember information for a few seconds or a lifetime depends on how deeply we process the information. Information can be processed, or encoded, according to three different features:

Structural — Information is stored based on visual codes — what information "looks" like or its physical structure.

Phonemic — Information is stored based on acoustic codes — what it sounds like.

Semantic — Information is stored based on semantic codes — what it means. Most information appears to be stored in memory based semantic codes.

Levels of processing theory suggests that deeper levels of processing result in longer-lasting memory codes. The deepest level of processing appears to be semantic. Structural encoding is often a shallow level of processing and phonemic encoding is intermediate.

Allan Paivio's dual code theory suggests that information is better remembered when it is represented in both semantic and visual codes because this allows for storage of both the word and image.

STORAGE

The information processing theories of memory emphasize how information flows through a series of separate memory stores. One prominent information processing model that was proposed by Richard Atkinson and Richard Shiffrin describes this flow of information through the sensory memory to short-term memory and finally to long-term memory.

Sensory Memory

Sensory memory (sometimes referred to as **sensory register**) holds sensory information for a brief period after the physical stimulus is no longer available. It holds an exact copy of the sensory stimulus for only a few seconds. More information enters our sensory memory than will reach our short-term memory. George Sperling developed a partial report procedure to measure this. Subjects were to report only some of the items from a visual display that they saw for a very short period of time (e.g., 1/10th of a second). Sperling found that subjects were able to see more items than they could report and that subjects' memories of the visual display faded completely after about one second.

In general, sensory memory holds information just long enough to recognize and transfer it to short-term memory for further processing through a process called **selective perception** or **selective attention**. Selective perception/attention allows only specific information out of the many possible sensory messages bombarding us at any one time to enter into our conscious awareness. It is controlled by the focus of our attention and the set of expectancies we have prior to receiving the information.

Iconic sensory memories, or **icons**, are visual representations that last for only about one second in sensory memory. **Echoic sensory memories**, or **echoes**, are representations of sound sensory memories that may last for several seconds.

Short-Term Memory

Short-term memory (STM) is where conscious thinking and processing of information take place. Whatever you are thinking about right now is in your short-term memory.

Once information enters short-term or "**working memory**," it usually remains there for only about 20 to 30 seconds, because short-term memory is very sensitive to interruption or interference. John Brown and Lloyd and Margaret Peterson devised a method for measuring the duration of short-term memory. Subjects were presented with a stimulus and then asked to count backwards. This backward counting prevented active rehearsal of the previously presented stimulus. Brown and the Petersons found that by 20 seconds of backward counting, subjects could not remember the previously presented stimulus.

Unless the information is important and meaningful or is being actively rehearsed or repeated, it quickly leaves short-term memory and is "forgotten" when new information displaces it as we begin to think about something else. The material is forgotten because it was never learned. Displacement occurs, therefore, when new information enters short-term memory and pushes out existing material. For example, when you look up a number in a phone directory and dial it once, it is doubtful that you will "remember" the number at a later date. You held the number in your short-term memory while dialing. Within 20 seconds after dialing, however, the number was no longer consciously available and was "forgotten" as you began to think about something else.

In order to determine if certain information is in short-term memory, researchers have proposed that we could engage in a parallel search by examining all the information in short-term memory at once, or we could use a serial search, examining only one bit of information at a time. Research results indicate that the search process in short-term memory is serial.

Short-term memory is also limited in the amount of information it can hold. The average adult can hold between five to nine bits, or chunks, of information in short-term memory. George Miller proposed the magical number seven, plus or minus two as the capacity of short-term memory. The capacity of short-term memory can be increased by using bigger chunks of information or by what Miller referred to as chunking. **Chunking** involves organizing or grouping separate bits of information into larger units or chunks. For example, 5 8 1 2 7 8 6 3 could be chunked into 58 12 78 63. This transforms eight bits of information into four, thereby freeing up space in short-term memory.

Memory span is a measure of the capacity of short-term memory. It is the largest number of items that can be recalled perfectly from short-term memory after only one presentation and no time for study.

Although various types of memory codes can be used in short-term memory, it appears that acoustic coding dominates, especially for verbal information.

Information in short-term memory may be new information coming in from the sensory store or it may be old information coming in from long-term memory in order to be thought about and used.

Long-Term Memory

If enough repeated rehearsal or practice occurs, information may be transferred from short-term memory into long-term memory. **Long-term memory (LTM)** is our permanent storehouse of information. For instance, all the knowledge we have accumulated, all the skills we have learned, and all of our memories of past experiences are stored in our long-term memories. The more meaningful the information is, the more easily it can be stored in long-term memory. Some information is stored automatically from short-term memory into long-term memory without effort, usually because this information is highly meaningful. Most information, however, must be actively rehearsed in order to be transferred from short-term to long-term memory.

Unlike short-term memory, long-term memory appears to have unlimited storage capacity.

Information in long-term memory appears to be organized. Research has suggested that new facts are learned by fitting them into a network of pre-existing knowledge.

Propositional network theory suggests that we store meanings in propositional representations in long-term memory. A **proposition** is the smallest unit of information that makes sense. Each proposition is represented by an oval or circle, called a node, which is connected to the components of the proposition by arrows, called links. For instance, the proposition "dog" might be connected to the nodes "bark," "fur," and "four legs."

Research shows that there are at least two broad types of memory circuits in long-term memory:

Declarative Memory — "Fact" memories such as names, dates, events; related to thinking and problem solving; accessible to conscious awareness; can often be rapidly learned and rapidly forgotten; has been subdivided into **semantic memory** (store of factual information) and **episodic memory** (store of our personal or autobiographical experiences).

Procedural Memory — "Skill" memory such as remembering how to ride a bike, play a musical instrument, or eat with a fork; learned by repetition and practice and are hard to unlearn; often performed without conscious thought.

Some long-term memories seem to be visual. An extreme and rather rare example is eidetic memory. **Eidetic memory** is characterized by relatively long-lasting and detailed images of scenes that can be scanned as if they were physically present. They are rare in adults and occur more frequently during childhood.

Human memory is so complicated that long-term memory storage and retrieval do not appear to be limited to just one brain structure, although the exact process is not completely understood. When a memory is stored, communication at existing synapses is improved, and the structure of neuron parts near the synapse is changed. Research has shown that the hippocampus is somehow important in storing and retrieving memories, as are the amygdala and the thalamus. The hippocampus, amygdala, and thalamus all send nerve fibers to the cerebral cortex, and it is in the cortex that memories are probably stored.

Neurotransmitters are also important in memory. For example, patients with Alzheimer's disease have decreased amounts of the neurotransmitter acetylcholine. Drugs that interfere with acetylcholine neurotransmission impair memory. Drugs that increase its production sometimes improve memory.

Mnemonics

Mnemonics are strategies for remembering information. They work because they add meaning and context to hard-to-remember information. Several different mnemonics are described below.

Rehearsal — Repeating (or writing or reading) the information over and over. This is a primitive method for remembering. Other methods are more effective and efficient.

Elaboration — Thinking about how new material is connected or related to information already in long-term memory. This results in deeper levels of processing than simple rehearsal.

Method of Loci — Used to remember a list of items. Think of a familiar path or route and then visualize each item you have to remember at different locations along this path or route. For instance, you could visualize one item in your driveway, another in your garage, another at your door, etc.

Peg Word System — Can be used to remember a list of items in a set order. First, you memorize a list of words that will serve as "memory pegs" (such as "one is a bun," "two is a shoe") and then you create a visual image between the peg word and what you need to remember. For instance, if you need to remember the terms "dog and tree," you could visual a dog in between a hot dog bun and a Christmas tree that is decorated with old tennis shoes.

Organization — Reorganizing information into meaningful groupings. For instance, organizing spelling words for study based on identical prefixes.

SQ3R — Series of five steps that can be used to learn reading material. These steps include surveying, questioning, reading, reciting, and reviewing. This is also known as the **PQRST method**: preview, question, read, self-recitation, and test.

Overlearning — Studying or practicing material beyond mastery — beyond the point where it can be repeated or carried out without error.

Metamemory — An effective way to improve one's memory is to become aware of it. Metamemory is our awareness of memory — how it works, its limitations, strategies for remembering, etc.

Spaced Practice — Short study sessions spread out over an extended period of time lead to better learning than does **massed practice** (one long learning or cramming session).

Retrieval

Retrieval involves bringing information from long-term memory to short-term memory so that it can be used or examined. Thus, whenever we remember anything, we are *retrieving* that memory from where it is stored. Retrieval is generally preceded by an internal process called **memory search**. **Retrieval cues** help us gain access to a memory and can be any stimulus or bit of information that aids in the retrieval of information from long-term memory.

Two basic methods of measuring retrieval are:

Recall — Material must be remembered with few or no retrieval cues (e.g., essay tests).

Recognition — Task is loaded with retrieval cues; material must be remembered through identification of the correct response (e.g., multiple-choice tests).

Encoding specificity principle states that retrieval cues are more efficient when they are coded when the information is learned, and that retrieval success is most likely if the context at the time of retrieval approximates that during encoding. For instance, people remember more material when their psychological state or physical location is similar to what it was when the material was originally learned. This is referred to as **state dependent** and **locus dependent learning**, respectively. According to **locus dependent learning** we should study or learn in a location or context that is as similar as possible to where we will be tested in order to maximize retrieval cues. The same is true of psychological state. If we are in a happy state when we learn material, we will be more likely to retrieve this information in the future if we are happy according to **state dependent learning.**

It is easier to retrieve beginning and ending items in a list and most difficult to remember the middle items. Recall being better for items at the beginning and end of a sequence is known as the **serial position effect**. Information at the beginning of a sequence is likely to be retrieved because it has already been placed in long-term memory. This is known as the **primacy effect**. Information at the end of the sequence is likely to still be in short-term memory and easily recalled, known as the **recency effect**. Middle items are least likely to be retrieved because they are neither in long-term memory nor in short-term memory.

The **tip-of-the-tongue experience** occurs when we are confident that we know information but cannot retrieve it. Even though the correct information cannot be recalled, it often can be recognized. This is because recognition tests provide retrieval cues about the needed information.

Forgetting

There are several theories that attempt to explain why forgetting occurs.

Decay Theory — If information in long-term memory is not used, it gradually fades over time until it is lost completely.

Interference Theory — Information in long-term memory is forgotten because other learning gets in the way of what needs to be remembered. Two types of interference have been described: **Proactive interference** occurs when old information in long-term memory interferes with remembering new information. **Retroactive interference** occurs when new memories interfere with remembering old memories.

Retrieval Failure — Not enough retrieval cues are available to prompt remembering.

Encoding Failure — The information was never learned; that is, the information never made it from short-term memory into long-term memory for permanent storage.

Consolidation Failure — Memories new to long-term memory take time to consolidate or be firmly implanted. Any disruption in the consolidation process can prevent a permanent memory from forming. Examples include a grand mal seizure, blow to the head, or anything that causes the loss of consciousness. **Retrograde amnesia** is the term used to describe a loss of memory for events occurring for periods of time *prior* to a brain injury. **Anterograde amnesia** is used to describe a loss of memory for events that occurred *after* a brain injury.

Motivated Forgetting — This occurs when disturbing, anxiety producing, or otherwise unpleasant memories are no longer consciously available because it would be disturbing to remember them. We tend to remember pleasant events better than unpleasant ones.

Hermann Ebbinghaus (1850–1909) was the first to plot a forgetting curve. He personally memorized lists of nonsense syllables (consonant-vowel-consonant trigrams, such as "wuf" and "rit") and later tested his own recall. He found that the longer the list of nonsense syllables, the more learning trials required. Ebbinghaus also found that most forgetting occurs immediately after learning, and then the rate of forgetting slows down considerably. This is what his forgetting curve documents. Ebbinghaus also measured savings, or the finding that relearning the same material is quicker and easier the second time. The concept of savings is used as evidence that forgetting is never complete.

6 LANGUAGE DEVELOPMENT

MAJOR PROPERTIES OF SPOKEN LANGUAGE

Language and thinking are two abilities that make us uniquely human. A spoken language requires the use of signs and symbols within a grammar. Grammar determines how the various signs and symbols are arranged and is a set of rules for combining the symbols, or words, into sentences. Language also allows us to use the signs and symbols within our grammar to create novel constructions.

Some characteristics of spoken language include:

Phonemes — The smallest unit of sound that affects the meaning of speech. The English language consists of 53 phonemes. By changing the beginning phoneme, the word "hat" comes "cat."

Morphemes — The smallest unit of language that has meaning. When speaking of more than one bat, we add the morpheme "s." Morphemes are often referred to as roots, stems, prefixes, and suffixes. Words are usually sequences of morphemes but one morpheme can constitute a whole word.

Semantics — The study of meaning in language.

Syntax — The set of rules that determine how words are combined to make phrases and sentences.

Phonetics — The study of how sounds are put together to make words.

Grammar — A broader term than syntax; it includes both syntax and phonetics.

Pragmatics — Includes the social aspects of language, including politeness, conversational interactions, and conversational rules.

Psycholinguistics — The study of the psychological mechanisms related to the acquisition and use of language.

Noam Chomsky distinguished between a sentence's **surface structure** (the words actually spoken) and its **deep structure** (its underlying meaning).

Two sentences, therefore, could have different surface structures but similar deep structures. An example would be, "The dog bit the boy" and "The boy was bitten by the dog." The surface structure of a sentence could also have more than one deep structure (e.g., "Visiting relatives can be boring."). When we hear a spoken sentence, we do not retain the surface structure, but instead transform it into its deep structure. Chomsky referred to this theory as **transformational grammar theory**.

Speech perception is guided by both bottom-up and top-down perception. **Bottom-up processing** in perception depends on the information from the senses at the most basic level, with sensory information flowing from this low level upward to the higher, more cognitive levels. For instance, the phoneme "c" in the word "cat" is perceived, in part, because our ears gather precise information about the characteristics of this sound. **Top-down processing** emphasizes the kind of information stored at the highest level of perception and includes concepts, knowledge, and prior knowledge. We are so skilled at top-down processing, for example, that we sometimes believe that we hear a missing phoneme. Warren and Warren found that subjects reported they heard the word "heel" in the following sentence where the * indicates a coughing sound: "It was found that the *eel was on the shoe." Subjects thought they heard the phoneme "h" even though the correct sound vibration never reached their ears. This is an example of top-down processing because prior knowledge and expectations influenced what subjects perceived they had heard.

LANGUAGE DEVELOPMENT

An outline of language development follows.

Cooing and Crying

↓

Babbling

↓

One-Word Stage

↓

Two-Word Stage

↓

Telegraphic Speech

↓

Verb Tenses, Meaning Modifiers, Pronouns, etc. Added

↓

Syntax Acquired

The first vocalizations that infants make include cooing and crying. At about four months of age, infants begin to babble. Their babblings are comprised of a repetition of syllables (e.g., "mamamama"). By six months of age, an infant is more likely to babble when an adult is talking to the infant. Babbling appears to be an innate ability because even deaf infants usually babble.

Infants usually begin to understand several individual words that caregivers are saying by five to eight months of age. A child's first words are ordinarily spoken between 10 to 12 months of age. This is referred to as the one-word stage because they can usually only use one word at a time. The first words that children use tend to be concrete nouns and verbs. Children often underextend and overextend the meanings of their first words. Underextension occurs when a child only uses a word in a specific context (e.g., only says "duck" when in the bathtub with a toy duck but never refers to this toy by name when outside the bathtub). Overextension or overgeneralization occurs when a child uses a word to mean more than an adult speaker would. For instance, a child who calls *all* four-legged, furry animals (cats, dogs, etc.) "doggie" is overextending or overgeneralizing.

Some researchers have referred to children's one-word utterances as holophrases — that is, this one word could be interpreted to mean an entire phrase. For instance, a child points at an object and says "Cookie." This one-word could possibly mean, depending on context, "I want a cookie," "There is a cookie," or "Is that a cookie?"

Children from 18 to 20 months of age are in the two-word stage of language development because they are now making short, two-word sentences (e.g., "More milk," "Where ball?"). Their vocabulary is also expanding rapidly during this stage. They may learn several new words each day.

Telegraphic speech quickly follows the two-word stage and consists of sentences that do not contain any morphemes, conjunctions, prepositions, or any other function words. Telegraphic speech only contains the content words necessary to convey meaning, similar to a telegram (e.g., "Doggie kiss Jeff."). Children's first sentences follow the subject-verb-object sequence, and children often rely on this word order to make their meaning clear.

Eventually, children add verb endings, adjectives, auxiliary verbs, and morphemes to their utterances. Interestingly, initially children tend to use the correct verb tenses, even the exceptions (e.g., "went," "ran"). By age four or five, however, they are often using incorrect forms ("goed," "runned"). These errors seem to indicate that children are acquiring general rules about their language and for a period of time they overgeneralize these rules to the exceptions. Eventually children use the exceptions appropriately. By age five, children have acquired most of the syntax of their native language.

When speaking to infants and older language-learning children, older children and adults typically use motherese. **Motherese** is speech that contains short sentences that are often repeated. This speech tends to consist of concrete nouns and active verbs. Pronouns, adjectives, conjunctions, and past tenses are usually absent. The sentences are enunciated clearly, often in a high-pitched voice. Many researchers believe that motherese helps children learn language.

An ongoing nature vs. nurture debate has been whether language is basically an innate, biological process or a learned phenomenon. Many researchers hold the view that children are somehow biologically programmed to learn language. According to Chomsky, the language acquisition device gives children an *innate* ability to process speech and to understand both the fundamental relationships among words and the regularities of speech. Researchers have also proposed a critical period for language learning during childhood. If exposed to language during this critical period, language learning will take place. After the critical period has passed, however, language learning will be much more difficult.

B. F. Skinner and other learning theorists proposed that language learning takes place similar to other forms of learning. That is, parents selectively reinforce and shape babbling sounds into words. When parents speak to their children, children receive attention and often affection as well. Children then try to make these reinforcing word sounds themselves and try to imitate their parents because it is reinforcing to do so.

7 INTELLIGENCE

INTELLIGENCE TESTING

Aptitude tests attempt to measure a person's capability for mastering an area of knowledge. (For instance, what is your potential or aptitude for learning a foreign language?) **Achievement tests** assess the amount of knowledge someone has already acquired in a specific area (such as math achievement, reading achievement, etc.). Because intelligence is a hypothetical construct, psychologists have disagreed on how to define it. Different intelligence tests, therefore, ask different questions and may measure different abilities.

Some definitions of intelligence include:

- The capacity to acquire and use knowledge.

- The total body of acquired knowledge.

- The ability to arrive at innovative solutions to problems.

- The ability to deal effectively with one's environment.

- Knowledge of one's culture.

- The ability to do well in school.

- The global capacity of the individual to act purposefully, to think rationally, and to deal effectively with the environment.

- Intelligence is what intelligence tests measure.

A major question related to intelligence has been "does intelligence consist of a single core factor or does it consist of many separate, unrelated abilities?" Responses to this include:

Charles Spearman	Concluded that cognitive abilities could be narrowed down to one critical **g-factor**, or general intelligence. (The **s-factors** represent specific knowledge needed to answer questions on a particular test.)
J. P. Guilford	Proposed that intelligence consists of 150 distinct abilities.

L. L. Thurstone	Used a statistical technique known as factor analysis to find seven independent primary mental abilities: numerical ability, reasoning, verbal fluency, spatial visualization, perceptual ability, memory, and verbal comprehension.
Raymond B. Cattell	Argued that a g-factor does exist, but cognitive ability consists of **fluid intelligence** (reasoning and problem solving) and **crystallized intelligence** (specific knowledge gained from applying fluid intelligence).
Robert Sternberg	Proposed a **triarchic theory of intelligence** that specifies three important parts of intelligence: **componential intelligence** (includes metacomponents, performance components, and knowledge-acquisition components), **experiential intelligence** (abilities to deal with novelty and to automatize processing), and **contextual intelligence** (practical intelligence and social intelligence).
Howard Gardner	**Theory of multiple intelligences** proposed seven different components of intelligence that include not only language ability, logical-mathematical thinking, and spatial thinking but also musical, bodily kinesthetic, interpersonal, and intrapersonal thinking.

History of Intelligence Testing

Early interest in intelligence testing dates back to the eugenics movement of Sir Frances Galton. Galton believed that it is possible to improve genetic characteristics (including intelligence) through breeding.

The first effective test of intelligence was devised in the early 1900s by French psychologist Alfred Binet. Binet was appointed by the French Ministry of Public Instruction to design an intelligence test that would identify children who needed to be removed from the regular classrooms so that they could receive special instruction.

Binet and his colleague Theodore Simon devised an intelligence test consisting of 30 subtests containing problems of increasing difficulty. The items on the test were designed to measure children's judgment, reasoning, and comprehension. This first test was published in 1905 and then revised in 1908 and 1911.

The 1908 revision of the Binet and Simon scale introduced the notion of mental age. **Mental age** is a measure of a child's intellectual level that is independent of the child's **chronological age** (actual age).

Shortly after Binet's original work, Lewis M. Terman of Stanford University and his colleagues helped refine and standardize the test for American children. Their version came to be the Stanford-Binet Intelligence Scale, and its latest revision is still being used today. (A further discussion of this scale can be found later in this chapter.)

Terman and others (e.g., L. William Stern of Germany) developed the idea of the IQ, or intelligence quotient (sometimes referred to as ratio IQ score).

To calculate IQ, a child's mental age (MA) (as determined by how well he or she does on the test) is divided by his or her chronological age (CA) and multiplied by 100. That is,

$$IQ = \frac{MA}{CA} \times 100$$

The major advantage of the IQ score over simple MA is that it gives an index of a child's IQ test performance relative to others of the same chronological age. The major problem with the ratio IQ score is that most people's mental development slows in their late teens. But as MA may remain fairly stable throughout adulthood, CA increases over time. Using CA as the divisor in the IQ formula, therefore, results in an individual's IQ score diminishing over time (even though MA has not changed).

David Wechsler corrected this problem with ratio IQ scores by devising the **deviation IQ score**. This deviation IQ score is calculated by converting the raw scores on each subtest of the test to standard scores normalized for each age group. These standard scores are then translated into deviation IQ scores.

Wechsler reasoned that intelligence is normally distributed, or follows the bell-shaped curve—that is, the majority of people score at or around the mean, or average, score of 100 and progressively fewer people will achieve scores that spread out in either direction of the mean. A group of IQ scores can be portrayed as a normal, bell-shaped curve with an average score of 100 and a **standard deviation** (average deviation from the mean) that is the same (i.e., 15) at every age level.

The advantage of the deviation IQ is that the standing of an individual can be compared with the scores of others of the same age, and the intervals from age to age remain the same. **Deviation IQ scores**, therefore, indicate exactly where a test taker falls in the normal distribution of intelligence.

Terman adopted the deviation IQ as the scoring standard for the 1960 revision of the Stanford-Binet Intelligence Scale, although he chose a standard deviation of 16 rather than 15. Almost all other intelligence tests today use deviation IQ scores.

Current Intelligence Tests

The two most widely used versions of intelligence tests today are described next. These tests are individually administered, which means that they are given only by trained psychologists to one test taker at a time.

The first Stanford-Binet Intelligence Scale was published in 1916 by Lewis Terman and his colleagues. It was revised in 1937, 1960, and 1986 and remains one of the world's most widely used tests of intelligence (although there are criticisms of the scale). It can be used with individuals from age two through adulthood.

In its latest revision, Stanford-Binet Intelligence Scale: Fourth Edition, the term *intelligence* has been replaced by *cognitive development*. The terms *intelligence*, *IQ*, and *mental age* are not used; instead the term *Standard Age Score (SAS)* is used. The fourth edition measures four areas of cognitive development and a SAS can be calculated for each area as well as an overall composite score. The four areas measured are called verbal reasoning, abstract/visual reasoning, quantitative reasoning, and short-term memory.

Because the Stanford-Binet initially appeared to be unsatisfactory for use with adults, in 1939 David Wechsler published a test designed exclusively for adults. This test has since been revised and is now known as the WAIS-R or Wechsler Adult Intelligence Scale, Revised.

Eventually, Wechsler published two scales for children and these are now known as:

WPPSI-R   Wechsler Preschool and Primary Scale of Intelligence, Revised (for children 4 to 6 years of age)

WISC-III   Wechsler Intelligence Scale for Children, third edition (for children 6 to 16 years of age)

The Wechsler scales were known for at least two major innovations when they were first developed. First, they were less dependent on verbal ability than the Stanford-Binet and included many items that required nonverbal reasoning. His tests allow the computation of three scores, a verbal IQ score, a performance IQ score, and an overall full scale IQ score. For example, subtests from the verbal and performance sections of the **WAIS-R** include:

Verbal Subtests	Performance Subtests
Information	Digit Symbol
Comprehension	Picture Completion
Arithmetic	Block Design
Similarities	Picture Arrangement
Digit Span	Object Assembly
Vocabulary	

Second, Wechsler developed the deviation IQ score based on the normal distribution of intelligence and abandoned the notion of intelligence quotient.

Wechsler's scales of intelligence are still widely used and respected today.

Intelligence tests, as with any other test, must fit certain requirements in order to be of good quality.

Reliability. Most intelligence tests used today (e.g., Stanford-Binet and Wechsler scales) demonstrate good reliability or consistency of scores.

Validity. The validity of intelligence tests depends on the criterion being used. For example, they do a good job of predicting success in school. Although intelligence test scores correlate with occupational attainment, they do not predict performance within a given occupation.

Stability. Intelligence test scores can and do change over time. For instance, infant and preschool scores are not good predictors of intelligence in later childhood, adolescence, or adulthood. It is not until late elementary school (e.g., after ages 8–10) that intelligence test scores begin to stabilize. It is also possible, however, to make substantial gains or losses in intelligence during adolescence and adulthood.

Determinants of Intelligence

The nature vs. nurture debate related to intelligence addresses whether heredity or environment determines one's intellectual skills.

Heritability is an estimate of how much of a trait in a population is determined by genetic inheritance.

In the late 1960s, Arthur Jensen argued that intelligence is approximately 80 percent due to heredity. He felt that the difference in mean intelligence scores for different races, nationalities, and social classes was due more to heredity than to environment.

Correlational studies with twins suggest that heredity influences the development of intelligence. For instance, the correlation of intelligence test scores for identical twins (who have identical genetic make-up) is higher than the correlation for fraternal twins. Even identical twins reared apart have more similar IQs than fraternal twins reared together in the same household.

There is research evidence, however, to indicate that environment also exerts a strong influence on intelligence. Sandra Scarr and other researchers have shown that underprivileged children placed in homes that provide an enriching intellectual environment have shown moderate but consistent increases in intelligence. Children placed in various enrichment programs have also shown gains in IQ. The IQs of identical twins reared together in the same environment are more similar than those for identical twins reared apart.

The term reaction range has been applied to the nature vs. nurture debate of intelligence. **Reaction range** implies that genetics may limit or define a potential range of IQ, but that environment can influence where along this range an individual's IQ score falls. For instance, children in an enriched environment should score near the top of their potential IQ range.

Racial and cultural differences in IQ are very small when compared to the range of genetic differences within each group. Research has suggested, for example, that the differences between mean intelligence test scores for black and white Americans may be due to differences in parental education, nutrition, health care, schools, and motivation for doing well on the test.

Many have argued that intelligence tests are culturally biased because they have been developed by white, middle-class psychologists. There is some research evidence to support this claim. Attempts have been made to produce language-free, culture-fair tests of intelligence. The Raven's Progressive Matrices is one such test.

8 SOCIAL DEVELOPMENT

Social development refers to the development of behaviors the child engages in when he interacts with others. This area of study includes such topics as games, morality, and learning the rules of society.

ATTACHMENT

Attachment is the close emotional relationship between an infant and his or her caretakers.

Initially, infants attempt to attract the attention (usually through crying, smiling, etc.) of no one in particular. Eventually infants develop the ability to discriminate familiar from unfamiliar people. Shortly thereafter, they may cry or otherwise become distressed when preferred caregivers leave the room. This is referred to as **separation anxiety**. Separation anxiety may begin as early as 6 months of age, but it usually peaks around 18 months and then gradually declines. Mary Ainsworth and her colleagues found they could distinguish three categories of attachments based on the quality of the infant-caregiver interactions.

Secure Attachments   Children use parent as secure base from which they explore their environment. They become upset if parent leaves the room but are glad to see the parent when parent returns.

Insecure Attachments

Anxious-Ambivalent   Tend not to use parent as a secure base (and may often cling or refuse to leave parent). They become very upset when parent leaves and may often appear angry or become more upset when parent returns.

Avoidant   These children seek little contact with parent and are not concerned when parent leaves. Usually avoid interaction when parent returns.

Parents of securely attached infants are often found to be more sensitive and responsive to their child's needs. Some studies have found a relationship between attachment patterns and children's later adjustment. For instance, one study found that securely attached infants were less frustrated and happier at two years of age than were their insecurely attached peers. Some researchers have suggested that temperament, genetic characteristics, and "goodness of fit" may be important for both the type of attachment bond formed and a child's later developmental outcome.

AGGRESSION

Aggression is defined as intentionally inflicting physical or psychological harm on others.

About one-third of studies show that males are more aggressive than females, and the differences are larger with children than adults and with physical rather than verbal aggression.

The **frustration-aggression hypothesis** states that frustration produces aggression and that this aggression may be directed at the frustrater or **displaced** onto another target, as in **scapegoating**. However, frustration does not always cause aggression.

According to social learning theory, people learn to behave aggressively by observing aggressive models and by having their aggressive responses reinforced. For instance, parents who are belligerent with others or who use physical punishment to discipline their children tend to raise more aggressive offspring.

According to social learning theory, exposure to role models in the mass media, especially television, can influence aggression. Some research demonstrates that adults and children as young as nursery-school age show higher levels of aggression after they view media violence.

ALTRUISM

Altruism, or **prosocial behavior**, is the selfless concern for the welfare of others that leads to helping behavior. One of the most widely studied aspects of altruism is **bystander intervention**—whether individuals will intervene and come to the aid of a person in distress. In 1964, a young woman named Kitty Genovese cried out as she was being brutally murdered outside her apartment building in Queens, New York. Thirty-eight neighbors watched and yet no one helped or even called the police. The Kitty Genovese case motivated social psychologists to study why bystanders will or will not intervene and help another individual.

The **bystander effect** states that people are less likely to help someone in an emergency situation when others are present. That is, when several people witness an emergency, each one thinks someone else will help. This appears to be due to diffusion of responsibility. **Diffusion of responsibility** is the tendency for people to feel that the responsibility for helping is shared or diffused among those who are present. The more people that are present in an emergency, therefore, the less personally responsible each individual feels. People tend to think that someone else will help or since no one is helping, possibly the person does not need help.

According to Latane and Darley, certain steps will occur before a person helps.

- They notice or observe the emergency event.

- They interpret the event as one that requires help.

- They assume responsibility for taking action. (It is here where diffusion of responsibility is likely to take place.)

- After individuals assume responsibility for helping, the decision must next be made concerning what to do.

- They take action and actually help.

Some social psychologists use a rewards-costs approach when explaining helping behaviors. The **rewards-costs approach** states that before a bystander is likely to help, the perceived rewards of helping must outweigh the costs.

Other research has found that individuals who are high in **empathy**— an emotional experience that involves a subjective grasp of another person's feelings—are more likely to help others in need. According to the **empathy-arousal hypothesis**, empathy has the power to motivate altruism.

Other factors that encourage altruism include a realization that help is necessary, being in a good mood, and seeing someone else helping.

Men are more likely to help strangers when an audience is present or when the task is especially dangerous for women. In other situations, however, men and women are equally helpful.

WORK VS. PLAY

Work and play are not distinguished by the specific activities they involve since these can be similar. Rather, work and play are distinguished by their end results. Play is engaged in for the pleasure—it is rewarding in and of itself. Work, on the other hand, is engaged in for the purpose of gaining a desired goal. Work can be enjoyable, but enjoyment is only incidental. The goal of more work is the attainment of monetary or material reward.

The child engages in three major categories of play: sensorimotor play, imaginative play, and parallel or cooperative play, which is based on the existence of the interaction among the players. Sensorimotor play is engaged in during infancy. It involves the manipulation of objects. This manipulation provides the child with pleasurable stimulation. Sensorimotor play can consist of motor activities such as crawling, walking, running, or waving.

Imaginative play involves games of make-believe. The child may imagine that he or she is someone or something else, that the activities he or she engages in are something other than what they really are, or possibly he or she imagines that objects that he or she is playing with are something different than what they appear to be. Daydreaming is a major form of imaginative play. Daydreaming, however, involves no physical activity as compared to the other types of play. It is pure imaginative thinking.

The third type of play consists of two sequential types. Each is named and described in terms of the existence of interaction among the players. The first type, parallel play, begins shortly after infancy. Here, children play side by side but do not interact. They might use the same play materials but any sharing is unintentional. Between the ages of two and five, children begin to act out fantasies, pretending that they are various characters. When children find that they share knowledge of various characters or fantasies, they engage in cooperative play as they act out fantasies together. Any type of play that involves interaction and cooperation among the players is called cooperative. One special type of cooperative play is called sociodramatic play. This type requires that the child's imagination and perception be highly active and alert—quick to pick up cues from the other players. It is comparable to the improvisation of professional actors. Through sociodramatic play, the child learns how to behave in society. In addition, the groundwork is laid for interpersonal relationships.

During the period of cooperative play, quarreling among players arises. This quarreling becomes especially common between the ages of three and four. Such quarreling marks the beginning of competitiveness, a quality that is highly reinforced in preschoolers in this culture.

In addition to teaching the child how to interact socially, play is also an influencing factor in cognition. Sutton-Smith (1967) considered play an activity in which the infant can work through new responses and operations and increase his or her range of responses. Sutton-Smith called play a mechanism for the "socialization of novelty." Children whose play is varied are given a chance to experience situations that increase their ability to respond appropriately to novel situations that may arise in the future. Children whose play is restricted are less able to respond in unfamiliar situations. Thus, play enlarges a child's repertoire of responses and thereby allows him or her to adjust quickly to new situations.

KOHLBERG'S THEORY OF MORAL DEVELOPMENT

Lawrence Kohlberg developed a model of moral development based on an individual's responses to moral questions called **moral dilemmas**. Kohlberg's theory attempts to explain how children develop a sense of right or wrong. Kohlberg was influenced by Piaget's theory and therefore felt that moral development was determined by cognitive development. The figure below is an example of Kohlberg's theory.

Kohlberg's theory describes how individuals pass through a series of three levels of moral development, each of which can be broken into two sublevels, resulting in a total of six stages.

Level I. Preconventional Morality

Stage 1.	**Punishment orientation**	A person complies with rules during this stage in order to avoid punishment.
Stage 2.	**Reward orientation**	An action is determined by one's own needs.

Level II. Conventional Morality

Stage 3.	**Good-girl/Good-boy orientation**	Good behavior is that which pleases others and gets their approval.
Stage 4.	**Authority orientation**	Emphasis is on upholding the law, order, and authority and doing one's duty by following societal rules.

Level III. Postconventional Morality

Stage 5.	**Social contract orientation**	Flexible understanding that people obey rules because

| | | they are necessary for the social order but that rules can change if there are good reasons and better alternatives. |
| **Stage 6.** | **Morality of individual principles orientation** | Behavior is directed by self-chosen ethical principles. High value is placed on justice, dignity, and equality. |

Criticisms of Kohlberg's theory of moral development include that it may be better at describing the development of male morality than of female morality, and development may not be as orderly and uniform as his theory suggests. For instance, it is not unusual to find individuals who are reasoning at several adjacent levels of moral reasoning at the same time. Also, Kohlberg's theory describes moral reasoning but does not predict moral behavior.

GENDER ROLE DEVELOPMENT

Gender roles are our set of expectations about appropriate activities for females and males. Research has shown that even preschoolers believe that males and females have different characteristics. They also believe it is inappropriate to act like a member of the other gender.

Theories that explain gender role development include:

| **Social Learning Theory** | Proposes that children learn gender roles because they are rewarded for appropriate behavior and punished for inappropriate gender role behaviors. Children also watch and imitate the behaviors of others. |
| **Cognitive Theory** | Kohlberg argued that children learn about gender the same way that they acquire other cognitive concepts (see Piaget's theory for more detail). First, preschool children acquire **gender identity**—that is, they identify themselves as male or female. Then children classify others, activities, objects, etc. as male or female. Once these gender concepts are acquired, children engage in gender-typed behavior—they prefer same-gender playmates, activities, etc. Kohlberg also proposed that |

preschool children lack **gender constancy**. That is, they do not understand that a person's gender stays the same despite changes in outward physical appearance.

Psychoanalytic, or Freud's, Theory   Freud's theory proposes that children establish their gender role identity as a result of identification with their same sex parent during the Phallic stage.

INTERPERSONAL ATTRACTION

Interpersonal attraction refers to our close relationships with others and those factors that contribute to a relationship being formed.

Friendship

Studies of friendships have found three factors that are important in determining who will become friends.

Similarity   People are generally attracted to those who are similar to themselves in many ways—similar in age, sex, race, economic status, etc.

Proximity or Propinquity   It is easier to develop a friendship with people who are close at hand. Proximity also increases the likelihood of repeated contacts and increased exposure can lead to increased attraction; the **mere exposure effect**. In a classic study at Massachusetts Institute of Technology, Festinger found that friends of women who lived in married student housing were most likely to live in the same building. In fact, half of all friends lived on the same floor.

Attractiveness   Physical attractiveness is a major factor in attraction for people of all ages. We tend to like attractive people.

Love

Overall, the same factors connected with friendships (similarity, proximity, and attractiveness) are also related to love relationships.

Similarity	Dating and married couples tend to be similar in age, race, social class, religion, education, intelligence, attitudes, and interests.
Proximity	We tend to fall in love with people who live nearby.
Attractiveness	We tend to fall in love with people whose attractiveness matches our own according to the **matching hypothesis**.

Researchers believe that love is a qualitatively different state than merely liking someone. Love includes physiological arousal, self-disclosure, all-encompassing interest in another individual, fantasizing about the other, and a relatively rapid swing of emotions. Unlike liking, love also includes passion, closeness, fascination, exclusiveness, sexual desire, and intense caring.

Some researchers have distinguished two main types of love.

Passionate or Romantic Love	Predominates in the early part of a romantic relationship. Includes intense physiological arousal, psychological interest, sexual desire, and the type of love we mean when we say we are "in love" with someone.
Companionate or Affectionate Love	The type of love that occurs when we have a deep, caring affection for a person.

Robert Sternberg has proposed a **triangular theory of love** that consists of three components:

Intimacy	The encompassing feelings of closeness and connectedness in a relationship.
Passion	The physical and sexual attraction in a relationship.
Decision/ Commitment	Encompasses the initial cognition that one loves someone and the longer-term feelings of commitment to maintain the love.

According to Sternberg's theory, complete love only happens when all three kinds of love are represented in a relationship. Sternberg called this complete love "**consummate love**." **Fatuous love** is based on passion and commitment only and is often short-lived. Research has shown that successful romantic relationships that last for many years are based on the expression of love and admiration, friendship between the partners, a commitment to the relationship, displays of affection, self-disclosure, and offering each other emotional support.

9 FAMILY AND SOCIETY

PARENTING STYLES

Diana Baumrind found that she could classify parents according to the following:

Authoritative Parents

Affectionate and loving.
Provide control when necessary and set limits.
Allow children to express their own point of view—engage in "verbal give and take."
Their children tend to be self-reliant, competent, and socially responsible.

Authoritarian Parents

Demand unquestioning obedience.
Use punishment to control behavior.
Less likely to be affectionate.
Their children tend to be unhappy, distrustful, ineffective in social interactions, and often become dependent adults.

Permissive Parents

Make few demands.
Allow children to make their own decisions.
Use inconsistent discipline.
Their children tend to be immature, lack self-control, and explore less.

ADOLESCENCE

Adolescence is that time in development that occurs between childhood and adulthood.

Physical Changes: **Puberty** refers to rapid physical growth that occurs with hormonal changes that bring sexual maturity. **Secondary sex characteristics** (the physical features associated with gender but not directly involved in reproduction, such as male facial hair) emerge at this time. **Menarche** refers to girls' first menstrual period. The peak growth spurt during puberty occurs earlier for girls than for boys.

Social Concerns: The main task for adolescents is to establish an identity. Adolescents are in Erikson's identity versus role confusion stage. Adolescents enter what Erikson called a psychosocial moratorium, which relates to the gap between the security of childhood and the autonomy of adulthood, where a person is free from responsibilities and can experiment with different roles.

At the turn of the century, psychologist G. Stanley Hall characterized adolescence as a time of storm and stress. Current research suggests that most adolescents make it through this time without any more turmoil than they are likely to encounter at other points in their lives.

Cognitive Skills: Cognitively, adolescents begin entering Piaget's stage of formal operations. Adolescent egocentrism may occur whereby adolescents believe that others are as preoccupied with them as they are with themselves.

ADULTHOOD

Certain events mark adult attainment in our society. Such events include leaving one's family, supporting oneself, getting married, and having children. Many of these transitions into adulthood involve changes in family relationships and responsibilities.

Early Adulthood

Early adulthood extends from approximately 20 to 40 years of age.

Physical Changes: Reaction time and muscular strength peak in the early to mid-twenties. External signs of aging begin to show in the thirties when the skin loses elasticity and hair becomes thinner and begins to turn gray. A gain in weight is common because a lowered metabolic rate contributes to increased body fat relative to muscle.

Social Concerns: Social development during early adulthood is focused on forming intimate relationships. Individuals are in Erikson's intimacy versus isolation stage.

Cognitive Skills: Intellectual abilities and speed of information processing are relatively stable and gains in intellectual skills are possible during early adulthood. Some studies have shown that approximately 50 percent of all adults have reached Piaget's stage of formal operations.

Middle Adulthood

Middle adulthood lasts from approximately 40 to 65 years of age.

Physical Changes: During middle adulthood the number of active brain cells declines, but the significance of this loss is unclear. In vision, far-sightedness increases. Sensitivity to high-frequency sounds decreases. In women, **menopause** (ending of monthly menstruation) occurs at around 51 years of age. The **male climacteric** includes decreased fertility and decreased frequency of orgasm. For both sexes, sexual activity declines, although capacity for arousal changes only slightly.

Social Concerns: Over time, individuals become more aware of their own mortality and the passage of time and enter Erikson's generativity versus stagnation stage. Those in middle adulthood are often caught between the needs of their children and those of their own aging parents and are thus referred to as the **sandwich generation**.

There has been much debate concerning whether or not most people go through a **midlife crisis**. Many studies have failed to find increased emotional turbulence at midlife.

Cognitive Skills: Effectiveness of retrieval from long-term memory begins a slow decline but is often not noticeable until after age 55. Despite a decreased speed in cognitive processing, intelligence and problem-solving skills usually remain stable. Career development peaks.

INFLUENCES OF DIVORCE AND SINGLE-PARENTHOOD

There have been three major trends facing the developing family over the past three decades: an increase in divorce, an increase in single-parent families, and an increase in working mothers. Because every household is different, it is difficult to generalize the effect of divorce or single-parenting on the family. There are general trends, however, that do appear.

Certain factors contribute to the stability of family members involved in divorce or single-parenthood. A parent who is secure and rewarded in the work place deals better with the situation. A positive network of friends and family provides support, lending a more positive aspect to the situation. When both parents play a role in raising the child there is a more positive outcome.

There are five aspects that affect the development of a child dealing with divorce. They are levels of stress and amount of support at the time;

sex of the child; the age of the child; the amount of time since the change; and the parents' response to the change.

A difference has been found in a family's development and the case of single parenthood. If a child lives in a single-parent home caused by death there tends to be more acceptance, support, and trust for people of same sex as deceased. However, if single-parenthood is caused by divorce it has been found that there is less acceptance and a general bitterness towards the opposite sex of the parent with custody.

10 PERSONALITY AND EMOTIONS

TEMPERAMENT

Temperament refers to a child's characteristic mood and activity level. Even young infants are temperamentally different from one another. The New York Longitudinal Study (1956), carried out by Stella Chase, Alexander Thomas, and Herbert Birch, is a research project that investigated temperament.

A **longitudinal** study is one that repeatedly observes and follows-up the same group of individuals as they mature. For example, a group of children could have their temperament assessed when they are three months old, and again when they are two years old, five years old, and ten years old.

A **cross-sectional** study involves different groups of individuals who are at different ages at the same point in time. A group of three-month-olds, two-year-olds, and five-year-olds may be assessed for temperament. In cross-sectional studies, therefore, the same individuals are not retested but instead are measured only once, and group averages are used to demonstrate developmental changes.

The New York Longitudinal Study followed 140 children from birth to adolescence. Thomas, Chess, and Birch interviewed parents when the infants were between two and three months of age and rated the infants based on activity level, rhythmicity, approach/withdrawal, adaptability, intensity of reaction, and quality of mood. Thomas, et al. found that they could classify infants into different groups based on temperament.

Easy Infants
(40 percent)

adaptable to new situations;
predictable in their rhythmicity or schedule;
positive in their mood;

Difficult Infants
(10 percent)

intense in their reactions;
not very adaptable to new situations;
slightly negative mood;
irregular body rhythms;

Slow-to-Warm-Up Infants
(15 percent)

initially withdraw when approached, but may later "warm up";
slow to adapt to new situations;

Average Infants   did not fit into any of the above categories
(35 percent)

Thomas, et al. found that temperament was fairly stable over time. For instance, they found that 70 percent of the difficult infants developed behavior problems during childhood, while only 18 percent of the easy infants did so. There were, of course, individual differences in whether specific children showed continuity or dramatic changes in their temperament over time.

Although early temperament appears to be highly biologically determined, environment can also influence temperament. Researchers have used the term **goodness of fit** to describe an environment where an infant's temperament matches the opportunities, expectations, and demands the infant encounters.

MOTIVATION

Psychologists study motivation because they want to know why a behavior occurs. Motivation is the process that initiates, directs, and sustains behavior while simultaneously satisfying physiological or psychological needs. A **motive** is a reason or purpose for behavior.

Theories of Motivation

Several theories describe the basis for motivation. An **instinct** is an inborn, unlearned, fixed pattern of behavior that is biologically determined and is characteristic of an entire species. The idea of attributing human and animal behavior to instincts was not seriously considered until Charles Darwin suggested that humans evolved from lower animals.

William McDougall believed that instincts were "the prime movers of all human activity." He identified 18 instincts, including parental instinct, curiosity, escape, reproduction, self-assertion, pugnacity, and gregariousness. However, psychologists do not agree on what and how many human instincts there are. While McDougall suggested 18, others have suggested even more.

Instinct theory was widely accepted by psychologists for the first 20 or 30 years of the twentieth century. Today, the idea that motivation is based on instincts has been replaced by other theories, because psychologists recognized that human behavior is too diverse and unpredictable to be consistent across our species. Further, there is no scientific way to prove the existence of instincts in humans. Many feel that instinct theory provides a description rather than an explanation of behavior.

Drive-reduction theory was popularized by Clark Hull and suggests that motivation results from attempting to keep a balanced internal state.

Homeostasis is the built-in tendency to maintain internal stability or equilibrium. Any deviation from homeostasis creates a need. A need results in a drive for action. A **drive**, therefore, is a psychological state of tension or arousal that motivates activities to reduce this tension and restore homeostatic balance.

Primary drives are drives that arise from biological needs. **Secondary drives** are learned through operant or classical conditioning. Drive-reduction theory can be diagrammed as:

Lack of Homeostasis

↓

Need

↓

Drive

↓

Motivation to Act

↓

Homeostasis

For instance, homeostasis works to maintain a constant internal body temperature in humans of approximately 98.6 degrees Fahrenheit. If body temperature goes above this average temperature, our bodies automatically respond (e.g., perspiration) to restore equilibrium. These automatic responses may not be sufficient by themselves, and we may be motivated to take other actions (e.g., remove some clothing).

The nervous systems are involved in maintaining homeostasis. For instance, the parasympathetic branch acts to counteract heat and the sympathetic branch responds to cold. Both of these branches are governed by the hypothalamus, a structure found near the base of the forebrain that is involved in the regulation of basic biological needs (e.g., temperature, hunger, thirst).

Drive theories, however, cannot explain all motivation. Motivation can exist without drive arousal. For instance, we often eat when there is no need to eat (i.e., we are not physically hungry). **Incentive theories** propose that external stimuli regulate motivational states (e.g., the sight of a hot fudge sundae motivates eating), and that human behavior is goal-directed. That is, anticipated rewards (i.e., the taste of the sundae) can direct and encourage behavior. Rewards, in motivational terms, are incentives, and behavior is goal-directed to obtain these rewards. Incentives vary from person to person and can change over time. Many psychologists believe that instead of contradicting each other, drive and incentive theories may work together in motivating behavior.

Arousal theory suggests that the aim of motivation is to maintain an optimal level of arousal. **Arousal** is a person's state of alertness and mental and physical activation. If arousal is less than the optimal level, we do something to stimulate it. If arousal is greater than the optimal level, we seek to reduce the stimulation. The level of arousal considered optimal varies from person to person.

The **Yerkes-Dodson law** states that a particular level of motivational arousal produces optimal performance on a task. Research suggests that people perform best when arousal is moderate. On easy or simple tasks, people can perform better under higher levels of arousal. On difficult or complex tasks, the negative effects of over-arousal are particularly strong.

Richard Solomon proposed an **opponent-process theory** of motivation. This theory argues that one emotional state will trigger an opposite emotional state that lasts long after the original emotion has disappeared. That is, an increase in arousal will produce a calming reaction in the nervous system, and vice versa. It is the opponent process, not the initial reaction, therefore, that maintains the motivation to carry out certain behaviors.

For instance, opponent-process theory suggests that the fear that skydivers feel when risking their lives will trigger an extremely positive emotional response. As a consequence, the motivation to skydive increases. This theory has also been used to explain the motivation behind risky, dangerous behaviors as well as drug addiction.

Abraham Maslow, a humanistic theorist, proposed a hierarchy of needs to explain motivations. According to Maslow, human needs are arranged in a hierarchy. People must satisfy their **basic** or **physiological needs** before they can satisfy their **higher-order needs**. Individuals progress upward in the hierarchy when lower needs are satisfied, but they may regress to lower levels if basic needs are no longer satisfied. As one moves up the hierarchy, each level of need becomes less biological and more social in origin.

For instance, Maslow proposed that the basic, fundamental needs for survival, such as food, water, stable body temperature, etc. must be met first. When a person satisfies a level of physiological needs, this satisfaction activates needs at the next level. This means that after basic physiological needs are met, safety and security needs become motivating. Following this pattern, only when the basic physiological and safety needs are met can a person consider fulfilling higher-order needs, consisting of **love and belonging**, **esteem and self-esteem**, and **self-actualization**.

Love and belonging needs include the need to obtain and give affection and to be a contributing member of society. **Esteem and self-esteem** relate to the need to develop a sense of self-worth by knowing that others are aware of one's competence and value. The highest need in Maslow's motivational hierarchy is the need for **self-actualization**, which is the need to fulfill one's potential. According to Maslow, people will be frustrated if they are unable to fully use their talents or pursue their true interests. A state of self-actualization provides a sense of satisfaction with one's current state of affairs.

Psychologists feel that Maslow's theory is important because it highlights the complexity of human needs. It also emphasizes that basic biological needs must be met before people will be concerned with higher-order needs. Criticisms of Maslow's theory include that it is difficult to test empirically; terms such as self-actualization are difficult to measure and study.

Burton White proposed the notion of **intrinsic motivation**, or the desire to perform an activity because we find it inherently enjoyable. For example, a person reads several books per month because he or she finds it enjoyable. Activities carried out because of curiosity are also examples of intrinsic motivation. **Extrinsic motivation** occurs when an activity is performed in order to obtain a reward or to avoid an undesirable consequence.

Human Needs

Motives for several of the most important human needs—hunger, thirst, sexuality—have been studied by psychologists. What motivates us to eat? What motivates us to stop eating once we have begun? How do we know we are hungry? Psychologists have attempted to answer these and other questions related to hunger and motivation.

Researchers have found that people report that they are hungry even when their stomachs have been removed for medical reasons. The explanation for hunger, therefore, is more complex than an empty stomach. A feeling of hunger seems to be related to both the brain and body chemistry as well as to external factors.

Glucose is a simple sugar nutrient that provides energy. When the level of glucose in our bloodstream is low, we feel hungry. When glucose levels are high, we feel full. Blood glucose levels appear to be monitored by **glucostats**, neurons that are sensitive to glucose levels. Where these glucostats are located is not clear, although it seems likely that the hypothalamus receives messages about glucose levels.

Another body chemical, insulin, is also related to hunger. **Insulin** is important for converting blood glucose into stored fat. Insulin is a hormone secreted by the pancreas. Research has shown that insulin influences hunger indirectly by decreasing glucose levels. Research has also shown that people with elevated insulin levels report feeling hungry and usually eat more than those with normal insulin levels.

The hypothalamus is the brain structure that appears to be primarily responsible for food intake. Injury to the hypothalamus, for instance, can cause radical changes in eating patterns. Laboratory rats whose lateral hypothalamus (LH, located at the side of the hypothalamus) was damaged would often literally starve themselves to death. When the rats' LH was stimulated, however, they would overeat.

Rats with injury to the ventromedial hypothalamus (VMH, located toward the center of the hypothalamus) became extreme overeaters. VMH stimulation caused animals to stop eating.

The **dual-center theory** maintains that the hypothalamus contains an "on" and an "off" switch for eating, located in two different regions, the LH and VMH. These switches can be activated by internal signals (e.g., damage or stimulation) and external signals (e.g., sight or taste of food).

Some researchers have suggested that injury to the hypothalamus affects the weight set point that regulates food intake. The **weight set point** is the particular, or target, weight that the body strives to maintain. Hunger or food intake adjusts to meet this set point. This means whenever we are below our set point, we feel hungry until we gain weight to match our set point.

Set point theory has been used as one explanation for obesity. According to set point theory, each person's body has a fixed number of **fat cells**, the cells that store fat. Fat cells may shrink in size when a dieter loses weight and increase in size when weight is gained. The number of fat cells does not change, only their size changes. Some researchers propose that the shriveled fat cells that result from dieting send hunger messages to the dieter's brain. To make matters worse, a dieter's **metabolism** (the rate at which energy is produced and expended by the body) may slow down as a result of a decrease in fat cell size. It is harder to lose weight with a slow metabolism.

Some individuals seem to have a naturally slow metabolism and, even though they eat small amounts of food, they gain weight readily. Those who gain weight easily are actually biologically more efficient because they easily convert food into body tissue.

Other individuals seem to have a naturally high metabolism rate and can eat as much as they want without weight gain. These individuals are inefficient in using the food that they eat and much of it is wasted.

There is also evidence that some people have a genetic predisposition to become obese. It seems likely that metabolic rate is an important inherited factor.

Other reasons for eating and overeating include:

Learned Preferences and Habits

We learn not only when to eat and how much to eat at one time but many taste preferences are the result of experience.

External Cues

External cues can influence eating. External cues can include the sight or smell of food as well as time of day.

Stress and Arousal

Several research studies have shown a relationship between heightened arousal and overeating for some people.

Because we lose a significant amount of water through sweating and urination, thirst represents an important motivational drive.

Three primary internal mechanisms produce thirst. First, when the concentration of salt cells in the body reaches a certain level, the hypothalamus is triggered to act in a way that results in the experience of thirst. A decrease in the total volume of fluid in the **circulatory system** also causes the sense of thirst. Finally, a rise in body temperature or a significant energy expenditure also produces thirst, probably because of a rise in the salt concentration of the body.

The dry mouth that accompanies thirst is a symptom of the need for water, but not the cause. The body does seem to have a kind of water meter in the mouth and stomach, however, that monitors the amount of water that has been consumed and immediately informs drinkers when they have had enough liquid to meet their needs.

Unlike food and water, sex is not necessary for individual survival, but is necessary for the survival of the species. Sexual motivation can arise out of social, cultural, and biological motives. Although not essential for survival, sexual motivation is very strong in humans. Even though social and cultural factors play a more important role in human sexual behavior, hormones have important organizational and activational effects. In humans, the hypothalamus controls the release of luteinizing hormone (LH) from the pituitary gland. LH controls the release of masculinizing (androgens) and feminizing (estrogens and progestins) hormones from the ovaries and testes. The hypothalamus, therefore, apparently plays a role in regulating the sex drive by sensing hormone levels and affecting their secretion through pituitary gland stimulation.

Hormonal factors affect sexual behavior less in more physiologically advanced species. Hormones do control sexual behavior in lower mammals—they mate only during **ovulation** (the monthly release of an egg from the ovary) when the female secretes pheromones, which attract the male.

Heterosexuals are attracted to individuals of the opposite sex. **Homosexuals** are attracted to individuals of the same sex. **Bisexuals** are attracted to people of the same and opposite sex. No one theory fully explains why people develop a particular sexual orientation. Some theories are **biological** in nature, suggesting that there may be a genetic or hormonal reason. Others have suggested that environmental factors play a key role. Still others argue that sex-role orientation is a learned behavior. Some feel that childhood experiences and family factors are important.

Achievement Motivation

Social motives are conditions that direct people toward establishing or maintaining relationships with others. Social motives are learned through socialization and cultural conditioning. **Social needs** are internal conditions related to feelings about self or others and establishing and maintaining relationships. The **need for achievement (nAch)** is a social need that directs a person to constantly strive for excellence and success.

Henry Murray identified a number of social motives or needs and believed that people have these social motives in differing degrees. He developed the Thematic Apperception Test (TAT) to measure the strength of these various needs. The need for achievement was included on Murray's list of needs and was defined as the need to accomplish something difficult and to perform at a high standard of excellence.

David McClelland and others have been interested in the effects of high or low needs for achievement. They found that people with a high nAch tend to set goals of moderate difficulty. They pursue goals that are challenging yet attainable. They actively pursue present and future successes and are willing to take risks. They persist after repeated failures, plan for the future, and take pride in their success.

Achievement motivation appears to be learned and related to child-rearing practices and values in the home. Parents may be more likely to have children with a high nAch if they give their children responsibilities, stress independence, and praise them for genuine accomplishments.

There is evidence that, at times, both men and women experience fear of success. Fear of success occurs when someone worries that success in competitive achievement situations will lead to unpleasant consequences (such as unpopularity).

Emotion includes a subjective conscious experience or cognitive component, bodily or physiological arousal, and overt or behavioral expressions.

As humans, we use our emotions to communicate our feelings to others. Emotions are automatic and involuntary. They also guide our behavior and appear to be more complex in humans than in any other animal.

ELEMENTS OF THE EMOTIONAL EXPERIENCE

Emotional reactions are associated with arousal of the autonomic nervous system (ANS). The **autonomic nervous system** is a division of the peripheral nervous system, which is concerned with involuntary functions of the body and regulates the activity of the glands, smooth muscles, and blood vessels. The autonomic nervous system is also responsible for the flight-or-fight response that occurs during emergency situations. When this response occurs, the pupils dilate, heart rate accelerates, respiration increases, adrenaline is secreted, and digestion is inhibited. The autonomic responses that accompany emotions, therefore, are controlled by the brain.

The **galvanic skin response (GSR)** describes an increase in electrical conductivity of the skin that occurs when the sweat glands increase their activity. GSR is often used as a measure of autonomic arousal and emotional reactions.

The polygraph or lie detector test is based on the assumption that there is a link between lying and emotions. Lie detector tests measure respiration, heart rate, blood pressure, and the galvanic skin response. Lie detectors do not detect lies; instead they detect nervousness, as measured by various physiological reactions. Usually lie detectors are accurate around two-thirds of the time, but many courts do not allow lie detector evidence. This is because some people may appear nervous when they are innocent and others may appear calm even though they are guilty.

THEORIES OF EMOTIONS

Various theories have attempted to explain the experience of emotions. William James and Carl Lange proposed that people experience physiological changes and interpret these changes as emotions. In other words, emotions follow behavior and not vice versa. For instance, you feel afraid after you begin to perspire. (You do not perspire because you are afraid.)

Stimulus ———➤ **Arousal/Behavior** ———➤ **Emotion**

(Snake) ———➤ (Perspiration) ———➤ (Fear)

Walter Cannon and a colleague, P. Bard, felt that the physiological changes in many emotional states were identical. Because of this, people cannot determine their emotional state only from their physiological state. The Cannon-Bard Theory argues that emotion occurs when the thalamus sends signals simultaneously to the cortex and to the autonomic nervous system.

                                                ➚ **Autonomic Arousal** (Perspiration)

Stimulus ———➤ Thalamus ⟨

(Snake) ➚   ➘ **Emotion** (Fear)

The **Common Sense Theory** argues that we react to emotions once they occur.

Stimulus ———➤ **Emotion** ———➤ **Reaction/Behavior**

(Snake) ———➤ (Fear) ———➤ (Perspiration)

Stanley Schachter's view of emotion is a cognitive approach. It is referred to as the **Schachter-Singer Theory**. This theory proposes that emotion occurs when physiological arousal causes us to search for reasons for this arousal. We examine the environment for an explanation for this arousal. Emotions are determined, therefore, by labeling our arousal based on what is occurring in our environment.

Physiological Arousal ——→ Appraise Environment ——→ Emotion

(Perspiration) ——→ (A snake is present) ——→ (Fear of snake)

or

(Perspiration) ——→ (I'm on a date) ——→ (I'm in love)

The **facial feedback theory** proposes that involuntary movements of the face send feedback to the brain about which emotion is being felt. This theory proposes that people universally show the same expressions when experiencing the same emotions. Five different universal facial expressions were suggested and include happiness, anger, disgust, sadness, and fear-surprise. For instance,

Facial expression ——→ Emotion

(Smiling) ——→ (Happy)

Robert Plutchik proposed that emotions evolved because they help a species to survive. He felt that emotions are inherited behavioral patterns, and modified by experience.

According to Plutchik, there are eight **primary emotions**: sadness, fear, surprise, anger, disgust, anticipation, joy, and acceptance. Other emotions are **secondary** (or composites of primary emotions). For instance,

Surprise + Sadness = Disappointment

Fear + Acceptance = Submission

Plutchik's theory has elements of both the Common Sense Theory and Schachter's theory, as outlined below.

Stimulus ——→ event	Cognitive ——→ assessment of stimulus event	Primary ——→ emotion	Behavior in response to primary emotion
(Snake) ——→	(You determine situation is dangerous.) ——→	(You feel ——→ fear.)	(You run away.)

ERIKSON'S PSYCHOSOCIAL STAGES OF DEVELOPMENT

Erik Erikson proposed eight stages of social-emotional/personality development. He is one of the few theorists to discuss development throughout the life span—infancy through old age.

Erikson was trained as a psychoanalytic or Freudian theorist. Erikson's theory, however, is very different from Freud's. For instance, Erikson believed that personality continues to develop over the entire life span (not just through childhood). Also, Erikson did not stress unconscious motives or desires. However, like Freud, Erikson did feel that events that occur early in development can leave a permanent mark on one's later social-emotional development.

A description of Erikson's eight stages of psychosocial development follows. Each stage represents a specific task or dilemma that must be resolved with some degree of success for further development.

ORAL-SENSORY (Birth-1 1/2 years)

Trust versus Mistrust   Infant's needs must be met by responsive, sensitive caretakers. If this occurs, a basic sense of trust and optimism develops. If not, mistrust and fear of the future results.

MUSCULAR-ANAL (1 1/2 – 4 years)

Autonomy versus Shame and Doubt   Children begin to express self-control by climbing, exploring, touching, and toilet training. Parents can foster a sense of autonomy by encouraging children to try new things. If restrained or punished too harshly, shame and doubt can develop.

LOCOMOTOR-GENITAL (4 – 6 years)

Initiative versus Guilt   Children are asked to assume more responsibility. Through play, children learn to plan, undertake, and carry out a task. Parents can encourage initiative by giving children the freedom to play, to use their imagination, etc. Children who are criticized or discouraged from taking the initiative learn to feel guilty.

LATENCY (6 – 11 years)

Industry versus Inferiority   In elementary school, children learn skills that are valued by society. Success or failure while learning these skills can have lasting effects on a child's feelings of adequacy.

ADOLESCENCE

Identity versus Role Confusion

The development of identity involves finding out who we are, what we value, and where we are headed in life. In their search for identity, adolescents experiment with different roles. If we establish an integrated image of ourselves as a unique person, then we establish a sense of identity. If not, role confusion results and can be expressed through anger and resentment.

YOUNG ADULTHOOD
Intimacy versus Isolation

At this time we are concerned with establishing intimate, long-term relationships with others. If we have successfully resolved the identity crisis, then we can be warm and open with others. If we are unsure of our identity or if we have developed an unhealthy identity, then we may avoid others or keep them at an emotional distance.

ADULTHOOD
Generativity versus Stagnation

This stage centers around a concern for the next generation. Successful development shows adults sharing their life-acquired wisdom and caring for the growth of the community. Complacency in this stage leads to stagnation and potentially to depression and loneliness.

MATURITY
Ego Integrity versus Despair

If a person looking back on his or her life can believe that it has been meaningful and relatively successful, then a sense of integrity develops. If all that is seen is wasted opportunities and meaninglessness, then the person will be disgusted. Despair will follow disgust if the person feels it is too late to change.

11 LEARNING

CLASSICAL CONDITIONING

Learning is defined as a relative permanent change in behavior as a result of experience, practice, or both. **Conditioning** is the process of forming associations. Learning and conditioning are inferred from behavior because they cannot be observed directly.

Classical conditioning always involves a **reflexive** or **respondent behavior**. This means that classical conditioning produces an automatic response to a stimulus. **Classical** or **respondent conditioning** occurs when a neutral stimulus that does not trigger a reflexive behavior is conditioned so that it will elicit an automatic response. Conditioning occurs because the neutral stimulus has been associated with a stimulus that automatically triggers a response.

It appears that both humans and animals may be biologically prepared to learn some associations more readily than others. The associations that are more readily learned may be ones that increase chances for survival.

Ivan Pavlov (1849–1936), a Russian physiologist, classically conditioned dogs using the salivary reflex. Dogs normally respond to food by salivating. They do not have to be conditioned to salivate to food. Dogs do not, however, automatically salivate to the sound of a bell ringing. This is what Pavlov conditioned them to do. He would ring the bell, present the food, and the dogs would salivate. He repeated this procedure until the bell alone would cause the dogs to salivate. They had learned to associate the sound of the bell with the presentation of food.

The terms used to describe classical conditioning include:

Unconditioned Stimulus (UCS) — The stimulus that automatically produces a reflex. (In Pavlov's study this was the food.)

Unconditioned Response (UCR) — An automatic response to the UCS; a natural response that does not require conditioning for it to occur. (In Pavlov's study this was salivation to the food.)

Conditioned Stimulus (CS) — A neutral stimulus that does not normally elicit an automatic response; only after pairing it repeatedly with the

UCS does the CS come to elicit a conditioned response. (In Pavlov's study this was the bell.)

Conditioned Response (CR) — The learned response that occurs when the CS is presented alone, without the UCS. (In Pavlov's study, the CR was salivation that occurred to the bell alone; no food was present.)

The standard classical conditioning paradigm is:

		UCS (food)	$\rightarrow$	**UCR** (salivation)
CS (bell)	+	**UCS** (food)	$\rightarrow$	**UCR** (salivation)
		CS alone (bell alone)	$\rightarrow$	**CR** (salivation)

Step 2 is repeated until the CS alone will prompt the CR.

The timing or **temporal relationship** between the conditioned stimulus (CS) and unconditioned stimulus (UCS) can vary:

Forward pairing — CS presented before UCS
Backward pairing — CS presented after UCS
Simultaneous pairing — CS and UCS occur at exactly the same time.

Research has indicated that forward conditioning leads to the best conditioning, especially if the CS precedes the UCS by about half a second. Backward and simultaneous conditioning are much less effective.

After classical conditioning has taken place, the conditioned stimulus (CS) must be paired with, or reinforced by, the unconditioned stimulus (UCS) at least some of the time or else the conditioned response (CR) will disappear. The process of eliminating the conditioned response (CR) by no longer pairing the unconditioned stimulus (UCS) with the conditioned stimulus (CS) is called **extinction**. Extinction will take place, therefore, if the conditioned stimulus (CS) is presented repeatedly without the unconditioned stimulus (UCS). Extinction is a method that is used intentionally to eliminate conditioned responses (CR).

The conditioned response might recover, however, if a rest period or break follows extinction. A rest period would occur if the conditioned stimulus (CS) is not presented for a period of time. After this rest period, the very next time the conditioned stimulus (CS) is presented the conditioned response (CR) is likely to occur (even though it was previously extinguished). If the conditioned response (CR) does reappear, this is called spontaneous recovery. **Spontaneous recovery** is, therefore, the reoccurrence of a conditioned response (CR) after a rest interval has followed extinction.

Reconditioning occurs after extinction has taken place and the conditioned stimulus (CS) and unconditioned stimulus (UCS) are again paired. Learning (i.e., responding with a CR when the CS is presented) is usually quicker during reconditioning than it was during initial conditioning.

Stimulus generalization occurs when a conditioned response (CR) occurs to a stimulus that only resembles or is similar to the conditioned stimulus (CS) but is not identical to it. For instance, Pavlov's dogs were classically conditioned to salivate to a bell (the CS), but if the first time they heard a buzzer they also salivated, this would be stimulus generalization. They were never conditioned with the buzzer, but they responded because the sound resembled that of the bell.

Stimulus discrimination occurs when the differences between stimuli are noticed and, thus, the stimuli are not responded to in similar ways. For instance, stimulus discrimination would occur if Pavlov's dogs did not salivate to the sound of the buzzer, even if it sounded similar to the bell. This would indicate that the dogs could discriminate these two sounds and, as a result, respond differently to each.

Researchers have used humans as well as animals in classical conditioning studies. In humans, emotional reactions occur sometimes as a result of classical conditioning because emotions are involuntary, automatic responses. For instance, **phobias** (intense, irrational fears) may develop as a result of classical conditioning.

The most famous classical conditioning study using a human subject was one conducted by American researcher John Watson (1878–1958). Although this study is considered unethical today and some have suggested that it is more myth or legend than fact, most textbooks mention the Little Albert study when discussing classical conditioning. Little Albert was an 11-month old infant who initially was not afraid of laboratory white rats. Watson classically conditioned Albert to fear these rats by pairing the presentation of the rat with a loud noise that scared the infant. The diagram of this study would be:

		Noise	→	Fear response
		(UCS)		(UCR)

Rat	+	Noise	→	Fear response
(CS)		(UCS)		(UCR)

eventually,

	Rat alone	→	Fear response
	(CS)		(CR)

Higher order conditioning occurs when a new neutral stimulus is associated with a conditioned stimulus (CS) and eventually comes to produce the conditioned response (CR). If after Albert was classically conditioned, a dog was always paired with the rat, eventually Albert would display the fear response to the dog. A diagram of this higher order conditioning example would be:

	Rat alone	→	Fear
	(CS)		(CR)

Dog	+	Rat	→	Fear
(new stimulus)		(CS)		(CR)

eventually,

	Dog alone	→	Fear
	(CS)		(CR)

OPERANT AND INSTRUMENTAL CONDITIONING

In **operant** or **instrumental conditioning**, responses are learned because of their consequences. Unlike classical conditioning, the responses learned in operant/instrumental conditioning are voluntary.

There are subtle measurement differences between operant and instrumental conditioning. Because both of these are similar in most respects, however, the term operant conditioning will be used to refer to both.

American psychologist Edward L. Thorndike's (1874–1949) **Law of Effect** states that a behavior that is rewarded tends to be repeated, while behavior that is not rewarded takes place only at random. What is learned during operant or instrumental conditioning is that certain responses are instrumental in producing desired effects in the environment.

Reinforcers are consequences for behavior and can be anything that increases the likelihood that a behavior will be repeated. Reinforcers can be positive or negative. Both positive and negative reinforcers have the potential to increase behaviors. Positive reinforcers are rewards or other positive consequences that follow behaviors and increase the likelihood that the behaviors will occur again in the future. Giving your dog a biscuit each time he sits on command is an example of positive reinforcement.

Negative reinforcers are anything a subject will work to avoid or terminate. Nagging behaviors are examples of negative reinforcement because we often will do something (anything!) to stop the nagging. For instance, a parent who buys a child a candy bar to stop a child's nagging in the grocery store is responding to negative reinforcement. **Escape conditioning** occurs when a subject learns that a particular response will terminate an aversive stimulus. The parent who buys a nagging child candy has escaped the nagging by purchasing candy. **Avoidance conditioning** occurs when a subject responds to a signal in a way that prevents exposure to an aversive stimulus. The candy counter at the store may become a signal that parents should buy candy if they want to avoid or prevent their child's nagging.

Reinforcers can also be primary or secondary. **Primary reinforcers** are necessary to meet biological needs and include such things as food, water, air, etc. **Secondary reinforcers** have acquired value and are not necessary for survival. Grades, money, pat on the back, etc. are examples of secondary reinforcers.

A reinforcer becomes less effective in promoting future behavior the longer the delay between a behavior and its reinforcement. The declining effectiveness of reinforcement with increasing delay is called the **gradient of reinforcement**.

Extinction can also occur in operant conditioning. The goal is the same as it is in classical conditioning, to decrease or eliminate a response. **Extinction** occurs in operant conditioning by removing the reinforcer. For example, the dog stops receiving dog biscuits for sitting or the child gets no candy for nagging. Once these reinforcers are removed, both sitting and nagging should decrease and/or be eliminated. **Spontaneous recovery** can also occur in operant conditioning.

How easily an operant response is extinguished is dependent, in part, on how often that response was reinforced, or its **schedule of reinforcement**. A continuous schedule of reinforcement happens when each and every response is reinforced (100 percent of the time). Each time your dog sits on command, he receives a biscuit. Behaviors that are continuously reinforced are easier to extinguish than behaviors that are not reinforced 100 percent of the time.

Behaviors that are not reinforced each time they occur are on an **intermittent**, or **partial**, **schedule of reinforcement**. There are four possible partial schedules of reinforcement:

Fixed ratio schedule: Reinforcement is given after a fixed number of responses (e.g., every third time your dog sits, he receives a biscuit). Being paid on a piece-rate basis is an example of a fixed ratio schedule. The fixed ratio schedule produces a high rate of responding with a slight pause after each reinforcement is given. Fixed ratio schedules produce the fastest rate of extinction because the subject realizes quickly that reinforcement has stopped.

Variable ratio schedule: Reinforcement is given after a variable number of responses. Thus, on one occasion, reinforcement may occur after 10 responses and on another occasion after 50, etc. The rate of reinforcement depends upon the rate of responding: the faster, the more reinforcers received. This schedule produces steady, high rates of responding and is extremely resistant to extinction. Slot machines are based on variable ratio schedules.

Fixed interval schedule: Reinforcement is given after the first response after a given amount of time has elapsed. This may mean a reinforcer every five minutes, for example. Being paid once per month is another example. Fixed interval schedules produce a low rate of responding at the beginning of each interval and a high rate toward the end of each interval.

Variable interval schedule: Reinforcement is given after the first response after a varying amount of time has elapsed. Pop quizzes often occur on a variable interval schedule. The variable interval schedule produces a steady, slow rate of responding.

In general, the ratio schedules produce higher response rates than the interval schedules. Variable schedules are usually harder to extinguish than are fixed schedules because variable schedules are less predictable.

American behaviorist B. F. Skinner (1904–1990) devised a chamber, known as a **Skinner box**, to study the effects of various schedules of reinforcement on the behavior of small animals such as rats and pigeons. During acquisition, or learning, each time a lever in the Skinner box was pressed, a food pellet was dispensed into a food dish. A speaker or light signal was also used to indicate conditions of reinforcement or extinction. In some studies, the grid floor was electrified, and the electric current could be turned off by pressing the lever. The speaker or lights signaled when the current would be turned on and, in avoidance trials, the animal had a certain amount of time to press the lever to avoid the shock.

Shaping involves systematically reinforcing closer and closer approximations of the desired behavior. When a rat is first placed in the Skinner box, it doesn't know that pressing the lever will result in a food reward and may never press the lever on its own. Lever pressing can be conditioned through shaping — each step closer to the lever results in a food reward.

Discriminative stimuli serve as cues that indicate a response is likely to be reinforced. The light in the Skinner box can be a discriminative stimulus. When the light is on, lever pressing results in a food reward. When it is off, lever pressing is not reinforced. The animal will eventually learn to discriminate and to press the lever only when the light is on.

Punishment is also an operant conditioning technique. The goal of punishment is to decrease behavior. Punishment involves the presentation of an **aversive stimulus**, or undesirable consequence, after a behavior has occurred. Something negative can be added or something positive can be taken away. Receiving a ticket for speeding and being placed on house restriction are two examples of punishment.

Timing is very important for punishment to be effective — the sooner the punishment is delivered after the undesired behavior occurred, the better the learning. Even very short delays can reduce the effectiveness of punishment. Punishment must also be severe enough to eliminate the undesirable response.

Punishment may have undesirable side effects. Punishment often provides a model of aggressive behavior, and the person punished may learn that aggression is a method for solving problems. Punishment alone does not teach appropriate behavior. The person providing the punishment can become a feared agent to be avoided. Punishment can get out of hand and become abusive. Many behaviorists today suggest that punishment be avoided as a method used for conditioning. Instead, they recommend the use of extinction to weaken an inappropriate response and reinforcement to increase appropriate behaviors.

OBSERVATIONAL LEARNING

Observational learning occurs when we learn new behaviors by watching others. This is sometimes called social learning, vicarious conditioning, or modeling.

Observational learning is guided by four processes.

Attention — Attention must be paid to the salient features of another's actions. Prestige or status of a model can influence whether another's actions are noticed.

Retention — Observed behaviors must be remembered in order to be carried out.

Reproduction of Action — We must be able to carry out the behavior that we observed.

Motivation — There must be some reason for carrying out the behavior. Observing someone being rewarded for a behavior increases the likelihood that the behavior will be performed.

Vicarious learning occurs when we learn the relationship between a response and its consequences by watching others. **Vicarious reinforcement** occurs when we observe the model receiving reinforcement. **Vicarious punishment** happens when we observe the model being punished for engaging in a behavior.

Edward Tolman (1886–1959) differentiated between learning and performance. **Latent learning** is learning that is not demonstrated at the time that it occurs. For instance, we may learn a behavior when we observe it, but never display the behavior. Thus, we may learn behavior but never perform it. Tolman maintained that behavior may not be demonstrated until it is motivating to do so.

The classic research on observational learning was conducted by **Albert Bandura** and his colleagues. This research included children watching and imitating an adult's aggressive behavior toward a Bobo doll. Bandura found that children learned the aggressive behavior even when the adult was not reinforced for this behavior. Later research indicated that children who watched an aggressive model being reinforced were much more aggressive in a similar situation than children who saw the model punished for the aggressive actions. Through his research, Bandura has demonstrated that both classical and operant conditioning can take place through observational learning — by observing another's conditioning.

12 SCHOOLING AND INTERVENTION

DAY CARE

Even though more children than ever before are attending day care, there have been relatively few well-controlled studies that have looked at the effects of day care on development. Summarized below are the most consistent findings to date.

Children who attend day care usually score higher than children who do not attend day care on tests of intelligence. Non-day care children, however, usually catch up once they enter kindergarten and elementary school.

Children in day care tend to be more socially skilled—more cooperative, more confident, and better able to take the perspective of another. Day care children also tend to be more aggressive and noncompliant (less likely to carry out an adult's request). Some have suggested this is because day care children have learned to think for themselves, not a symptom of maladjustment. There is a slight tendency for day care children to be classified as insecurely attached (36 percent vs. 29 percent for home care children). Although statistically significant, some have questioned the practical significance of a 7 percent difference.

APPLICATION OF DEVELOPMENTAL PRINCIPLES WITHIN THE SCHOOL

It is one thing for teachers to have command of their subject matter. It is a given that English teachers will be able to write well, that math teachers will be able to compute and calculate, that science teachers will know and understand science, and so forth. However, it is something else—and something at least as important—that teachers know how to teach.

When teachers understand learners, that is, when teachers understand developmental processes common to all learners and how environmental features and learning styles—varied and diverse—affect learning, then teachers are better able to design and deliver effective instruction. Although there may be some intuitive aspects to teaching (and it seems that some people were born to teach), teaching skills can be acquired through processes of introspection, observation, direct instruction, self-evaluation, and experimentation.

How teachers teach should be directly related to how learners learn. Theories of cognitive development describe how learners learn new information and acquire new skills. There are many theories of cognitive development, two of which will be included in this review: the Piagetian (or Neo-Piagetian) theory and the information processing theory.

Piagetian theory (including Neo-Piagetian theory), describes learning in discrete and predictable stages. Therefore, teachers who understand this theory can provide students with developmentally-appropriate instruction. This theory also describes learners moving from simpler ways of thinking to more complex ways of problem-solving and thinking. For teachers, there are many important implications of this theoretical perspective. For example, teachers must create enriched environments that present learners with multiple opportunities to encounter new and unfamiliar stimuli—be they objects or ideas. Teachers must also provide learners with opportunities to engage in extended dialogue with adults; according to Piaget's theory, conversational interactions with adults are a key component in cognitive development, especially the acquisition of formal operations (or higher-ordered thinking skills). Moreover, it is important that adults (and teachers in particular) model desired behaviors. Teachers must reveal their own complex ways of thinking and solving problems to students.

On the other hand, information processing theories of human development take a different approach to describing and understanding how learners learn. Based on a computer metaphor and borrowing computer imagery to describe how people learn, information processing theories begin by determining the processing demands of a particular cognitive challenge (or problem to solve). This necessitates a detailed task-analysis of how the human mind changes external objects or events into a useful form according to certain, precisely-specified rules or strategies; this is similar to the way a computer programmer programs a computer to perform a function. Thus, information processing theories focus on the process, how the learner arrives at a response or answer.

A brief analysis of one information processing theory will serve to illustrate this point. Sternberg's (1985) triarchic theory of intelligence is a theory taking into account three features of learning. Those three features are (1) the mechanics or components of intelligence (including both higher-ordered thinking processes, such as planning, decision making and problem solving, and lower-ordered processes, such as making inferences, mapping, selectively encoding information, retaining information in memory, transferring new information in memory, and so forth); (2) the learner's experiences; and (3) the learner's context (including the adaptation to and the shaping and selecting of environments).

According to Sternberg, learners' use of the mechanics of intelligence is influenced by learners' experiences. To illustrate, some cognitive processes (such as those required in reading) become automatized as a result of continued exposure to and practice of those skills. Learners who come from homes where parents read and where there are lots of different reading materials tend to be more proficient readers; certainly, learners who read a lot become more proficient readers. Those learners who are exposed to reading activities and who have ample opportunities to practice reading have greater skill and expertise in reading. In a cyclical manner, students who have skills in reading like to read. Conversely, those who lack reading skills don't like to read. Students who don't like to read, don't read; thus, their reading skills, lacking practice, fail to improve.

An information processing approach acknowledges that not only are individuals influenced by their environments which they then adapt to, but individuals also are active in shaping their own environments. In other words, a child who wants to read but who has no books at home may ask parents to buy books, may go to the library to read, or may check out books to read at home.

Information processing theory is of interest to educators because of its insistence on the idea that intelligent performance can be facilitated through instruction and direct training. In sum, intelligent thinking can be taught. Sternberg has urged teachers to identify the mental processes that academic tasks require and to teach learners those processes. He challenges teachers to teach learners what processes to use, when and how to use them, and how to combine them into strategies for solving problems and accomplishing assignments.

Teachers who wish to follow Sternberg's advice might choose to begin teaching by identifying **instructional objectives**, that is, what students should be able to do as a result of instruction. Second, these teachers would analyze the objectives in terms of identifying the **instructional outcomes**, the tasks or assignments that students can perform as a result of achieving the instructional objectives. Third, teachers would analyze instructional outcomes in terms of the **cognitive skills**, or mental processes, required to perform those tasks or assignments. After following these three steps and identifying instructional objectives, instructional outcomes, and cognitive skills involved, the teachers would be ready to conduct a

preassessment (or pretest) to determine what students already know.

Instruction is then based on the results of the preassessment, with teachers focusing on teaching directly the cognitive skills needed in order for students to perform the task(s). Following instruction, teachers would conduct a **post-assessment** (or post-test) to evaluate the results of instruction. Further instruction would be based on the results of the post-assessment, that is, whether or not students had achieved expected outcomes and whether or not teachers had achieved instructional objectives.

Regardless of which theoretical perspective is adopted by teachers, and teachers may sometimes find themselves taking a rather eclectic approach and borrowing elements from several theoretical bases, it is helpful for teachers to consider if they are structuring their classrooms to satisfy learners' needs or merely their own needs as teachers. Furthermore, if the teachers' goal is to increase teaching effectiveness by facilitating learners' knowledge and skill acquisition, then teachers will engage continuously in a process of self-examination and self-evaluation.

INTERVENTION PROGRAMS AND SERVICES

Childhood intervention programs were originally developed by U.S. government and private educational agencies acting on the supposition that intelligence is strongly influenced by environment, and therefore poor and culturally deprived people are at a great disadvantage academically. The best known of these intervention programs is Project Headstart. In accordance with the theory of environmental influence, underprivileged children ready to enter first grade—about five years old—were given experience with toys, books, and games with which most middle-class children are familiar. It began as a summer program and lasted eight weeks.

Project Headstart was not completely successful. The children made immediate gains in IQ, but these gains were unstable: the children's IQs returned to the pre-intervention level as soon as the program ended. Opponents of Headstart, who believe that intelligence is determined genetically, used this information to support racist claims that blacks had less innate intellectual ability than did whites.

Owing to its poor organization, however, Headstart was destined to fail from its inception. It simply was not designed to play an important enough role in the lives of the children. Mainly, the children's experience in the program was isolated from their family environments. The enrichment did not extend to the rest of the family, the unit that has the most significant influence on a child. In addition, an eight-week intervention program cannot compensate for the cultural deprivation a five-year-old minority child has experienced. Intervention programs must begin earlier, last longer, and make more complete changes in a child's life.

The new philosophy of childhood intervention is to involve the mothers of the children in the programs: mothers are taught how to be effective teachers. This kind of intervention has been extremely successful. Children's IQ scores rise, thus lessening the disparity in group IQs. Moreover, there is a secondary benefit to this kind of intervention. When a mother is involved as the teacher, her self-esteem is raised, her cooperation increases, she becomes closer to her child, and she can spread her learning to other mothers in the area.

In view of the new program's positive results, the evidence against the efficacy of intervention programs is insubstantial. Even the best intervention programs, however, cannot affect the pervasive deprivation that exists in poverty areas. Pre-natal care is often inadequate, and nutrition is often insufficient. Self-respect is frequently low. All these factors have negative effects on a child's intellectual development. Nevertheless, even if intervention programs are not completely successful, it cannot be concluded that the environment is not an important factor in the determination of intelligence.

TRAINING IN PARENTING SKILLS

Studies show that behaviors, positive and negative, are passed down through generations. Often subconsciously, a parent reacts to a situation in the manner in which he or she saw his or her parent respond. This is particularly threatening in the case of abusive or neglectful behavior.

Today, it is commonly believed that the best way to end a cycle of poor parenting is through parental retraining. Parents are taught through discussion and role play how to deal successfully with stressful situations arising in the family. These situations vary from dealing with a crying baby to dealing with a rebellious teenager using inappropriate language. Because their initial response was learned vicariously through watching their parents, the adults need to be retrained in the more appropriate methods of parenting. Parenting classes have proven effective for both male and female parents.

13 ATYPICAL DEVELOPMENT

DEFINING PSYCHOLOGICAL DISORDERS

This section describes how psychological disorders are defined and diagnosed and presents explanations of their possible causes. Because it is often difficult to distinguish normal from abnormal behavior, there have been several approaches for defining abnormal behavior. None of the definitions presented, however, is broad enough to cover all instances of abnormal or psychological disorders.

Deviation from Average (Statistical Approach)	A statistical definition. Behaviors that are infrequent or rare are considered abnormal. The problem is that not all rare behaviors (e.g., genius) are abnormal.
Deviation from Ideal (Valuative Approach)	Considers standard behavior or what most people do. Abnormal behavior occurs when behavior deviates from the norm or what most people do. Problems with this definition are that norms change over time and people don't always agree on what ideal behavior is.
Subjective Discomfort (Personal Approach)	Behavior is abnormal if it produces distress or anxiety in an individual. A problem with this definition is that people may be feeling no distress but may be engaging in bizarre behaviors.
Humanistic-Existential Model (Phenomenological Model)	Abnormal behaviors occur as a result of failure to fulfill one's self-potential. Emphasizes the effects of a faulty self-image. Client-centered and Gestalt therapies are used to increase self-acceptance.
Cognitive Model	Faulty or negative thinking can cause depression or anxiety. Focus of treatment is on changing faulty, irrational, or negative thinking.

DIAGNOSING AND CLASSIFYING PSYCHOLOGICAL DISORDERS

A number of schemes have been developed for classifying and diagnosing psychological disorders. No scheme is perfect, however, and all have been criticized.

One standard system, used by most professionals, is the **Diagnostic and Statistical Manual of Mental Disorders (DSM), Fourth Edition**. Published by the American Psychiatric Association, DSM describes more than 300 specific mental disorders. An historical overview of the DSM follows.

DSM   Published in 1952 according to a format that had been used by the army during World War II.

DSM-II   In 1968 the DSM was revised to conform with different classifications used by the World Health Organization.

DSM-III   A 1977 revision that described mental disorders in greater detail.

DSM-III-R A revision of the third edition that was published in 1987, which clarified and updated the previous revision.

DSM-IV   A revised edition was published in 1994.

DSM-IV-TR Released in 2000, this text revision saw most of its changes in Associated Features and Disorders; Specific Culture, Age, and Gender Features; Prevalence; Course; and the Familial Pattern sections.

DSM-IV-TR evaluates each individual according to five dimensions, or axes, and is therefore considered a multiaxial system of classification.

Axis I   Describes any mental disorder or clinical syndrome that might be present.

Axis II   Describes any personality disorder that might be present.

Axis III   Describes any physical or medical disorder that might be present.

Axis IV   Rates severity of psychosocial stressors in the individual's life during the past year.

Axis V   Assesses level of adaptive functioning currently and during the past year.

The major categories of mental disorders described in DSM-IV-TR are described in the remaining sections of this section.

ANXIETY DISORDERS

Description. Intense feelings of apprehension and anxiety that impede daily functioning. Approximately 8–15 percent of adults in this country are affected by anxiety disorders.

Types. Different types of anxiety disorders include:

Generalized Anxiety Disorders	Characterized by continuous, long-lasting uneasiness and tension. Person usually cannot identify a specific cause.
Panic Disorders	Recurrent attacks of overwhelming anxiety that include heart palpitations, shortness of breath, sweating, faintness, and great fear. Often referred to as **panic attacks**.
Phobic Disorders	Intense, irrational fears of specific objects or situations. Common phobias include fears of snakes, insects, spiders, and mice/rats. **Agoraphobia** is the fear of being in public places (or away from home) and is often associated with panic disorders.
Obsessive-Compulsive Disorders	**Obsessions** are persistent, unwanted thoughts that are unreasonable (e.g., worry over germs). **Compulsions** are repetitive behaviors performed according to certain rules or rituals (e.g., repetitive counting or checking).

Causes. No one theory or model adequately explains all cases of anxiety disorders. **Genetic factors** play a role; if one identical twin has a panic disorder, for example, there is a 30 percent chance that the other twin will have it also. Chemical deficiencies in the brain (low levels of certain neurotransmitters) and an overreaction to lactic acid may produce some kinds of anxiety disorder, especially obsessive-compulsive disorder. Anxiety can also be a learned response to stress. These disorders can also be inappropriate and inaccurate cognitions about one's world.

SOMATOFORM DISORDERS

Description. Patterns of behavior characterized by complaints of physical symptoms in the absence of any real physical illness. About 1 person in 300 has a somatoform disorder, and they are slightly more common in women than in men.

Types. Hypochondriasis and conversion disorder are the two main types of somatoform disorders.

Hypochondriasis

Involves a constant fear of illness, and normal aches and pains are misinterpreted as signs of disease.

Conversion Disorder

An appearance of a physical disturbance or illness that is caused by psychological reasons. Usually has a rapid onset. Numbness or paralysis, such as glove anesthesia, for example.

Cause. Conversion disorders seem to occur when an individual is under some kind of stress. The physical condition allows the person to escape or reduce the source of this stress.

MOOD DISORDERS

Description. **Mood disorders** involve moods or emotions that are extreme and unwarranted. These disturbances in emotional feelings are strong enough to intrude on everyday living.

Types. The most serious types of mood disorders are major depression and bipolar disorders.

Major Depression

Characterized by frequent episodes of intense hopelessness, lowered self-esteem, problems concentrating and making decisions, changes in eating and sleeping patterns, fatigue, reduced sex drive, and thoughts of death. Occurs twice as frequently among females as males. Can occur at any time during the life cycle; an estimated 5–8 percent of all Americans will suffer from major depression at least once in their lifetime. Approximately one-half of people who attempt suicide are depressed.

Dysthymic Disorder

More common and less severe than major depression. Similar symptoms as for major depression, but they are less intense and last for a longer period (at least two years).

Seasonal Affective Disorder (SAD)

Depressive symptoms occur during the winter months when the periods of daylight are shorter. An affected person usually craves extra sleep and eats more carbohydrates.

Bipolar I Disorder	Characterized by two emotional extremes—depression and mania. **Mania** is an elated, very active emotional state. Manic episodes alternate every few days, weeks, or years with periods of deep depression. Sometimes mood swings and behavior are severe enough to be classified as psychosis.
Bipolar II Disorder	Also characterized by extreme mood swings. Episodes include depression and at least one episode of **hypomania** (mania that is not severe enough to interfere with everyday life).
Cyclothymia	A slightly more common pattern of less extreme mood swings than bipolar disorder.

Causes. Both psychological and biological theories have been proposed to explain the cause of mood disorders. There is evidence that both are correct.

Traditional **psychodynamic theory** states, for example, that depression is more frequent in people with strong dependency needs and represents anger or aggression turned inward at oneself. Other theorists have related mood disorders to cognitive or learning factors. For instance, Martin Seligman suggested that depression results from **learned helplessness**, or a state where people feel a lack of control over their lives and believe that they cannot cope and escape from stress so they give up trying and become depressed. Aaron Beck proposed that faulty thinking, or cognition, causes depression because depressed people typically see themselves as losers, blaming themselves when anything goes wrong. **Learning theorists** propose that depression is learned through reinforcement or imitation of depressive behaviors.

Biological factors also appear to play a role in mood disorders. For instance, there is evidence that depression can be caused by a chemical imbalance in the brain because the norepinephrine and serotonin systems are malfunctioning. The cyclical nature of many mood disorders suggests that abnormalities in biological rhythms may play a role. Genetics may also be part of it. This appears especially true for bipolar disorder. For example, if one member of an identical-twin pair develops bipolar disorder, 72 percent of the other members usually develop the disorder. Children with depressed parents are also more likely to develop depression.

DISSOCIATIVE DISORDERS

Description. Characterized by a loss of contact with portions of consciousness or memory, resulting in disruptions in one's sense of self. They appear to be an attempt to overcome anxiety and stress by dissociating oneself from the core of one's personality and result in a loss of memory, identity, or consciousness.

Types. The major dissociative disorders are:

Psychogenic Amnesia	Either partial or total memory loss that can last from a few hours to many years. Usually remembers nonthreatening aspects of life. There appears to be no physical cause but often results from stress. (That is, one "doesn't remember" stressful aspects of one's life.)
Psychogenic Fugue	People suddenly leave or "flee" their present life and establish a new, different existence and identity in a new location. Their former life is blocked from memory. Often they return from their fugue state to their former life just as suddenly as they left.
Multiple Personality Disorder	One person develops two or more distinct personalities.

Cause. Dissociative disorders allow people to escape from an anxiety-producing situation. The person either produces a new personality to deal with the stress or the situation that caused the stress is forgotten or left behind. For instance, researchers have found that about 94 percent of people with multiple personalities were abused as children. Not all abused children, however, exhibit multiple personalities.

PERSONALITY DISORDERS

Description. **Personality disorders** are patterns of traits that are long-standing, maladaptive, and inflexible and keep a person from functioning properly in society. Behavior often disrupts social relationships. Personality disorders are coded on Axis II of the DSM-IV-TR system for diagnosing mental disorders.

Types. Representative types of personality disorders are described following.

Antisocial   Displays no regard for moral or ethical rules and continuously violates the rights of others. Is manipulative, impulsive, and lacks feelings for others. Also appears to lack a conscience or guilt.

Narcissistic   An exaggerated sense of self and self-importance; preoccupied with fantasies of success. Lacks empathy. Often expects special treatment.

Paranoid   Continual unjustified suspicion and mistrust of people. Often appears cold and unemotional. Easily offended.

Histrionic   Overreacts and overdramatic in response to minor situations. Often seen as vain, shallow, dependent, or manipulative.

Avoidant   Tends to be a "loner," or social snob. Oversensitive to rejection or possible humiliation. Has low self-esteem.

Schizotypal   Not disturbed enough to be diagnosed as schizophrenic. Strangeness in thinking, speech, and behavior.

Causes. Suggested causes for personality disorders range from problems in family relationships to a biological inability to experience emotions. A growing body of evidence indicates that biological problems may be the cause of many personality disorders.

SCHIZOPHRENIC DISORDERS

Description. **Schizophrenia** is a serious psychotic disorder (i.e., one is out of touch with reality). Schizophrenia is not the same as multiple personality disorder, described previously with the dissociative disorders. Schizophrenia includes disorders of thought. Schizophrenics display problems in both how they think and what they think.

Schizophrenic thinking is often incoherent. For instance, they sometimes use **neologisms**, or words that only have meaning to the person speaking them (e.g., the word "glump"). **Loose associations**, where thought appears logically unconnected, is another characteristic that is sometimes seen. **Word salad** describes a jumble of words that are spoken that do not make sense.

The content of a schizophrenic's thinking is also disturbed. Various kinds of delusions are common. **Delusions** are false beliefs that are maintained even though they are clearly out of touch with reality. Common delusions are beliefs that they are being controlled by someone else, that someone is out to get them, that they are a famous person from history (e.g., the President of the United States), and that their thoughts are being broadcast so that others are able to know what they are thinking.

A person with schizophrenia may also experience **hallucinations**, or the experience of perceiving things that do not actually exist. The most common hallucination is hearing voices that do not exist. Schizophrenics also tend to display **flat** (absent) or **inappropriate affect**. Even dramatic events tend to produce little or no emotional reaction from a schizophrenic. The emotional responses they do display are often bizarre and unexpected. A person with schizophrenia usually has little interest in others and appears socially withdrawn. **Abnormal motor behavior** may also occur, such as unusual pacing back and forth, rocking constantly, or being immobilized for long periods of time. Schizophrenia usually involves a noticeable deterioration in functioning. That is, the person used to function adaptively (and did not display symptoms of schizophrenia) but now the quality of work, social relations, and personal care have deteriorated. Their previous level of functioning has broken down.

Types. Five major subtypes of schizophrenia are described in DSM-IV-TR.

Disorganized	Severe deterioration of adaptive behavior. Speech incoherent. Strange facial grimaces common. Inappropriate silliness, babbling, giggling, and obscene behavior may be displayed. Includes 5 percent of schizophrenics.
Catatonic	Characterized by disordered movement. Alternates between extreme withdrawal where the body is kept very still and extreme excitement where movement is rapid and speech incoherent. **Waxy flexibility** describes the odd posturing. Makes up about 8 percent of all cases.
Paranoid	Delusions of persecution or grandeur. Judgment is impaired and unpredictable. Often includes anxiety, anger, jealousy, or argumentativeness. Hallucinations are common. Tends to appear later in life than the other types. Onset is often sudden. Less impaired. Makes up about 40 percent of all schizophrenics.

Undifferentiated	No one subtype dominates. About 40 percent of all schizophrenics receive this diagnosis.
Residual	Has had a prior episode of schizophrenia but currently is not displaying major symptoms. Subtle indications of schizophrenia may be observed, however.

Causes. Genetic, biological, psychological, and environmental factors have been used to explain the origin of schizophrenia. No one theory, however, can adequately account for all forms of schizophrenia.

Twin studies have suggested a hereditary or genetic component to schizophrenia. When one identical twin is identified as schizophrenic, the other twin has a 42–48% chance of also developing schizophrenia. Children of schizophrenics who are adopted by nonschizophrenics also have a higher incidence of schizophrenia than control populations. Schizophrenia, therefore, does run in families.

Most people with schizophrenic relatives, however, do not develop schizophrenia. This has led researchers to conclude that what might be inherited is a **predisposition**, or genetic vulnerability, for schizophrenia. What is needed for schizophrenia to develop is this genetic predisposition plus environmental stress. This is often referred to as the **predisposition** or **vulnerability model** and the **diathesis-stress model**.

Neurochemical factors are also related to schizophrenia. Schizophrenia appears to be accompanied by changes in the activity of one or more neurotransmitters in the brain. The **dopamine hypothesis** suggests that schizophrenia occurs when there is excess activity in those areas of the brain using dopamine to transmit nerve impulses. Excessive dopamine appears related to delusions.

Some researchers have suggested that structural abnormalities in the brain are linked to schizophrenia. Studies have suggested that schizophrenic individuals have difficulty focusing their attention and display bizarre behaviors because of brain abnormalities. Such structural abnormalities might include shrinking or deterioration of cells in the cerebral cortex that cause enlargements of the brain's fluid-filled ventricles, reduced blood flow in parts of the brain, and abnormalities in **brain lateralization**, or in the ways the hemispheres of the brain communicate with each other.

Psychoanalytic theorists propose that schizophrenia represents a regression to earlier stages in life when the id was the most dominant aspect of personality.

Other theorists assert that schizophrenia is a learned behavior and consists of a set of inappropriate responses to social stimuli. This is sometimes referred to as the **learned-inattention theory**. Defective or faulty communication patterns within the family may also be learned and therefore result in schizophrenia. Such faulty communication might include unintelligible speech, stories with no ending, extensive contradictions, and poor attention to child's attempts at communicating.

The **two-strike theory** suggests a prenatal link to schizophrenia. According to this theory, the **first strike** is an inherited susceptibility of the fetal brain to be disrupted by exposure to the flu virus during the second trimester of pregnancy. The **second strike** occurs when exposure to the flu virus actually occurs during the second trimester of pregnancy. Microscopic examination of the brains of schizophrenics does indicate that whatever is going wrong in their brains probably occurred during the second trimester of pregnancy.

It appears, therefore, that schizophrenia is associated with several possible causes. Schizophrenia is probably not caused by a single factor but by a combination of interrelated variables.

EXTREMES OF INTELLIGENCE

Two basic extremes of intellectual performance are demonstrated on the extreme left and right of the normal distribution for intelligence.

In order to be considered **mentally retarded**, an individual must meet all three of the essential features described below:

1. Intellectual functioning must be significantly below average. Today intelligence test scores of below 70—or 2 standard deviations below the mean—are considered significantly below average.

2. Significant deficits in adaptive functioning must be evident. Adaptive functioning refers to social competence or independent behavior that is expected based on chronological age.

3. Onset must be prior to age 18.

Four general categories or ways of classifying mental retardation include the following:

Category	Percentage	IQ Range	Characteristics
Mild	80 percent	50 – 70	May complete sixth grade academic work; may learn vocational skills and hold a job; may live independently as an adult.
Moderate	12 percent	35 – 49	May complete second grade academic work; can learn social and occupational skills; may hold job in sheltered workshop.
Severe	7 percent	20 – 34	May learn to talk or communicate; through repetition may learn basic health habits; often needs help for simple tasks.
Profound	1 percent	less than 20	Little or no speech; may learn limited self-help skills; requires constant help and supervision.

There are hundreds of known causes of mental retardation. Many of them are biological, genetic, chromosomal, prenatal, perinatal, and postnatal in origin. Mental retardation can also result from environmental influences, such as sensory or maternal deprivation. In some cases (especially mild mental retardation), the cause of an individual child's mental retardation is unknown.

Giftedness is often defined as having an intelligence of 120 to 130 or higher (or having an IQ in the upper 2 to 3 percent of the population). Lewis Terman began a longitudinal study of gifted children in the 1920s. That is, he and others followed the lives of these children as they grew up and became adults. The study will not be completed until the year 2010. The average intelligence score was 150 for the approximately 1,500 children in this study. The findings of this study have challenged the commonly held belief that the intellectually gifted are emotionally disturbed and socially maladjusted. In fact, just the opposite was found. As adults, this group was also more academically and professionally successful than their non-gifted peers.

Creativity is the ability to think about something in novel and unusual ways and to come up with unique solutions to problems.

▼

PRACTICE TEST 1

This test is also on CD-ROM in our special interactive CLEP Human Growth & Development TEST*ware®*. It is highly recommended that you first take this exam on computer. You will then have the additional study features and benefits of enforced timed conditions, individual diagnostic analysis, and instant scoring. See page 2 for guidance on how to get the most out of our CLEP Human Growth & Development book and software.

CLEP HUMAN GROWTH AND DEVELOPMENT
Test 1

(Answer sheets appear in the back of this book.)

TIME: 90 Minutes
90 Questions

DIRECTIONS: Each of the questions or incomplete statements below is followed by five possible answers or completions. Select the best choice in each case and fill in the corresponding oval on the answer sheet.

---

1. According to Piaget, a person who CANNOT consistently use abstract logic has not reached the stage of

    (A) concrete operations.

    (B) preoperational development.

    (C) formal operations.

    (D) initiative vs. guilt.

    (E) extrovert vs. introvert.

QUESTIONS 2 and 3 refer to the following passage:

Suppose you are playing "Monopoly" with a group of children. These children understand the basic instructions and will play by the rules. They are not capable of hypothetical transactions dealing with mortgages, loans, and special pacts with other players.

2. According to Piaget, these children are in which stage of cognitive development?

    (A) Sensorimotor stage

    (B) Formal operations stage

(C) Preconceptual preoperational stage

(D) Concrete operational stage

(E) Intuitive preoperational stage

3. What are the probable ages of these children?

(A) 8-13

(B) 4-7

(C) 2-4

(D) 7-11

(E) 5-10

4. Modeling is a technique used in

(A) behavior therapy.

(B) logotherapy.

(C) client-centered therapy.

(D) psychoanalysis.

(E) rational-emotive therapy.

5. The ego, in contrast to the id,

(A) mediates between wish-fulfilling desires and the outer reality.

(B) is composed of only wish-fulfilling desires.

(C) mediates between reality and internal rules.

(D) cannot mediate with the superego.

(E) is innate, not learned.

6. According to Freud, a developmental halt due to frustration and anxiety is referred to as

(A) depression.

(B) fixation.

(C) regression.

(D) neurosis.

(E) learned helplessness.

7. Freud believed that the primary driving force in an individual's life was

(A) the superego.

(B) psychosexual development.

(C) sexual urge.

(D) bodily functions.

(E) domination.

8. According to Carl Rogers, the structure of the personality is based upon

(A) introversion and extroversion.

(B) being and non-being.

(C) the organism and the self.

(D) the will to meaning and the will to power.

(E) expectations and reality.

9. According to Alfred Adler, man is striving for

(A) self-actualization.

(B) power.

(C) superiority and goals.

(D) leadership.

(E) distinction.

10. Which of the following is the most widely accepted significance level for demonstrating significance in experimental results?

(A) .5

(B) .05

(C) .55

(D) 5.0

(E) .10

11. A stimulus that elicits a response before the experimental manipulation is a (an)

(A) response stimulus (RS).

(B) unconditioned stimulus (UCS).

(C) generalized stimulus (GS).

(D) conditioned stimulus (CS).

(E) specific stimulus (SS).

12. Correlational studies

    (A) indicate causality.

    (B) are more valid than laboratory studies.

    (C) involve manipulations of independent variables.

    (D) indicate some relationship between two variables.

    (E) All of the above.

QUESTIONS 13 and 14 refer to the following passage:

A classical experiment in conformity research done by Muzafer Sherif involved the effects of group judgments on "the autokinetic phenomenon." A light projected on the wall appears to move although this movement is actually due to the movement of the subject's eyes. It was found that individuals' judgments of the rate of movement of the light were influenced very much by the opinions of others. Even when the group was no longer present, the individual estimates were still in agreement with previous group opinions.

13. The fact that the subjects still agreed with the confederate group although they were no longer present shows that

    (A) compliance took place.

    (B) private acceptance took place.

    (C) internalization has occurred.

    (D) Both A and B.

    (E) All of the above.

14. All of the following choices are advantageous of field research except

    (A) "real people" are studied.

    (B) reactions of subjects are more natural.

    (C) it has more impact than lab studies.

    (D) behavior is not influenced by the psychologist.

    (E) there is an appropriate control involved.

QUESTIONS 15 and 16 refer to the following passage:

The cerebellum is greatly involved in planning movements as well as in coordinating them. It develops new motor programs that enable slow and deliberate movements to become rapid and automatic after practice. Damage to the cerebellum can lead to inability to perform rapid alternating movements and difficulty in making eye movements.

15. Which of the following is NOT controlled by the cerebellum?

    (A) Speaking

    (B) Writing

    (C) Playing the piano

    (D) Walking

    (E) Playing basketball

16. The fact that a blind infant would smile for the first time at about the same age as a sighted infant is evidence that smiling is

    (A) learned.

    (B) imitative behavior.

    (C) congenital.

    (D) nurtured behavior.

    (E) innate.

17. Neurons are unique among cells in that they

    (A) cannot conduct impulses.

    (B) cannot reproduce.

    (C) have a nucleus containing genetic material.

    (D) are surrounded by a membrane.

    (E) All of the above.

18. Which of the following best describes the major function(s) of the spinal cord?

    (A) Acts as a messenger to the brain

    (B) Filters sensory impulses

    (C) Directs simple actions independent of brain

    (D) Both A and B.

    (E) Both A and C.

19. The reticular formation of the brain

    (A) has definite boundaries.

    (B) is critical for wakefulness and alertness.

    (C) can only be activated by certain stimuli.

    (D) is important for conveying precise information.

    (E) All of the above.

20. The function of the vestibular organs is to provide

    (A) auditory conduction to the brain.

    (B) visual conduction to the brain.

    (C) a kinesthetic response.

    (D) electrical transmission to receptor cells.

    (E) a sense of balance.

21. The thalamus serves which of the following functions?

    (A) Relay center for sensory impulses

    (B) Relay center from spinal cord to cerebrum

    (C) Regulates external expression of emotion

    (D) All of the above.

    (E) None of the above.

22. Which of the following effects does adrenaline have on the human body?

    (A) Constriction of the pupils

    (B) Increased rate of digestion

    (C) Accelerated heartbeat

    (D) Increased hormone production

    (E) Decreased hormone production

23. Which of the following are NOT innervated by the autonomic nervous system?

(A) Leg muscles   (D) Pituitary glands

(B) Pupillary muscles   (E) Heart muscles

(C) Adrenal glands

24. The retina

    (A) is the round opening in the center of the eye through which light passes.

    (B) consists of photosensitive nerve cells located at the back of the eye.

    (C) bends and focuses light rays.

    (D) protects the internal parts of the eye.

    (E) is the muscle holding the pupil in place.

25. In auditory sensation, pitch

    (A) is the only variable by which we distinguish sounds.

    (B) is closely related to the loudness of sound.

    (C) is closely related to the frequency of sound.

    (D) is closely related to the intensity of sound.

    (E) is measured in decibels.

26. When light changes from bright to dim, the iris of the eye

    (A) dilates.   (D) changes in color.

    (B) constricts.   (E) thickens.

    (C) remains the same.

27. In sensory systems, a minimum difference between two stimuli is required before we can distinguish between them. This minimum threshold, which can be measured, is called the

    (A) interstimulus difference (ISD).

    (B) differential threshold (DL).

    (C) signal detectability threshold (TSD).

    (D) comparison stimulus threshold (CST).

    (E) subdifferential threshold (SDL).

28. In perceiving the distance a sound has traveled, a person depends heavily upon

    (A) loudness and intensity.   (D) saturation.

    (B) resonance.   (E) frequency.

    (C) brightness and hue.

29. The greatest concentration of cones occurs in the

    (A) pupil.   (D) fovea.

    (B) blind spot.   (E) ganglion.

    (C) optic nerve.

30. The short-term memory can hold how many items at one time?

    (A) Seven items, plus or minus two

    (B) Ten items, plus or minus two

    (C) Ten items, plus or minus five

    (D) Five items

    (E) None of the above.

31. The type of learning that is unique for humans is

    (A) classical conditioning.

    (B) operant conditioning.

    (C) verbal learning.

    (D) discrimination learning.

    (E) motor task learning.

32. Children learning the alphabet is a common form of

    (A) rehearsal.   (D) repetition.

    (B) pairing.   (E) serial learning.

    (C) mediation.

33. The ethologist who spent several years studying the problem-solving abilities of chimpanzees was

    (A) Margaret Mead.

    (B) Wolfgang Kohler.

    (C) Joy Adamson.

    (D) Aldous Huxley.

    (E) Erik Erikson.

34. One effect of anxiety on learning is

    (A) the removal of mental blocks.

    (B) a reduction in performance on difficult tasks.

    (C) a reduction in the ability to discriminate clearly.

    (D) more interference with familiar material than with new material.

    (E) reduction in the ability to perform any task.

35. Which of the following problems would require divergent thinking?

    (A) Adding a column of numbers

    (B) Deciding whether to turn left or right at an intersection while driving a car

    (C) Choosing the best move in a card game

    (D) Repairing a broken typewriter

    (E) Both A and D.

36. According to Bruner's theory of cognitive development, the iconic stage is

    (A) concerned with language development.

    (B) concerned with the use of visual images to understand the world.

    (C) concerned with the use of action to understand the world.

    (D) concerned with symbolism in the understanding of the world.

    (E) representative of egocentric activity.

37. The theory of selective attention was proposed by

    (A) Selfridge.

    (B) Bruner.

    (C) Broadbent.

    (D) Lockhart and Craik.

    (E) Tolman.

38. Items that are most likely to be forgotten are those

    (A) that are "concrete."

    (B) with the least digits/letters.

    (C) at the beginning of a long list.

    (D) at the middle of a long list.

    (E) at the end of a long list.

39. A model in which the internal representation of a pattern is structurally similar to the stimulus pattern is called a

    (A) visual feature model.   (D) specific feature model.

    (B) constructive model.   (E) pandemonium model.

    (C) template matching model.

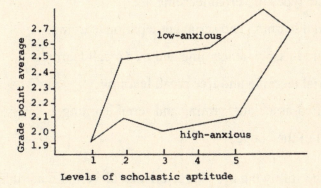

40. According to the above diagram, which of the following statements is true?

    (A) Levels of scholastic aptitude are not related to grade point average.

    (B) Low-anxiety students have higher grade point averages and higher scholastic aptitudes.

    (C) High-anxiety students have higher grade point averages and higher scholastic aptitudes.

    (D) Both A and B.

    (E) Both A and C.

41. An important function of rehearsal in verbal learning is

    (A) mediation.

    (B) transference of material from short-term to long-term memory.

    (C) acclimation to the meaning of the material.

    (D) Both A and B.

    (E) All of the above.

42. The Language Acquisition Device was proposed by

    (A) Piaget.   (D) Chomsky.

    (B) Bruner.   (E) Mednick.

    (C) Kohler.

43. The basic types of verbal learning are

    (A) serial learning and serial anticipation learning.

    (B) paired-associate learning and free recall learning.

    (C) serial learning and free recall learning.

    (D) paired-associate learning and serial learning.

    (E) All of the above.

44. All of the following are characteristics of verbal materials that influence how effectively we learn them EXCEPT

    (A) list length.   (D) similarity.

    (B) item position.   (E) meaningfulness.

    (C) word length.

45. The utterance "a" is an example of

    (A) a morpheme.   (D) prosody.

    (B) a phoneme.   (E) a kernel.

    (C) syntax.

46. In linguistic terminology, the term "boy" is a (an)

    (A) morpheme.   (D) prosody.

    (B) phoneme.   (E) example of syntax.

    (C) stereotype.

47. According to Noam Chomsky's theory of transformational grammar, a "kernel" is

    (A) the surface structure of a sentence.

    (B) the smallest unit of meaning in a language.

    (C) the deep structure of a sentence.

    (D) the connotation of a sentence.

    (E) the basic declarative thought of the sentence.

48. Intelligence tests are NOT considered reliable

    (A) at any age.

    (B) before seven years of age.

    (C) before puberty.

    (D) before twenty years of age.

    (E) None of the above.

49. A "normal" average I.Q. score is

    (A) 85.   (D) 110.

    (B) 100.   (E) None of the above.

    (C) 115.

50. Which of the following does NOT describe a true relationship between environmental factors and the stability of the I.Q.?

    (A) There is an increasing stability of the I.Q. with age.

    (B) Prerequisite learning skills contribute to the stability of the I.Q.

    (C) Changes in family structure have no effect on the I.Q.

    (D) Emotional stability has a beneficial effect on the I.Q.

    (E) Parental concern over the child's welfare has a stabilizing effect on the I.Q.

51. Which of the following concepts helps to explain the bystander effect, as exemplified in the Kitty Genovese murder case?

    (A) Cognitive dissonance

    (B) Tragedy of the commons

    (C) Risky shift

    (D) Actor-observer bias

    (E) Diffusion of responsibility

52. Shortly after birth a duck will follow the first object that walks by it. This illustrates

    (A) conditioned responses.   (D) imprinting.

    (B) super stimuli.   (E) shaping.

    (C) sign stimuli.

53. Suppose that psychosurgery is tried to remedy the uncontrollable violent behavior of a convicted serial murderer. Which brain structure should probably be operated on?

    (A) Thalamus   (D) Medulla

    (B) Cerebellum   (E) Amygdala

    (C) Pituitary

54. When we think of an extrovert, we automatically think of a person who is outgoing, assertive, and talks a great deal. We do so because of

(A) conformity.

(B) attribution bias.

(C) prototypes.

(D) actor-observer bias.

(E) prejudice.

55. As _____ increases, a person's need for social affiliation increases.

(A) cognitive dissonance   (D) depression

(B) fear   (E) None of the above.

(C) anxiety

56. The concept of social facilitation implies that

(A) friendships are easier to make in large groups than in small ones.

(B) prejudices are more easily overcome in sociable settings.

(C) the presence of other people improves individual performance.

(D) first impressions are formed more rapidly when many other people are present.

(E) conformity is greatest when other people are present.

57. Which of the following is NOT a factor that influences the degree to which two people like each other?

(A) Familiarity   (D) Conformity

(B) Physical attractiveness   (E) Proximity

(C) Similarity

58. Military strategists can plan a nuclear war, in which millions would be killed, without thinking about the human loss in a meaningful way. Which concept best explains how they can do this?

(A) Suppression   (D) Social reality

(B) Dehumanization   (E) Equity theory

(C) Prejudice

59. Konrad Lorenz contended that aggression is

    (A) socially learned.

    (B) the result of prejudice.

    (C) a direct result of territoriality.

    (D) a direct result of personal space.

    (E) an innate readiness to fight for survival.

60. Which of the following statements is false?

    (A) If a child is rewarded for random aggressive behavior, chances are good that the behavior will be repeated.

    (B) If a child is punished for acting aggressively, the likelihood of that behavior reoccurring is lessened.

    (C) If aggression is reinforced irregularly, the aggressive behavior is gradually discouraged.

    (D) Both B and C.

    (E) None of the above.

61. First-born children have been shown to

    (A) be more dependent than later-borns.

    (B) be more affiliative when fearful than later-borns.

    (C) be more intelligent than later-born children.

    (D) Both A and B.

    (E) All of the above.

62. You are watching television and see a commercial where one of your favorite movie stars is discussing a nutritional cereal that you should buy. Because we like the star's movies, there is a tendency to believe that the star is also an expert on cereals. This tendency is referred to as the _____ effect.

    (A) barnum   (D) halo

    (B) piezoelectric   (E) None of the above.

    (C) star

63. According to Baumrind's 1967 study of the family as a socializing agent,

    (A) children's personality was related to the type of discipline received from parents.

    (B) parental discipline was not related to a child's personality.

    (C) there was a correlation between parental personalities and children's personalities.

    (D) there was an inverse relationship between the amount of discipline the child received and the amount of behavioral control he or she exhibited.

    (E) None of the above.

64. According to social learning theory, one of the primary means of socializing our children is

    (A) taming their instincts.

    (B) developing their superegos.

    (C) helping them self-actualize.

    (D) observational learning.

    (E) providing minimum discipline.

65. According to Erich Fromm, man has needs that arise from conditions of his lonely existence. Which of the following did Fromm identify as a human need?

    (A) The need for a sense of individual identity

    (B) The need for belonging to a society

    (C) The need to relate satisfactorily to his fellow beings

    (D) All of the above.

    (E) None of the above.

66. Which of the following statements is false?

    (A) Nurture determines the extent to which potentialities for behavior will be realized.

    (B) The genotype sets fixed genetic limits for behavior.

(C) A deprived environment has a detrimental effect on intellectual development.

(D) A child's I.Q. can be raised with an improvement in environment.

(E) None of the above.

67. Which approach to psychology stresses the person's inner drive to develop to his or her full potential?

(A) Psychodynamic

(D) Cognitive

(B) Humanistic

(E) Psychobiological

(C) Behavioristic

68. Stanley Schachter has proposed that emotion is a product of _____ and _____ .

(A) instincts, physical states

(B) heredity, environment

(C) motivation, learning

(D) physiological arousal, cognitive appraisal

(E) testosterone levels, epinephrine levels

69. The social norms concerning the public expression of various emotions are called

(A) display rules.

(D) stereotypical rules.

(B) species-specific rules.

(E) affective rules.

(C) conformity rules.

70. An elderly person looking back on life is unlikely to feel futility or despair if he or she has achieved a sense of

(A) ego-integrity.

(D) identity.

(B) genital gratification.

(E) competence.

(C) generativity.

71. Suppose you believe that people are capable of developing personally throughout life and that, given the opportunity, they will achieve their full potential. Which approach to personality does this describe?

    (A) Humanistic   (D) Behavioristic

    (B) Cognitive   (E) Social learning

    (C) Psychodynamic

72. Maslow would contend that a person must first satisfy _____ needs before satisfying _____ needs.

    (A) cognitive, attachment

    (B) attachment, esteem

    (C) aesthetic, esteem

    (D) safety, biological

    (E) transcendence, self-actualization

73. Which theorist distinguished between deficiency motivation and growth motivation?

    (A) Maslow   (D) Bandura

    (B) Jung   (E) Rogers

    (C) Kelly

74. Ivan P. Pavlov is famous for his research on

    (A) teaching machines.   (D) classical conditioning.

    (B) perceptual learning.   (E) backward conditioning.

    (C) forward conditioning.

75. A stimulus that elicits a response before the experimental manipulation is a (an)

    (A) response stimulus (RS).

    (B) unconditioned stimulus (UCS).

    (C) generalized stimulus (GS).

    (D) conditioned stimulus (CS).

    (E) specific stimulus (SS).

76. In which form of conditioning is the conditioned stimulus (CS) presented after the unconditioned stimulus (UCS)?

    (A) Higher-order conditioning

    (B) Forward conditioning

    (C) Backward conditioning

    (D) Second-order conditioning

    (E) Delayed conditioning

77. The role of imitation in social learning was first systematically observed by

    (A) Miller and Dollard.   (D) B.F. Skinner.

    (B) Bandura and Walters.   (E) J.B. Watson.

    (C) Stanley Milgram.

78. In our society, money is an example of a

    (A) primary reinforcer.

    (B) secondary (conditioned) reinforcer.

    (C) socio/reinforcer.

    (D) negative reinforcer.

    (E) simple operant.

79. The reinforcement schedule that produces the highest rates of performance is a

    (A) fixed-interval schedule.

    (B) variable-interval schedule.

    (C) fixed-ratio schedule.

    (D) variable-ratio schedule.

    (E) None of the above.

80. Second-order conditioning is an important phenomenon because it demonstrates how an originally neutral CS used in the first-order conditioning can assume the properties of a (an)

(A) first-order conditioning stimulus.

(B) instrumental stimulus.

(C) reinforcer.

(D) positive reward.

(E) negative reward.

81. According to the actor-observer bias, which of the following would likely occur after a student fails a professor's exam?

(A) The student would blame himself for not being intelligent.

(B) The student would blame the professor for creating too difficult an exam.

(C) The student would blame himself for not trying hard enough.

(D) The professor would blame himself for creating too difficult an exam.

(E) The professor would blame the university for a classroom that is too noisy for taking exams.

82. Suppose you teach preschool and you break Joe's candy bar into three pieces and Mike's candy bar into two pieces. Mike complains that he received less than Joe. What does Mike lack?

(A) Conservation   (D) Egocentrism

(B) Constancy   (E) Accommodation

(C) Object permanence

83. Mary is a bright student but she is constantly disrupting the class by trying to draw the teacher into a power struggle for control. The school psychologist might advise the teacher to do all of the following EXCEPT

(A) not show Mary the anxiety she is causing.

(B) ignore the student's disruptive behavior.

(C) verbally embarrass the student until she is more cooperative.

(D) suggest psychotherapy to the parents.

(E) reinforcing the student when she engages in more productive behavior.

84. One of the major contrasts between the suburban and urban school settings that a school psychologist should be aware of is

   (A) less interest in the education of children in urban settings.

   (B) there is more diversity among students in suburban schools.

   (C) there is more peer pressure to conform in urban schools.

   (D) crime, delinquency, and similar problems are more prevalent in urban schools.

   (E) teachers tend to be more experienced in urban schools.

85. Test scores and data analyses of group intelligence tests employ all of the following methods of data presentation EXCEPT

   (A) letter ratings.

   (B) standard error of the mean.

   (C) percentile values.

   (D) sigma scores.

   (E) stanine scores.

86. A key component of the clinical profile of paranoia is usually

   (A) an organized delusional system with jealous content.

   (B) the presence of tactile hallucinations.

   (C) the experiencing of vivid auditory hallucinations.

   (D) the presence of a "dual" personality.

   (E) the experiencing of vivid visual hallucinations.

87. The major affective disorders are characterized by

   (A) extreme and inappropriate emotional responses.

   (B) severe depression.

   (C) withdrawal and emotional distortion.

   (D) chronic experience of depression.

   (E) delusional emotional experiences.

88. Individuals rated as "High Anxious" on the Manifest Anxiety Scale

    (A) have a high potential for developing an anxiety disorder at some point in their lifetime.

    (B) display some signs of the learned helplessness phenomenon.

    (C) do better on verbal learning tasks than "Low Anxious" individuals.

    (D) have a shorter attention span than "Low Anxious" individuals.

    (E) None of the above.

89. In a test situation, the examiner wants there to be only one independent variable—the individual being tested. To ensure this, the examiner administers a(n)

    (A) item analysis.   (D) normal test.

    (B) standardized test.   (E) individual test.

    (C) factor analysis.

90. The psychiatrist who has written several influential books questioning the use of the term "mental illness" is

    (A) Bruno Bettelheim.   (D) Jose Delgado.

    (B) B.F. Skinner.   (E) Anna Freud.

    (C) Thomas Szasz.

CLEP HUMAN GROWTH
AND DEVELOPMENT
TEST 1

1.	(C)	23.	(A)	46.	(A)	69.	(A)
2.	(D)	24.	(B)	47.	(E)	70.	(A)
3.	(D)	25.	(C)	48.	(B)	71.	(A)
4.	(A)	26.	(A)	49.	(B)	72.	(B)
5.	(A)	27.	(B)	50.	(C)	73.	(A)
6.	(B)	28.	(A)	51.	(E)	74.	(D)
7.	(C)	29.	(D)	52.	(D)	75.	(B)
8.	(C)	30.	(A)	53.	(E)	76.	(C)
9.	(C)	31.	(C)	54.	(C)	77.	(A)
10.	(B)	32.	(E)	55.	(B)	78.	(B)
11.	(B)	33.	(B)	56.	(C)	79.	(D)
12.	(D)	34.	(B)	57.	(D)	80.	(C)
13.	(D)	35.	(C)	58.	(B)	81.	(B)
14.	(E)	36.	(B)	59.	(E)	82.	(A)
15.	(D)	37.	(C)	60.	(C)	83.	(C)
16.	(E)	38.	(D)	61.	(E)	84.	(D)
17.	(B)	39.	(C)	62.	(D)	85.	(B)
18.	(E)	40.	(B)	63.	(A)	86.	(A)
19.	(B)	41.	(B)	64.	(D)	87.	(A)
20.	(E)	42.	(D)	65.	(D)	88.	(C)
21.	(D)	43.	(E)	66.	(B)	89.	(B)
22.	(C)	44.	(C)	67.	(B)	90.	(C)
		45.	(B)	68.	(D)		

DETAILED EXPLANATIONS
OF ANSWERS

TEST 1

1. **(C)** The stage of formal operations is noted for the ability of the individual to deal with abstract problems and concepts. It usually begins around puberty but research shows that some people never develop these skills and continue to function at the level of concrete operations for life.

2. **(D)** Based on the description of the way these children understood the game rules, one could determine that they are in the concrete operational stage of development. This stage emphasizes concrete understanding of rules and logical thinking as it relates to real concrete objects. Abstract and hypothetical thinking are largely undeveloped.

3. **(D)** The concrete operational stage lasts from ages seven to eleven years. This is the usual age span, but it may be shorter or longer in an individual child.

4. **(A)** In modeling, an individual learns by observing and then imitating the behavior of others. For example, to rid a client of a dog phobia, the therapist exposes the client to both live and filmed displays of people interacting fearlessly with dogs. The client then imitates behavior, eventually overcoming his fear of dogs. As a number of research programs have shown, this kind of learning helps people acquire new resources in a relatively short time.

5. **(A)** The ego is the intermediary between the id and reality. It develops between the ages of eight months and eighteen months, as the child acquires an understanding of what is possible in the outer world. The ego also distinguishes between long-range and short-range goals and decides which activities will be most profitable to the individual. The id and ego work together to determine the individual's goals.

6. **(B)** According to Freud, fixation results from abnormal personality development. Freud stated that a person feels a certain amount of frustration and anxiety as he passes from one stage of development to the next. If that frustration and anxiety become too great, development may halt and the person becomes fixated at the stage he is trying to grow out of. For example, an overly dependent child is thought to be fixated. Development has ceased at an early stage preventing the child from growing up and becoming independent.

7. **(C)** Freud believed that the primary driving force in an individual's life is the sexual urge (the libido). His theory of motivational development was particularly concerned with sexual gratification, as it changed in relation to the child's body. His theory of personality constructs (the id, ego, and superego) also deals with the sexual urge, as it confronts the constraints of the outer world.

8. **(C)** Roger's personality constructs are the organism and the self. The organism is conceived to be the locus of experience; experience includes everything available to the awareness and all that occurs within the organism. The self or self-concept refers to the organized and consistent set of perceptions that are self-referential, i.e., that refer to "I" or "me." It also includes the perceptions of the relationships between the self and the rest of the world. In addition to the self, there is an ideal self that represents what the individual aspires to be.

9. **(C)** To Adler, the goal of behavior is to compensate for a subjectively perceived sense of inferiority by achieving superiority. Therefore, an individual cannot fully comprehend his life without understanding the goal he or she is striving for.

10. **(B)** The appropriate significance level is .05. This is the usual cutoff point for determining the significant difference between two means. At the .05 level the difference between the means is considered so great that it is unlikely that it could have occurred by chance. A p value of .05 means that the results obtained could have occurred by chance in only 5 out of 100 replications of the experiment.

11. **(B)** In classical conditioning the stimulus that elicits a response before any conditioning begins is called the unconditioned stimulus. It reliably elicits the unconditioned response (UCR) before the experiment. During the experimental manipulation the unconditioned stimulus (UCS)

is paired with a conditioned stimulus (CS) that originally does not elicit a response. After several such pairings the subject will elicit a conditioned response (CR) to the conditioned stimulus (CS) that is very similar to the unconditioned response (UCR). After this conditioned response (CR) is learned, the unconditioned stimulus (UCS) may be removed, but the subject will keep responding to the conditioned stimulus (CS).

12. **(D)** Correlations are indicative of a relationship between two variables. The higher the absolute value of the correlation, the stronger the relationship between the variables. Correlation measures how well the existence of a variable or some aspect of a variable is predictive of another variable. Unfortunately, correlation tells us nothing about which of the two variables has an effect on the other. Many times, it is a third variable that is affecting both variables together.

13. **(D)** Compliance refers to a change in external behavior, while private acceptance refers to a change in attitude. In the presence of a group, the subjects conform with their beliefs outwardly; that is, they show compliance. The fact that they continue to do so in the group's absence shows that private acceptance also takes place. Internalization is a very strong social response based on a desire to be "right." Once a belief is internalized it is highly resistant to change.

14. **(E)** The issue of control in field research is problematic. Control is not an advantage of field studies because there isn't appropriate control involved in these types of studies. Control is a tradeoff for the other advantages in field research.

15. **(D)** The cerebellum controls the ballistic movements of speaking, writing, playing an instrument, and performing most athletic skills. The basal ganglia control the slower, more gradual movements that are modified by sensory feedback while the movement is still occurring. The basal ganglia are involved with postures and movements of the body as a whole.

16. **(E)** Since the blind baby has never seen a smile, it can't be imitating it. Likewise, it cannot be a learned or nurtured behavior. Smiling when we are pleased or content must therefore be an innate (inborn) characteristic in humans. Congenital refers to factors being present at birth. Smiling usually doesn't occur for the first few months.

17. **(B)** Neurons are the basic structural and functional units of the nervous system. There are many types, each having a specific function. Despite their diversity, there are certain characteristics common to all neurons. They all conduct impulses and consist of a cell body, an axon, and dendrites. They are different from all other types of cells in the body in that they cannot reproduce.

18. **(E)** The spinal cord has two major functions. It acts as a messenger, relaying information from the body to the brain and back to the body. It also directs simple reflex actions without input from the brain.

19. **(B)** The reticular formation is critical for wakefulness and alertness. The input and output of the reticular formation are diffuse. The area appears more irregular and disorderly than most of the rest of the brain. Any strong stimulation activates the system and thus diffusely activates the entire cerebral cortex.

20. **(E)** Our vestibular organs provide us with a sense of balance. They do this through information about the movements and position of the head. There are two groups of vestibular organs. These are the semicircular canals and the otolith organs, both located in the inner ear. The three semicircular canals are fluid-filled and respond to the changes in rate of motion of the head. The otolith organs are small stone-like crystals that respond to the actual position of one's head.

21. **(D)** The thalamus serves a number of functions. It serves as a relay center for sensory impulses. Fibers from the spinal cord and parts of the brain synapse here with other neurons going to the various sensory areas of the cerebrum. The thalamus seems to regulate and coordinate the external signs of emotion. The thalamus is in the forebrain, located on top of the hypothalamus.

22. **(C)** Adrenaline is a hormone that stimulates the sympathetic nervous system. One of the many resulting effects of adrenaline on the body is the stimulation of the heart. When stimulated, the sympathetic branch to the muscles of the heart causes the heart to beat more rapidly and vigorously. Thus, adrenaline has the effect of accelerating and strengthening the heartbeat.

23. **(A)** The leg muscles are innervated by the somatic nervous system. The other choices are innervated by the autonomic nervous system. The somatic nervous system includes the sensory nerves that bring all sensory

information into the central nervous system, plus the motor nerves that control the activity of the skeletal muscles. The autonomic system directs the activity of smooth and cardiac muscles and of glands.

24. **(B)** The retina is composed of photoreceptor nerve cells (rods and cones) that form a photosensitive curtain at the back of the eye. Over 120 million photoreceptor cells are found in the retina of each eye.

25. **(C)** Pitch is closely related to the frequency of the stimulus. Sound is basically vibrations of particles in the air. These vibrations are wavelike and are called soundwaves. The frequency of a vibration is a measure of how many times it goes up and down in a single period of time. We generally experience high frequency waves as high-pitched tones. Waves with low frequencies correspond to low-pitched tones; therefore, pitch is closely related to the frequency of sound.

26. **(A)** The iris responds to dimmer light by dilating. This adjusts the amount of light entering the eye through the pupil. When the light dims, the iris opens more to allow more light in. Conversely, when the light becomes brighter, the iris constricts to reduce the amount of light entering the pupil.

27. **(B)** The concept of a differential threshold (DL) is basic to understanding sensory systems. The differential threshold is not considered constant, even for a specific sensory system. For example, if you are in a room with one person talking, you will definitely notice when a second person begins talking. That additional sound energy will be above the DL. If you are in a room where 20 people are talking, you may not notice if one other person begins to speak. In this case the DL is higher; a greater amount of sound energy is needed in order for the addition to be noticed. In general, the greater the intensity of the original stimulus, the greater is the differential threshold.

28. **(A)** The loudness of a sound is closely related to the intensity of the physical stimulus. Intensity is a measure of the amount of physical energy a stimulus sends to our senses, in this case our auditory system. We experience a high-intensity sound as being loud. Hence, in perceiving the distance of a sound, loudness and intensity are important factors. In addition to these factors, previous psychological and physical experience with the sound is of great importance.

29. **(D)** Cones are located primarily in the fovea. There are about 6 to 7 million cones in each eye. Cones require a large amount of light energy to respond to a stimulus.

30. **(A)** Short-term memory (STM) is very limited in its capacity. It can only hold about seven items (plus or minus two items) of information at a time. This brief memory span requires deliberate rehearsal to prevent a specific memory from decaying over time.

31. **(C)** While all of the choices are types of human learning, the most distinctly human and significant type of learning is verbal learning. Verbal learning provides an important link between elementary non-verbal learning processes, language, and thought. All formal and informal education in older children and adults involves verbal learning.

32. **(E)** Whenever items of a list are learned in sequence, serial learning takes place. Associations may be formed between the items, or the proper order of the items may be learned by linking them to a particular position in the list.

33. **(B)** Kohler spent years studying the problem-solving behavior of chimps. He observed that the animals often exhibited "insight," i.e., the sudden solution to a problem without the use of trial-and-error learning.

34. **(B)** Anxiety is an emotional state characterized by non-specific fears and various autonomic symptoms. The effect of anxiety is different for different learning tasks. One major finding is that anxiety does not hinder the learning of simple tasks, such as discrimination learning, but does hinder the learning of more complicated, less familiar tasks.

35. **(C)** In choosing the best move in a card game, one must be able to generate a number of possible solutions; therefore, divergent thinking is the process being utilized. Divergent thinking requires flexibility, fluency of ideas, and originality.

36. **(B)** The iconic mode is the second stage in Bruner's theory of cognitive development. In this stage, knowledge of the world is based heavily on images that stand for perceptual events. A picture, for example, may stand for an actual event. While the emphasis is usually on visual images, other sensory images are possible.

37. **(C)**   The theory of selective attention was proposed by Broadbent. Broadbent's approach also became known as the filter theory, because it generally hypothesized that certain sensory inputs are rejected, while others are "allowed in" for further processing. According to the theory, information passes through a selective filter that only attends to the important aspects of stimuli. This filtered information then passes through channels into a limited-capacity short-term memory bank where it is retained by the processing system.

38. **(D)**   Generally, the items that are forgotten are those in the middle of the list. This is because what is learned first usually interferes with what comes later (productive interference) and what is learned later usually interferes with what came earlier (retroactive interference). Thus, the items in the middle are most susceptible to being forgotten because they are subject to both kinds of interference.

39. **(C)**   Template matching theories purport that each pattern is recognized by noting its similarity with a basic, internal model. It is considered a problematic theory due to its rigidity. For example, people recognize an "R" even if it is upside down, very small, or huge. The template theory would have to be expanded to include a new template for every possible size and orientation of the letter, to provide a viable explanation of the capabilities of the human, pattern-recognition system.

40. **(B)**   Based on the reading of the graph in the diagram, low-anxiety students have higher grade point averages and higher levels of scholastic aptitude than high-anxiety students. Notice the performance jump from level 1 to level 2 of scholastic aptitude. Usually, the more anxious a person is, the lower his performance level on a verbal learning task.

41. **(B)**   Rehearsal serves two functions. It allows items in short-term memory to be retained. Also, it appears to facilitate material from the short-term to long-term memory. In transference of most contents, rehearsal is necessary for learning.

42. **(D)**   Noam Chomsky believes that children are born with a certain "something," a certain genetic predisposition that enables them to learn grammar. Chomsky called this predisposition the Language Acquisition Device (LAD). It is believed to exist at birth. Chomsky used this concept to explain the relative ease with which normal children learn grammar.

43. **(E)** Serial learning occurs when a list of items is memorized and recalled in a particular order. In serial-anticipation learning, a series of items—usually nonsense syllables—are presented one at a time for a standard time interval. The first time the list is presented, the subject will not know which successive syllables are correct. Beginning with the second trial, he is asked to anticipate the syllable that follows the one he is looking at. This method provides immediate feedback to the subject about accuracy of response. In paired-associate learning, the subject must learn a list of paired items. The left-hand item of the pair is the stimulus item and the right-hand item is the response item. After learning the pairs, the subject should be able to produce the response item when given the stimulus item. Free recall learning is the learning and recall of a list of items. The retrieved items do not need to be in any specific order.

44. **(C)** Word length is not an important characteristic influencing the learning of verbal material.

45. **(B)** Phonemes are the smallest units of sound in a language. They are single vowel and consonant sounds found in every language. English has 45 phonemes. Phonemes are the first sounds that an infant makes.

46. **(A)** A morpheme is the smallest unit of meaning in a given language. In English, morphemes can be whole words, such as "boy"; prefixes such as "anti-"; or suffixes such as "-ing." There are more than 100,000 morphemes in English.

47. **(E)** Noam Chomsky (1957) was the first to distinguish between surface and deep structure in language; he constructed a theory of transformational grammar based on these structures. In this system, a "kernel" of a sentence is the basic, declarative thought of the sentence. For example, "The boy hit the girl" could be a kernel sentence. This kernel sentence can be transformed to: "The girl was hit by the boy," "Did the boy hit the girl?," or "Wasn't the girl hit by the boy?" The kernel sentence, along with its transformations, comprises the basic patterns of surface structure.

48. **(B)** In general, humans do not have the life experience, cognitive, verbal, and motor skills required to complete an I.Q. test before the age of seven. Few people question the reliability of I.Q. tests. The validity of these tests, however, *has* been questioned.

49. **(B)** A "normal" I.Q. score is considered to be about 100, while 98 percent of the people who take I.Q. tests fall in the range between 60 and 140. Someone who scores above 140 is considered a genius.

50. **(C)** Changes in family structure, such as divorce, loss of parents, adoption, and severe or prolonged illness of a family member, have a negative effect on the child's intellectual development. In general, these changes disrupt the stability of the child's intelligence quotient by acting as stressors in the child's life.

51. **(E)** The bystander effect refers to individuals watching a brutal attack without helping the victim, calling the police, or in any way intervening. One factor that helps account for this social phenomenon is diffusion of responsibility. No one feels personally responsible for taking action because each person believes someone else should handle the situation. Two other relevant factors are that people (1) judge the costs of intervening as too high and (2) incorrectly assume that because no one else is intervening there really is not a problem, despite appearances. Ironically, helping is more likely when there is only one witness than when there is a group of witnesses.

52. **(D)** Konrad Lorenz observed that newborn ducks would follow him if they saw him before encountering their mother. He termed this phenomenon "imprinting" and argued that it illustrated the importance of instinctual behavior. This concept, along with sign stimuli that release fixed patterns, comprised some of the central ideas of ethnology.

53. **(E)** The amygdala is a portion of the limbic system that plays a central role of aggression. Creating a lesion in the amygdala has actually been tried in violent prisoners for whom psychosurgery appeared to be the last option available. The thalamus is a sensory center whereas the medulla is responsible for basic repetitive processes such as breathing. The cerebellum controls motor coordination. The pituitary is known as the master gland.

54. **(C)** A prototype is an ideal example of a concept or schema. It represents all the characteristics that are most typical of the concept. Prototypes are important in pattern recognition and memory. Beliefs about personality traits such as extroversion are also organized about prototypes.

55. **(B)** The need for social affiliation or a desire to be with other people is great when we are afraid. In a classic series of studies, Stanley Schachter manipulated the fear level of college women by leading them to believe they would receive electric shocks in a laboratory experiment. He then measured whether the women preferred to wait for the experiment to begin either alone or with others. Cognitive dissonance has no known effect on affiliation. Anxiety in general may or may not affect social affiliation, whereas depression decreases the desire to be with others.

56. **(C)** Social facilitation refers to improvements in an individual's performance when other people are present. This phenomenon occurs both when the person is competing with others and when there is no interaction with others at all. The effect is limited to well-learned tasks, however. The presence of others can increase arousal to non-optimal levels for difficult novel tasks.

57. **(D)** Research on social attraction indicates that proximity is important for the obvious reason that social interaction is more likely when two people live nearby. Physical attraction and similarity are critical factors. All else being equal, the greater the familiarity, the greater the social attraction.

58. **(B)** Dehumanization is a defense mechanism in which we strip away human qualities of those we aggress against. We refuse to admit that our enemies share the same thoughts, beliefs, fears, and values that we do. We begin to regard the enemy as subhuman animals who are not worthy of living. Obviously dehumanization can be one consequence of extreme prejudice. Suppression is another defense mechanism in which a person tries to forget an anxiety-provoking event.

59. **(E)** Konrad Lorenz, the well-known ethnologist, contended that aggression was an instinctive readiness to fight for one's own survival. He studied how most species engage in aggression, though serious injury or death is usually avoided (unlike the case with human aggression). Other ethnologists view aggression as a derivative of territoriality. All ethnological views contrast with the frustration-aggression hypothesis of learning theory.

60. **(C)** According to the social learning theory of aggression, if a child is rewarded for random aggressive behavior, it is highly probable that the behavior will occur again. On the other hand, if a child is punished

for acting aggressively, the likelihood of that behavior occurring again is reduced. It has been found that the schedule of reinforcement is particularly important in the learning of aggressive responses. For example, if aggression is reinforced irregularly, the aggressive behavior will tend to last longer than if the reinforcement is continuous.

61. **(E)**   All of these are characteristics of first-born children. Although none of these relationships is especially strong, they do exist and have raised many questions about the factors contributing to them. Schachter and Zajone have suggested that these effects may be due to parents giving more specialized attention to their first-born children than to later-born children.

62. **(D)**   Humans tend to believe that if a person is proficient in one area, then they are competent in other areas. This is the halo effect. Teachers tend to think that a student who is earning an "A" in their class is an overall "A" student.

63. **(A)**   In his study, Baumrind (1967) found a relationship between type of discipline and child's personality. Children in a preschool were categorized into three personality groups. The children who were friendly, self-controlled, and self-reliant were found to have parents who were demanding, controlling, and loving. Children who were withdrawn and unhappy were found to have demanding but unaffectionate parents. The children who lacked self-control and self-reliance had parents who were both permissive and affectionate.

64. **(D)**   In behaviorism, the environment shapes our behavior through the use of rewards and punishments. We also learn by observing other people who serve as models for us. Choices (A) and (B) represent the Freudian approach, while choice (C) comes from the humanistic approach.

65. **(D)**   Erich Fromm believed that man has five basic needs that result from conditions of a lonely existence. Three of these needs were listed in the question. The five needs are the following: having a sense of identity; feeling that one belongs to society; transcending animal nature as a creative human being; relating to fellow beings; and maintaining a stable and consistent frame of reference.

66. **(B)**   The genotype, nature, does not set fixed genetic limits for behavior. Limits do not exist because the genotype must act through the

environment to produce a particular behavior. Nature or inheritance sets the potentialities for behavior, and nurture or the environment determines the extent to which potentialities will be realized. A deprived environment can greatly retard intellectual development, and an enriched environment can enhance intellectual abilities.

67. **(B)** The humanistic approach, as exemplified by theorists such as Carl Rogers and Abraham Maslow, stresses the self-actualization of an individual's potential. Psychodynamic theory stresses the inner conflicts of personality, whereas behaviorism focuses on the external shaping of personality by the environment. The cognitive approach stresses the active construction of knowledge and beliefs about the world, and the psychobiological approach focuses on neural mechanisms of behavior.

68. **(D)** Schachter proposed and reported evidence in favor of a two-factor theory of emotion. General, undifferentiated arousal from sympathetic activation is the first factor. The second is our cognitive appraisal about the causes of our bodily arousal. If the arousal is attributed to emotional sources, then emotion is experienced.

69. **(A)** Display rules are norms for how to express an emotion in a particular public setting. Research suggests that some aspects of emotional expression are present at birth or are common across cultures. For example, facial expressions of happiness, sadness, anger, fear, surprise, and disgust are universal. However, different cultures hold different norms for the public display of emotion.

70. **(A)** Erikson's final stage of development in late adulthood is the crisis of ego integrity versus despair. A successful coping with this crisis involves achieving a sense of satisfaction and wholeness with life. Failure to do so leads to negative views on life and despair.

71. **(A)** The humanistic approach, as exemplified by the work of Rogers, stresses the process of self-actualization. The cognitive approach, as seen in George Kelly's personal construct theory, stresses the construction of meaning, interpretations, and beliefs. The Freudian psychodynamic approach stresses unconscious conflicts. The behavioristic approach, as seen in Skinner's writings, stresses environmental stimulus control of behavior. Lastly, Bandura's social learning theory stresses the importance of self-regulation of behavior.

72. **(B)**   Maslow's hierarchy of needs consists of the following: air, food, water, and shelter; safety and security; love and belonging; esteem and self-esteem; and self-actualization. Theoretically, a person must satisfy basic needs before moving up the hierarchy to satisfy higher order needs.

73. **(A)**   Abraham Maslow presumed that people are motivated in two ways. Deficiency motivation refers to restoring physical or psychological equilibrium. Growth motivation refers to moving beyond stability to new challenges and satisfactions.

74. **(D)**   Ivan P. Pavlov (1849–1936) virtually discovered the phenomenon of classical conditioning and was the first to investigate it systematically. In Pavlov's experiments with the salivating response of his dogs, he established the basic methodology and terminology still used today in classical conditioning experiments. Pavlov referred to food as the unconditional stimulus (UCS) because it naturally and consistently elicited salivation, which he called the unconditioned response (UCR). Pavlov later taught dogs to salivate to light. This was accomplished by presenting the light just prior to presenting the food. After a series of such pairings, the dogs would salivate in response to the light. In this case, the light was a conditioned stimulus (CS) and the salivation in response to the light was a conditioned response (CR). Hence, Pavlov's research elucidated the process of classical conditioning.

75. **(B)**   In classical conditioning, the stimulus that elicits a response before any conditioning begins is called the unconditioned stimulus. It reliably elicits the unconditioned response (UCR) before the experiment. During the experimental manipulation the unconditioned stimulus (UCS) is paired with a conditioned stimulus (CS) that originally does not elicit a response. After several such pairings the subject will elicit a conditioned response (CR) to the conditioned stimulus (CS) that is very similar to the unconditioned response (UCR). After this conditioned response (CR) is learned, the unconditioned stimulus (UCS) may be removed, but the subject will keep responding to the conditioned stimulus (CS).

76. **(C)**   In backward conditioning, the CS is presented after the UCS. Backward conditioning is not very effective, if at all. In a classical conditioning experiment, backward conditioning would take place if a light (CS) would be turned on shortly after the food (UCS) was delivered to the dog. This particular procedure has shown that no response is conditioned even though there exists a temporal contiguity between the CS and UCS.

77. **(A)** Experiments with children, in which they were rewarded for imitating a model, formed the basis of Miller and Dollard's conclusions concerning learning from model imitation. They concluded that imitation of social behavior probably derives strength from the fact that conformist behavior is rewarded in many situations, whereas nonconformist behavior often results in punishment.

78. **(B)** Conditioned, or secondary reinforcement, occurs when the reinforcing stimulus is not inherently pleasing or reinforcing, but becomes so through association with other pleasant or reinforcing stimuli. Money is an example of a secondary (conditioned) reinforcer. Coins and paper currency are not in themselves pleasing, but the things they buy are pleasing. Therefore, an association is made between money and inherently pleasing primary reinforcers, such as food and drink. Hence, the term "conditioned reinforcer" is used.

79. **(D)** With the highest rates of performance, the variable-ratio schedule elicits consistently high rates even after prolonged discontinuance of the reinforcement. In fact, once an operant learning response has been established with a variable-ratio reinforcement schedule, it is difficult to extinguish the response.

80. **(C)** In secondary reinforcement, a neutral stimulus is paired with the conditioned stimulus, after that conditioned stimulus can reliably elicit the conditioned response. When this is accomplished, the new or second conditioned stimulus will elicit the conditioned response even though it was never directly paired with the unconditioned stimulus. In this manner, the original, neutral CS comes to work as a reinforcer for the second-order conditioning response.

81. **(B)** The actor-observer bias provides a qualification to the fundamental attribution error. As observers of others, we overestimate the power of internal factors in controlling their behavior. As actors, however, we are less susceptible to this error in making attributions about our own behavior. In fact, psychologically healthy (nondepressed) individuals are likely to attribute their failure on an exam to an external factor, such as the professor creating too difficult an exam.

82. **(A)** Conservation is a Piagetian concept of recognizing the identity of number, mass, and volume despite transformations that alter their perceptual properties. Mike lacks conservation of mass in not realizing that

his candy bar is equal to Joe's despite the perceptual difference of two versus three pieces. Learning conservation is a key indicator of progression from the preoperational to the concrete operations stage of development. However, learning conservation in one domain, such as mass, does not imply that other domains, such as volume, are understood.

83. **(C)**   Power struggles with authority figures occur for a variety of reasons. Depending on verbally abrasive responses to punish usually results in alienation of the student and deterioration of class atmosphere.

84. **(D)**   Due to the greater density of people, wide range of economic bases, overcrowding and understaffing, and acceptable community norms, urban schools have more problems with teen gang behavior and criminality. There is less variability in race, religion, and family income in suburbs. Teaching posts in suburban schools are frequently earned after a teacher has spent years in an urban school.

85. **(B)**   Letter ratings are often assigned. For example, an "A" would represent all IQ scores above 118, and "B" would refer to scores between 110 and 117, etc. Sigma scores refer to a measure of standard deviation. The stanine system places scores in one of nine categories, stanine 9 (the highest 4 percent) to stanine 1 (the lowest 4 percent of the scores).

86. **(A)**   In the DSM, paranoid disorders are classified as psychoses and listed as one of the major categories of abnormal behavior. The essential features of this disorder are persistent persecutory delusions or delusions of jealousy. The persecutory delusions usually involve a single theme or an organized series of themes, such as being drugged, poisoned, conspired against, or harassed.

87. **(A)**   Affective disorders are characterized by a disturbance of mood accompanied by related symptoms. Mood is defined as a prolonged emotional state that colors the whole psychic life and generally involves either depression or elation. In affective disorders, mood tends to be at one extreme or the other. The patient may be depressed, may be manic, or may exhibit bipolar symptoms, an alternation between depression and mania.

88. **(C)**   The Manifest Anxiety Scale (MA) is a self-report inventory that determines an individual's arousal level in comparison to group scores on a test. Because anxiety and arousal level are thought to correlate with

drive level, learning theorists have been interested in the performance levels of High versus Low Anxious scorers. Many studies using this scale have shown that High Anxious individuals do better on verbal learning tasks than do Low Anxious individuals.

89. **(B)**   Standardization of a test implies that there is a uniformity of procedure in administering and scoring the test. If this uniformity (standardization) exists, then one can be assured of measuring only the one independent variable of interest—the person being tested. Without standardization, the examiner cannot be certain that the difference in test scores among individuals is attributable to true individual differences rather than chance factors in the testing environment.

90. **(C)**   Thomas Szasz, in books such as *Ideology and Insanity*, believes that mental illness as the term is used is a myth. "Illness" implies a disease model, yet no one has demonstrated that maladaptive behavior patterns are reliably the result of underlying neurological damage or malfunction.

▼
PRACTICE TEST 2

CLEP HUMAN GROWTH AND DEVELOPMENT
Test 2

(Answer sheets appear in the back of this book.)

TIME: 90 Minutes
90 Questions

DIRECTIONS: Each of the questions or incomplete statements below is followed by five possible answers or completions. Select the best choice in each case and fill in the corresponding oval on the answer sheet.

---

1. The theory that we all experience a series of psychosocial crises throughout our lives was proposed by

    (A) Freud.

    (B) Adler.

    (C) Sheldon.

    (D) Erikson.

    (E) Jung.

2. This theory deemphasizes the importance of _____ in the cognitive development of the child.

    (A) language

    (B) thinking

    (C) emotion

    (D) performance

    (E) using indexes

3. Which of the following psychoanalytic theorists proposed the need to move toward people, move against people, and move away from people?

    (A) Sullivan

    (B) Horney

    (C) Fromm

    (D) Anderson

    (E) Adler

4. According to Freud, the main function of dreams is

    (A) to bridge the unconscious with the conscious mind.

    (B) the assimilation of conscious memories into the unconscious.

    (C) the release of unconscious materials into preconscious.

    (D) wish fulfillment of the individual.

    (E) release of sexual and social tensions.

5. Which of the following developmental periods is characterized by indifference to sexually related matters?

    (A) Latency stage   (D) Tactile stage

    (B) Oral stage   (E) Phallic stage

    (C) Anal stage

6. "OEDIPUS COMPLEX" : "ELECTRA COMPLEX" ::

    (A) girl : boy.   (D) boy : father.

    (B) girl : mother.   (E) boy : girl.

    (C) id : ego.

7. The first stage of ego development is considered to be

    (A) id, ego, superego conflicts.

    (B) primary identification with the mother.

    (C) autonomous ego functions.

    (D) ego introjects.

    (E) ego boundary settings.

8. In Karen Horney's psychoanalytic theory, the fundamental concept is

    (A) basic anxiety.   (D) need to be loved.

    (B) need to love.   (E) libidinal instincts.

    (C) self-actualization.

9. According to psychoanalytic thinking, the personality structure consists of

(A) habits.

(B) drives.

(C) self.

(D) id, ego, and superego.

(E) consciousness.

10. A "positively skewed" distribution is

(A) a distribution that has a few extremely high values.

(B) a distribution that has a few extremely low values.

(C) a flat distribution, with a wide dispersion of values.

(D) a distribution that is very peaked and leptokurtic.

(E) a distribution that is both flat and leptokurtic.

11. A psychologist wants to observe language development. He studies five children over a ten-year period. This psychologist is performing a

(A) longitudinal study.

(B) case study.

(C) factor analysis.

(D) laboratory study.

(E) durational study.

12. By obtaining two scores for one subject with just one test, a researcher achieves

(A) test-retest reliability.

(B) alternate reliability.

(C) split-half reliability.

(D) parallel reliability.

(E) scorer reliability.

13. In drug research, a control group consisting of subjects administered a "fake" drug with no active ingredients is usually included. This "fake" drug is known as a

(A) phoneme.

(B) null drug.

(C) blind drug.

(D) null, dependent variable.

(E) None of the above.

14. Which of the following correlation values is the best predictor for a relationship between x and y?

(A) −.70   (D) .10

(B) +.60   (E) +7.0

(C) +5.0

15. The region at the base of the brain that is highly involved in most emotional and physiological motivation is the

(A) medulla.   (D) hypothalamus.

(B) rhinencephalon.   (E) actomyosin.

(C) pituitary gland.

16. Spinal nerves belong to the

(A) peripheral nervous system.

(B) central nervous system.

(C) antagonistic nervous system.

(D) residual nervous system.

(E) None of the above.

17. An EPSP causes the nerve cell to

(A) polarize.   (D) become less negative.

(B) contract.   (E) None of the above.

(C) become more negative.

18. The pituitary gland secretes which of the following hormones?

(A) TSH (thyroid-stimulating hormone)

(B) ACTH (adrenocorticotrophic hormone)

(C) FSH (follicle-stimulating hormone)

(D) LH (luteinizing hormone)

(E) All of the above.

19. The part of the brain that regulates and coordinates muscle movement is the

(A) cerebellum.   (D) medulla.

(B) pons.   (E) thalamus.

(C) ventricle.

20. The fourth ventricle is located in the

   (A) hypothalamus.   (D) pons.

   (B) medulla.   (E) ventricle.

   (C) spinal cord.

21. The part of the brain that coordinates muscle movements on the two sides of the body is the

   (A) thalamus.   (D) cerebellum.

   (B) hypothalamus.   (E) pons.

   (C) medulla.

QUESTIONS 22 and 23 refer to the following figure:

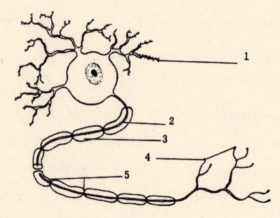

22. Which of the following choices identifies the synaptic boutons that contain neurotransmitters?

   (A) 1   (D) 4

   (B) 2   (E) 5

   (C) 3

23. Which of the following choices identifies the dendrites, neural fibers that receive electrical impulses?

   (A) 1   (D) 4

   (B) 2   (E) 5

   (C) 3

24. In humans, the _____ control(s) slow gradual movements that are modified by sensory feedback.

    (A) cerebellum

    (B) spinal cord

    (C) basal ganglia

    (D) hippocampus

    (E) hypothalamus

QUESTIONS 25 and 26 refer to the following passage.

Sensory feedback has been found to be vital in the control of movement. Walking produces many kinds of sensory feedback. It is possible to eliminate this feedback from arm and leg movements by means of surgery. One can cut all the sensory nerves for part of the body without harming the motor nerves because of their segregation. Sensory nerves enter the spinal cord in the dorsal root, and the motor nerves leave the spinal cord in the ventral root.

25. Cutting the sensory nerves in animal's limb to eliminate feedback is called

    (A) denervation.

    (B) deactivation.

    (C) deafferentation.

    (D) deefferentation.

    (E) decerebration.

26. If the sensory nerves of both forelegs of a monkey are cut, the animal will most probably

    (A) be paralyzed for life.

    (B) recover the use of the stronger limb.

    (C) have to be trained to walk again.

    (D) gradually recover the use of both limbs.

    (E) Both C and D.

27. The colored portion of the eye is called the

    (A) lens.

    (B) cornea.

    (C) pupil.

    (D) iris.

    (E) retina.

28. Receptor cells that are very sensitive to color are the

    (A) ganglion cells.   (D) bipolar cells.

    (B) rods.   (E) chromatic cells.

    (C) cones.

29. A person who has more difficulty hearing high-pitched tones than low-pitched tones probably has

    (A) nerve deafness.   (D) tone-specific deafness.

    (B) conduction deafness.   (E) tonotopic deafness.

    (C) functional deafness.

30. Selfridge's "Pandemonium" model of pattern recognition is an example of a (an) _____ theory.

    (A) template matching   (D) synthetic

    (B) feature analysis   (E) psycholinguistic

    (C) heuristic

31. According to consistency theories of motivation, imbalanced cognitive structures

    (A) are the result of negative learning.

    (B) tend to remain imbalanced.

    (C) will seek expression through contradictory behavior.

    (D) are a major cause of psychosis.

    (E) tend to change and become balanced.

32. According to Guilford, divergent thinking requires

    (A) one solution.   (D) categorization.

    (B) arithmetic reasoning.   (E) Both A and B.

    (C) fluency of ideas.

33. The stage of development within which a child can reliably demonstrate conservation of mass and number is the _____ stage.

(A) preoperational   (D) sensorimotor

(B) formal operations   (E) concrete

(C) operational

34. The phenomenon of backward masking provides evidence for

    (A) long-term memory.   (D) information processing.

    (B) short-term memory.   (E) iconic coding.

    (C) latent inhibition.

35. Material in long-term memory

    (A) may be lost if the person is interrupted while retrieving it.

    (B) is hypothesized to involve ongoing electrical processes in the brain rather than changes in the brain cells.

    (C) includes all memory that is not currently active.

    (D) may include information that never passed through short-term memory.

    (E) Both A and C.

36. Psychologists and educators have come to realize that creativity and intelligence are

    (A) synonymous.

    (B) not synonymous.

    (C) negatively correlated.

    (D) appear as bimodal functions.

    (E) both measured by I.Q. tests.

37. According to Piaget, a child capable of hypothetical thinking is in which developmental stage?

    (A) Sensorimotor stage

    (B) Preoperational stage

    (C) Intuitive preoperational stage

    (D) Concrete operations stage

    (E) Formal operations stage

38. According to Piaget's theory of cognitive development, middle child-hood is characterized by

    (A) hypothetical reasoning.   (D) egocentric thinking.

    (B) deductive thinking.   (E) INRC binary grouping.

    (C) concrete operations.

39. Which of the following is true of short-term memory (STM)?

    (A) It has a storage capacity of 10 items.

    (B) It does not require rehearsals.

    (C) STM is highly susceptible to interference.

    (D) Information always travels from STM to long-term memory.

    (E) It is a permanent record of experience.

40. With reference to short-term memory, rehearsal

    (A) assists in the transfer of information from short-term to long-term memory.

    (B) allows material to remain in short-term memory indefinitely.

    (C) is not primarily an acoustic phenomenon.

    (D) Both A and B.

    (E) Both B and C.

41. The critical period for language acquisition refers to the fact that

    (A) humans are not emotionally stable until they can communicate effectively.

    (B) after a certain age, language skills deteriorate.

    (C) if a person has not acquired a language by puberty, he or she may never learn to speak appropriately.

    (D) humans must acquire one language at a time.

    (E) the brain needs a time frame to develop language centers.

42. Retarded humans frequently show language deficits. Below a measured I.Q. of _____, language acquisition of simple statements and sentences is highly unlikely.

(A) 100   (D) 50

(B) 80   (E) 20

(C) 70

43. The best demonstrations of language acquisition by apes and chimps show that they function on a level equivalent to a human

   (A) three-year-old.

   (B) child between 7 and 11 years of age.

   (C) adolescent, between 12 and 15 years of age.

   (D) adolescent, between 16 and 20 years of age.

   (E) adult, 21 years of age or older.

44. Morphemes differ from phonemes in that

   (A) morphemes are utterances that have no meaning.

   (B) phonemes carry meaning while morphemes do not.

   (C) morphemes carry meaning while phonemes do not.

   (D) morphemes refer to animal sounds while phonemes are sounds made only by humans.

   (E) phonemes refer to speech sounds while morphemes refer to sign language gestures.

45. All of the following are morphemes EXCEPT

   (A) "pre-."   (D) "n."

   (B) " girl."   (E) "re-."

   (C) "-ing."

46. Bees can signal the location and distance of pollen to other bees. They communicate this information in the form of a dance. The Nobel Prize winner who spent years studying and deciphering the "bee dance" is

(A) Konrad Lorenz.   (D) Karl von Frisch.

(B) Charles Darwin.   (E) Niko Tinbergen.

(C) Edward Wilson.

47. The linguistic differences in the world's languages are produced by

(A) different combinations of morphemes.

(B) the fact that different races can produce different phonemes.

(C) the different syntax rules that were developed by different nations.

(D) different combinations of phonemes.

(E) All of the above.

48. According to Guilford's model of intelligence, how many dimensions of intelligence are there?

(A) Three dimensions

(B) A variable number depending on I.Q.

(C) 120 dimensions

(D) 10 dimensions

(E) None of the above.

49. According to Guilford's model of intelligence, which of the following is true?

(A) The Stanford-Binet test is wrong to use as a performance measure.

(B) Intelligence is a function of experience, not of genetic endowment.

(C) Intelligence consists of a specific set of traits that can be classified.

(D) Intelligence is a unitary characteristic.

(E) Intelligence is a function of contents × contexts.

50. Alfred Binet is famous for developing the first

(A) item analysis.

(D) fixed alternative test.

(B) adult intelligence test.

(E) child intelligence test.

(C) projective test.

51. Suppose a business executive decides it is morally wrong to dump his company's toxic waste in a rural wooded area because the law prohibits it. Kolhberg would say that he is at stage _____ of moral development.

(A) 3

(D) 6

(B) 4

(E) 7

(C) 5

52. During which stage of moral development, according to Kohlberg, are moral judgments based on a need for acceptance from others?

(A) 1

(D) 4

(B) 2

(E) 5

(C) 3

53. Complete social isolation of monkeys during their first six months of life can cause

(A) learned helplessness.

(B) delayed attachment with peers.

(C) delayed imprinting with mother.

(D) fear or aggression around mother.

(E) fear or aggression around peers.

54. Which of the following statement(s) about homosexuality is/are true?

    (A) It occurs more often in warmer climates.

    (B) It is caused by hormonal imbalances.

    (C) Many homosexuals have had heterosexual experiences.

    (D) Hormone shots can alter sexual preference.

    (E) All of the above.

55. In the Milgram obedience studies, the "teachers" would give painful electric shocks to the "learners" even though the learners begged them to stop. The results suggest that

    (A) people are basically sadists.

    (B) the subjects were ignorant about the dangers of electric shock.

    (C) people learn faster if they are punished with electric shock whenever they give a wrong answer.

    (D) people will obey legitimate authority even if the orders are against their moral codes.

    (E) corporal punishment does not work.

56. The fact that a crowd of people will stand by and watch a person on a building ledge consider suicide, and few of the people in the crowd will intervene or call the police, is an example of

    (A) diffusion of responsibility.

    (B) bystander intervention.

    (C) people's fascination with death.

    (D) Milgram's obedience law.

    (E) cognitive dissonance.

57. Harry Harlow raised monkeys with dolls instead of their natural mothers. One of the results of his studies suggested that

(A) the monkeys preferred the doll to their natural mothers.

(B) adult sexual receptivity and ability to nurture one's own children are learned early in life.

(C) there were no behavioral differences in animals raised with dolls relative to those monkeys raised with their mothers.

(D) the presence of the father was more important than that of the mother.

(E) the monkeys will refuse to eat and eventually die if raised only with dolls.

58. Children are shown a movie of an adult hitting and kicking a rubber doll. Later, they are given access to the doll. Videotapes of the children made with a hidden camera reveal that

(A) they treat the doll like they do their own toys.

(B) they hit and kick the doll.

(C) the boys hit the doll while the girls play gently with it.

(D) the children avoid the doll.

(E) the girls console the doll.

59. Which of the following is NOT an example of parental sex role development strategies?

(A) Pink for girls and blue for boys

(B) Refusing to buy a six-year-old boy a doll

(C) Teaching your daughter to defer to your son

(D) Buying your son a set of plastic tools

(E) Encouraging little girls to pretend that they are doctors

60. The factor that has been found to be the most predictive of interpersonal attraction is

(A) similarity.

(B) proximity.

(C) status.

(D) honesty.

(E) physical attractiveness.

61. Social comparison theory was first introduced by

    (A) Bandura.   (D) Festinger.

    (B) Krauss.   (E) Aronson.

    (C) Schachter.

62. Which of the following characteristics have been found to be strong predictors of conformity to social pressure?

    (A) Authoritarian personality

    (B) "External" personality

    (C) High need for approval

    (D) Both B and C.

    (E) All of the above.

63. Among the findings on Rotter's Locus of Control scale is the fact that

    (A) individuals with high achievement motivation are more internal in their dispositions.

    (B) individuals with low achievement motivation are more internal in their dispositions.

    (C) whites are less internal than blacks.

    (D) females are less external than males.

    (E) locus of control is an innate characteristic.

64. Research has shown that children who are reared by strict punishment usually

    (A) become criminals.   (D) enlist in the armed forces.

    (B) grow up to be passive.   (E) Both A and D.

    (C) grow up to be aggressive.

65. We usually recommend a film to friends if it started well and had a terrific ending, even though the middle was slow and boring. The film's producer is taking advantage of the _____ and _____ effect.

    (A) primacy, recency

    (B) cognitive, primacy

(C) cognitive, inertial

(D) recency, overgeneralization

(E) personal bias, halo

66. Which one of the following is a "Western" concept?

(A) Infancy

(B) Puberty

(C) Adolescence

(D) Teenagers

(E) Juvenile delinquency

67. Maslow and _____ both emphasized the concept of self-actualization.

(A) Kelly   (D) Fromm

(B) James   (E) Sullivan

(C) Rogers

68. The fact that people will work harder for a while after a supervisor speaks to them is an example of

(A) social loafing.   (D) social facilitation.

(B) obedience.   (E) deindividuation.

(C) peer compliance.

69. The part of the brain involved in emotional responses such as rage and aggression is the

(A) parasympathetic system.

(B) reticular activating system.

(C) limbic system.

(D) sympathetic system.

(E) Broca reflex loop.

70. People who take credit for their successes but blame others for their failures (for example, "I got an A in biology, she failed me in math") are using the ego defense mechanism of

(A) fantasy.

(B) rationalization.

(C) denial.

(D) projection.

(E) displacement.

71. The tendency to hold people totally responsible for their behavior and discount environmental factors (fat people have no self-control) is known as

(A) cognitive dissonance.

(B) the fundamental attribution error.

(C) the reference group misjudgment.

(D) an altruistic excuse.

(E) situational inducement.

72. The James-Lange theory of emotion claims that

(A) we run because we are afraid.

(B) we are afraid because we are running.

(C) we simultaneously run and are afraid.

(D) running and being afraid are not necessarily related.

(E) this theory really does not exist.

73. The eight basic emotional responses that an infant is capable of include

(A) fear and envy.

(B) joy and revenge.

(C) anger and distress.

(D) interest and guilt.

(E) guilt and joy.

74. The first systematic study of operant conditioning was performed in 1938 by

(A) E.L. Thorndike.

(B) B.F. Skinner.

(C) Miller and Dollard.

(D) A. Bandura.

(E) I. Pavlov.

75. The reinforcement schedule that yields the lowest performance is the

    (A) fixed-ratio schedule.

    (B) variable-ratio schedule.

    (C) fixed-interval schedule.

    (D) variable-interval schedule.

    (E) intermittent reinforcement schedule.

76. Extinction of a conditioned response occurs when

    (A) the CS is presented without the UCS several times.

    (B) the UCS is presented without the CS several times.

    (C) the CS is presented for more than five seconds before the start of the UCS.

    (D) the CS terminates before the onset of the UCS.

    (E) the CS begins after the UCS is terminated.

77. An approving comment made by a boss to an employee is an example of

    (A) generalized reinforcement.

    (B) conditioned reinforcement.

    (C) primary reinforcement.

    (D) social reinforcement.

    (E) positive reinforcement.

78. The repeated presentation of the CS without the UCS results in

    (A) spontaneous recovery.   (D) higher-order conditioning.

    (B) inhibition.   (E) negative reinforcement.

    (C) extinction.

79. In classical conditioning, the response that automatically occurs whenever the unconditioned stimulus is presented without any training is called a (an)

(A) behavioral response.   (D) unlearned response.

(B) unconditioned response.   (E) instinctive response.

(C) preconditioned response.

QUESTION 80 refers to the following passage.

A woman visits a psychologist because she is extremely afraid of pigeons and is overcome with fear and anxiety every time she sees one. She tells the psychologist that her fear is irrational and she cannot control it. She first remembers being afraid of pigeons at age eight when she fell off her bicycle in the street and landed on a dead pigeon. Her fear is growing more intense, and earlier that week a pigeon flew past her and sent her huddling in a doorway crying with fear.

80. Within a learning theory paradigm, the origin of this disorder could be explained by stating that fear associated with falling from the bike was the UCS and that the bird lying in the street was the

    (A) US.   (D) CS.

    (B) CR.   (E) SS.

    (C) UCR.

81. Which of the following is NOT a primary difference between dealing with an adolescent student and an elementary school student?

    (A) The tendency to act out

    (B) The necessity to get consent from the student to be treated

    (C) The advantages of using group therapy

    (D) The potential advantages of being counseled

    (E) The severity of the inappropriate behavior they engage in

82. The better "intelligence," "mental ability," and "learning aptitude" tests attempt to assess students across a (an) _____ year interval.

    (A) one-   (D) six-

    (B) two-   (E) eight-

    (C) four-

83. The Wechsler Intelligence Scale for Children differs from the Revised Stanford Binet test in

    (A) the age groups that can be tested.

    (B) the distribution of verbal and nonverbal tasks.

    (C) its applicability with psychotic students.

    (D) its accounting for cultural background differences.

    (E) All of the above.

84. All of the following are commonly used personality tests EXCEPT the _____ test.

    (A) Rorschach   (D) Sica Personality Inventory

    (B) Children's Apperception   (E) Bender Motor Gestalt

    (C) Michigan Picture Story

85. A third-grade transfer student scores a 66 on the Revised Stanford Binet test. This student would be placed in

    (A) an advanced class.

    (B) a class appropriate for his or her age.

    (C) a special education class.

    (D) a program for remedial visual motor training.

    (E) a program emphasizing math.

86. People who repeatedly wash their hands even when they are not dirty may be said to be suffering from

    (A) learned helplessness.

    (B) a conversion reaction.

    (C) an obsession.

    (D) a phobia.

    (E) a compulsion.

87. Transference neurosis is an aspect of the therapeutic process most common in

    (A) logotherapy.   (D) client-centered therapy.

    (B) implosive therapy.   (E) None of the above.

    (C) psychoanalysis.

88. An antisocial reaction is an example of

    (A) a depressive neurosis.   (D) delusional behavior.

    (B) a neurosis.   (E) a psychosis.

    (C) a conduct disorder.

89. Electroconvulsive shock therapy (ECT) has been demonstrated to be effective in the treatment of

    (A) severe depression.   (D) fugue.

    (B) schizophrenia.   (E) All of the above.

    (C) paranoia.

90. In reactive schizophrenia, the onset of symptoms is

    (A) inconsistent among this psychiatric population.

    (B) rapid and sudden.

    (C) slow and gradual.

    (D) indirectly related to the prognosis.

    (E) None of the above.

CLEP HUMAN GROWTH AND DEVELOPMENT TEST 2

1.	(D)	23.	(A)	46.	(D)	69.	(C)
2.	(C)	24.	(C)	47.	(D)	70.	(D)
3.	(B)	25.	(C)	48.	(A)	71.	(B)
4.	(D)	26.	(D)	49.	(C)	72.	(B)
5.	(A)	27.	(D)	50.	(E)	73.	(C)
6.	(E)	28.	(C)	51.	(B)	74.	(B)
7.	(B)	29.	(A)	52.	(C)	75.	(C)
8.	(A)	30.	(B)	53.	(E)	76.	(A)
9.	(D)	31.	(E)	54.	(C)	77.	(D)
10.	(A)	32.	(C)	55.	(D)	78.	(C)
11.	(A)	33.	(E)	56.	(A)	79.	(B)
12.	(C)	34.	(E)	57.	(B)	80.	(D)
13.	(E)	35.	(C)	58.	(B)	81.	(D)
14.	(A)	36.	(B)	59.	(E)	82.	(B)
15.	(D)	37.	(E)	60.	(B)	83.	(B)
16.	(A)	38.	(C)	61.	(D)	84.	(D)
17.	(D)	39.	(C)	62.	(E)	85.	(C)
18.	(E)	40.	(D)	63.	(A)	86.	(E)
19.	(A)	41.	(C)	64.	(C)	87.	(C)
20.	(B)	42.	(E)	65.	(A)	88.	(C)
21.	(E)	43.	(A)	66.	(C)	89.	(A)
22.	(D)	44.	(C)	67.	(C)	90.	(B)
		45.	(D)	68.	(D)		

DETAILED EXPLANATIONS
OF ANSWERS

TEST 2

1.   **(D)**   Erikson determined that there were eight developmental crises in our lives corresponding to the eight developmental periods. These crises in their developmental order are (1) trust vs. mistrust; (2) autonomy vs. doubt and shame; (3) initiative vs. guilt; (4) industry vs. inferiority; (5) identity crisis; (6) intimacy vs. isolation; (7) crisis of child rearing; and (8) integrity vs. despair in old age.

2.   **(C)**   You will notice in the passage that there is no mention of the emotional effects and experience of the child on its cognitive development. This theory is limited to looking at the progressive problem-solving ability in the child. It does not examine the emotional or psychosocial development of the child.

3.   **(B)**   Karen Horney, an analyst who broke from classical psycho-analysis, developed a theory concerning the neurotic needs of the individual. She identified 10 neurotic needs that fall under three general categories: (l) moving toward people; (2) moving away from people; and (3) moving against people. She thought most people achieve an integration and balance of these forces, but the neurotic individual lacks this balance and integration.

4.   **(D)**   Freud reasoned that the dream is a hallucinatory state that structures events not as they would be in reality, but as the dreamer wishes them to be. When unconscious desires conflict with conscious restraints, however, it is necessary for the "dream work" to pursue devious paths to express the wish.

5.   **(A)**   The latency stage lasts about five years, from ages six to eleven. During this period the child's identification with the parent of his or her own sex becomes stronger. The child also incorporates more of the beliefs and values of his or her culture; hence, the superego is developing

to a greater degree. The child comes to distinguish between acceptable and unacceptable behavior in his society. During this period children generally seek out more playmates of their own sex.

6.   **(E)**   The Oedipus Complex is to the Electra Complex as boy is to girl. In the Oedipal Complex, the boy wants his mother for himself and wants to be rid of the competing father, but he fears castration from the father. In order to deal with that fear, he represses it and identifies with his father. In the Electra Complex, the girl desires the father and wants to be rid of the mother, but with time, her devaluation of her mother and her jealousy fade, as she develops the female behaviors of appealing to the father and desiring a baby as a substitute for the penis she is lacking.

7.   **(B)**   Primary identification with the mother occurs during the first few weeks of life. At first, it is thought, the infant cannot distinguish himself from his mother. During this stage, the infant's level of differentiation between himself and the mother and himself and the environment increases. This early identification is a necessary part of the child's ego development, according to psychoanalytic theory.

8.   **(A)**   The fundamental concept in Karen Horney's psychoanalytic theory is basic anxiety. This is experienced in childhood as a feeling of isolation and helplessness in a potentially hostile world. The anxiety results from parental attitudes toward the child, which may take the form of dominance, lack of affection, lack of protective behavior, and many other negative affect states. Horney considers anxiety to be a learned response, not an innate response.

9.   **(D)**   The personality structure consists of id, ego, and superego. According to Freud, the id is the most fundamental component of personality and is comprised of drives, needs, and instinctual impulses. It is unable to tolerate tension, is obedient only to the pleasure principle, and is in constant conflict with the superego. The superego develops out of the ego during childhood. It contains values, morals, and basic attitudes as learned from parents and society. The ego mediates between the id and superego. The ego is sometimes called the executive agency of the personality because it controls actions and decides how needs should be satisfied.

10.   **(A)**   To state that a distribution is positively skewed is an attempt to describe the curve form of that frequency distribution. A few extreme higher values form a positively skewed graph.

11. **(A)** A longitudinal study is an extended examination of the same subject or subjects over a (usually long) period of time. This approach is particularly useful in examining the stability of a behavior characteristic over time or the development of a behavior over time.

12. **(C)** In split-half reliability the correlation between the two scores is the reliability coefficient. Usually, the examiner uses scores on odd and even items as the two scores. This procedure is preferred to comparing scores from the first and second half of the test due to practice effects and fatigue. The split-half reliability coefficient is often called the coefficient of internal consistency because the comparison of two scores on a test indicates whether the test has an underlying consistency.

13. **(E)** A "fake" drug is known as a placebo. A placebo is used to control the effects caused by the simple ingestion of a pill or injection of a drug. It is also used as a baseline measure against which the effects of the other drugs are compared. In order to demonstrate that a drug is effective, one must show that it had a greater effect on the subject than the placebo did.

14. **(A)** The correlation of –.70 is the best predictor. Correlations can have any value between –1.0 and +1.0. As the absolute value of the correlation approaches 1.0, the prediction based on the correlation becomes more accurate. A negative correlation shows an inverse relationship between x and y: as x goes up, y goes down, and vice versa. A positive correlation shows a direct relationship between x and y: as x goes up, y goes up, and vice versa.

15. **(D)** The hypothalamus, located under the thalamus, is a collection of nuclei concerned with homeostatic regulations. Electrical stimulation of certain cells in the hypothalamus produces sensations of hunger, thirst, pain, pleasure, or sexual drives. These are all important emotional and physiological motivators of behavior.

16. **(A)** Spinal nerves belong to the peripheral nervous system (PNS). They arise as pairs at regular intervals from the spinal cord, branch, and run to various parts of the body to innervate them. In humans, there are 31 symmetrical pairs of spinal nerves.

17. **(D)** An EPSP is an excitatory postsynaptic potential and refers to changes in a nerve cell's charge, relative to the environment. An EPSP occurs when stimulation makes the nerve cell less negative, as would occur if the cell membrane began to allow positive charges to pass

through. It is considered excitatory because if it is large enough, it may cause the nerve cell to become sufficiently positive in order to fire.

18. **(E)** The pituitary gland produces TSH, ACTH, FSH, and LH. TSH induces secretion of another hormone in the thyroid gland. ACTH stimulates the adrenal cortex to secrete cortisol. Both LH and FSH control the secretion of the sex hormones by the gonads. They also regulate the growth and development of sperm and ovum. Hence, the pituitary is in a sense a master gland that directs the hormone secretions to other glands and organs.

19. **(A)** The cerebellum is made up of a central part and two hemispheres extending sideways. The size of the cerebellum in different animals is roughly correlated with the amount of muscular activity. The cerebellum coordinates muscle contraction. Injury to the cerebellum results in the inability to coordinate muscle movements, although the muscles can still move.

20. **(B)** The medulla is connected to the spinal cord and is the most posterior part of the brain. Here the central canal of the spinal cord (spinal lumen) enlarges to form a fluid-filled cavity called the fourth ventricle. The medulla also has numerous nerve tracts that bring impulses to and from the brain.

21. **(E)** The pons is an area of the hindbrain containing a large number of nerve fibers that pass through it and make connections between the two hemispheres of the cerebellum, thus coordinating muscle movements on the two sides of the body. The pons also contains the nerve centers that aid in the regulation of breathing.

22. **(D)** Synaptic boutons, also called axonic terminals, are the end tip of the axon. They almost make contact with the dendrites of another neuron. The neurotransmitters produced in the boutons travel across the synaptic cleft to interact with the membrane of the receiving cell, changing the membrane permeability.

23. **(A)** Dendrites are numerous in the neuron. They receive information either from other neurons or directly from the environment and then divert the electrical impulses (information) toward the cell body of the neuron. Action potentials are not generated along the dendrites.

24. **(C)** The basal ganglia, which consist of the caudate nucleus, the putamen, and the globus pallidus, are important for slow, gradual move-

ments that can be modified by sensory feedback while the movement is occurring. Damage to the basal ganglia can lead to Parkinson's disease, a progressive deterioration of walking, standing, and other movements of the body as a whole.

25. **(C)** Cutting the sensory (afferent) nerves in a limb to eliminate feedback is referred to as deafferentation. The animal loses all sensation in the affected part of the body, but the motor nerves remain totally intact.

26. **(D)** In 1968, Taub and Berman cut all the afferent nerves from one arm of a monkey, after which the animal did not spontaneously use the limb for anything. However, when the afferent nerves of both forelimbs were cut, the monkey recovered use of both. It was concluded that if one forelimb is deafferented, the monkey does not use it only because it is easier to use the normal limb alone. When both are deafferented, the monkey is forced to use both, thus showing that voluntary movements are still possible after sensory feedback has been greatly reduced.

27. **(D)** The colored portion of the eye is called the iris. It is the tissue that surrounds the pupil and regulates its size. By contracting or dilating, the iris adjusts the amount of light entering the eye.

28. **(C)** Cones respond differentially to different color wavelengths, providing us not only with color perception but also an ability to sense fine gradations of color.

29. **(A)** A person suffering from nerve deafness will have more difficulty hearing high-pitched tones. This type of deafness results from damage to the auditory nervous system. Hair cells in the cochlea translate sound vibrations into electrical messages our brain can "understand." Specific hair cells respond to specific tones. If some are damaged, the vibrations of certain tones will not be properly translated into electrical messages.

30. **(B)** Feature analysis theories, of which the best known is the "Pandemonium" theory, describe mechanisms whereby the nervous system analyzes small details in sensory input. Feature analysis also describes the cognitive system as being hierarchically organized in its analysis of information.

31. **(E)** Consistency, or homeostatic, theories maintain that the principal motivating force of the organism is to maintain a consistent physical or

psychological state. The theory states that imbalanced relationships tend to change and become balanced.

32. **(C)** Divergent thinking involves generating a number of possible solutions. It requires a fluency of ideas, flexibility, and originality. The solution of complex chess problems, for example, requires divergent thinking. This is true because there are always many possibilities to consider before making a move.

33. **(E)** According to Piaget, concrete operations is the level of cognitive development in which children understand conservation. At this level, they can reason abstractly enough to realize that changing the shape of an object (rolling a ball of clay into a cigar shape, for example) doesn't change the amount of material they have to work with.

34. **(E)** In the backward masking procedure, a letter is flashed on a screen. After the letter is flashed, there is a brief period of time during which the impression can be completely erased by the flash of a bright light. This time period is about five seconds, but during this time, the image can be read as though the stimulus was still present. The backward masking effect demonstrates that the brief life of memory codes can be easily erased by input that is specific to the given sense modality.

35. **(C)** Long-term memory is complex and possesses a virtually limitless capacity. It is therefore difficult for theorists to study. Long-term memory can be slow and difficult. Past events that relate to a current situation have to be searched for out of billions of stored items. It usually requires effort to put new information into long-term memory. Material that is in long-term memory can be brought into active memory and will not be lost if it is interrupted.

36. **(B)** Specialists in the fields of psychology and education have come to recognize that creativity and intelligence are not synonymous. Creativity is certainly not measurable by standard I.Q. tests. Creativity is influenced by many non-intellectual, temperamental characteristics, such as a receptive attitude toward novel ideas, specific perceptual tendencies, and ideational fluency.

37. **(E)** The stage of formal operations is the final step in Piaget's system of cognitive development. It begins at about age 11 when the child begins to free him- or herself from the period of concrete operations. The child can now imagine hypothetical states and realize that there are many

possible solutions to a problem. Thinking becomes increasingly propositional, logical, and idealistic.

38. **(C)**   In Piaget's theory, an operation is a thought. Thought refers to
the mental representation of something that is not immediately perceived.
During this period of concrete operations, the child is capable of invoking
a mental representation or image of an object or event. This representation
is linked to a mental image of the "concrete" perceptual experience. It
must exist in the physical sense and not be hypothetical.

39. **(C)**   STM is highly susceptible to interference. For instance, when
a person begins dialing a telephone number but is interrupted, the number
may be forgotten or dialed incorrectly. Interference can disrupt STM because there is no rehearsal time after a response. Information may also be
interrupted because the interfering activity could also enter STM and
cause it to reach its capacity for stored items. In either case, displacement
of old, unrehearsed items will occur.

40. **(D)**   Rehearsal appears to serve two main functions. The first is to
allow material to remain in short-term memory indefinitely. The second
appears to be assisting in the transfer of information from short-term to
long-term memory. The limited capacities of short-term memory affect the
amount of information that can be successfully rehearsed. It is a relatively
small amount of material that can be remembered and kept alive through
rehearsal.

41. **(C)**   Humans are born prewired to acquire language. However, the
environment must provide the stimulation for the brain areas associated
with language to develop. Cases of children raised by animals or under
conditions of extreme language deprivation (e.g., kept locked in a room
and seldom spoken to) show that if a human doesn't acquire a language by
puberty, they will never acquire any reasonable mastery of language,
whether they are later provided with extensive remedial language training
or not.

42. **(E)**   Humans with an I.Q. of 20 or less barely make reliable contact
with their environments and seldom develop abilities beyond those of an
infant. Retarded individuals with an I.Q. of 50 or higher can learn to
comprehend and make simple statements.

43. **(A)**   Even with years of daily training, the number of vocabulary
words and the complexity of the statements that apes and chimps make

and comprehend are equivalent only to a human three-year-old. Most statements involve rewards such as "Give me apple." Further, they often act as if word order doesn't matter. "Give me apple," "Apple me give," and "Me apple give" are used interchangeably. In ape communications, syntax is limited.

44. **(C)** Phonemes are the 40 or so basic sounds that all humans are capable of making. The coos and babbling of a baby are phonemes. Morphemes are the smallest units of speech sounds that carry meaning. Prefixes such as "un," "pro," and "pre" are examples of morphemes.

45. **(D)** Morphemes are the smallest units of meaning in a language. All of the question choices were morphemes except "n," which is a phoneme. Phonemes combine to form morphemes. In English, morphemes can be whole words such as "girl" or prefixes and suffixes like "re-" and "-ing." There are more than 100,000 morphemes in the English language.

46. **(D)** Karl von Frisch demonstrated that bees dance around using particular muscular movements in order to communicate the location and distance of food to other members of the hive.

47. **(D)** Phonemes are the 40 or so speech sounds all humans are capable of making. Regardless of nationality or race, all humans are members of the same species. The differences in languages are the result of using phonemes in different combinations.

48. **(A)** The three dimensions of intelligence are operations, contents, and products. Operations help describe what mental activity a person is using to approach a problem, for example, memory or cognition. Operations like memory or cognition are performed on some specific kind of content, like reading material. Products are the end results of the operations. More specifically, a product is the form in which information is processed.

49. **(C)** Guilford's concept of intelligence is based on a multiple factor theory, which means that he describes intelligence as consisting of a specific set of traits, or factors. He classifies intelligence along three dimensions: operations, contents, and products.

50.   **(E)**   In 1904, the French government asked Alfred Binet to construct a test that would distinguish between normal children and children with severe learning disabilities. Binet conceived of intelligence as the relationship of mental ability and chronological age. For each age up to 15 years, there is a set of characteristic abilities that develop in the normal child. If they developed earlier than average, the child is more intelligent than average; if the abilities develop later, then the child is considered to be of below average intelligence.

51.   **(B)**   Stage 4 is a law and order orientation in which one is motivated to follow the rules laid down by authorities. The business executive behaves morally to avoid a fine and jail sentence imposed by criminal law. He has not yet achieved what Kohlberg calls the stages of principled morality. In stage 5, the beginning of principled morality, a person behaves morally to promote society's welfare.

52.   **(C)**   Stage 3 of Kohlberg's theory of moral development is part of the conventional morality level of ethical reasoning. The individual is motivated to be "good" so as to avoid the disapproval of others and gain their acceptance. Stage 2 is a cost-benefit orientation whereby one behaves morally to obtain rewards.

53.   **(E)**   Complete social isolation prevents the development of attachment and socialization in primates. Monkeys raised in complete social isolation either display fear or aggression when suddenly placed in the companionship of peers.

54.   **(C)**   Interviews with homosexuals reveal that many have had unsatisfactory heterosexual experiences. There is no evidence to indicate that it is caused by hormone imbalances. Human sexual behavior is not controlled by hormones as it is in lower species. Giving testosterone to a male homosexual produces a more muscular and aggressive homosexual, not a heterosexual. Throughout history, homosexuals have existed in all climates.

55.   **(D)**   Milgram was interested in how people can be induced to perform acts that are morally reprehensible to them or in contradiction to their dominant personality traits. His research indicates that a person will commit acts, including murder, if a legitimate authority orders it, and more importantly, if that authority figure accepts the responsibility and consequences of these acts. Hence, it is possible to turn a boy into a killing soldier within a few weeks of basic training.

56. **(A)** Diffusion of responsibility refers to the fact that the larger the group of people, the less any member of the group feels personally responsible for the events that are occurring. Members of lynch mobs, gangs, and crowds at sports events often act as spectators to events that they do not condone.

57. **(B)** Monkeys that are raised with "doll mothers" have had no model to demonstrate nurturing techniques. They have also been deprived of physical contact with their own species. As adults, they show little interest in sex. After they are artificially impregnated and give birth, they reject their young. The research suggests that there is no mothering instinct in primates or humans. Our parenting techniques are based on our own childhood experiences.

58. **(B)** Children imitate what they see and hear without making value judgments. They assimilate the habits, good or bad, of those around them. Children (boys and girls) who see an adult abusing a doll imitate the behavior when given the opportunity. Many parents do not let their children watch violent cartoons or shows like "The Three Stooges," because they practice what they see on their siblings, playmates, and parents.

59. **(E)** Sex role development refers to the fact that parents, primarily due to their own upbringing, believe that there are appropriate ways for children to act, depending on their sex. Boys are expected to be aggressive, dominant, and mechanically inclined. Girls are expected to be more submissive and gentle. Some parents reinforce their children for behaving in accordance with the sex stereotypes.

60. **(B)** The closer two individuals are geographically, the more likely it is that they will like each other. A repeated finding concerning mate selection is that individuals find mates who live close to them. Another function of proximity is that it makes possible the operation of other factors that can increase attraction, such as attitude similarity.

61. **(D)** Festinger (1954) proposed that all people have a drive to evaluate themselves. In situations lacking objective, nonsocial means of evaluation, people evaluate themselves by comparison with other people. This is the social comparison theory. Much research has been performed using this phenomenon, most notably Stanley Schachter's studies on emotion and affiliation.

62. **(E)** Three personality characteristics that have proven to be predictive of conformity behavior are the following:

(1)   An authoritarian person is greatly influenced by authority figures; thus, the more authoritarian a person is, the more he or she will conform.

(2)   People who believe that the circumstances of life are under their control are called "internals," while those that feel that what happens to them is beyond their control are "externals." "Externals" are more likely to conform than "internals."

(3)   People who are high in need for approval conform more than people who are low in this need.

63.   **(A)**   Rotter's Locus of Control scale attempts to measure the extent to which a person has an internal or external orientation. A person with an internal orientation tends to take responsibility for what happens to him or her, whereas the "external" sees life events as due to chance or some other factor beyond his or her control. Consistent findings include the following: people with high achievement motivation are generally more internal; males are more internal than females; and whites are more internal than blacks. Locus of control is a learned or acquired characteristic and can be changed by new experiences.

64.   **(C)**   This adverse effect has generally been attributed to the frustrating effect of severe punishment. Mild punishment is a far more effective tool for reducing aggression in children.

65.   **(A)**   The primacy and recency effects, respectively, refer to our remembering best the first and the last bits of information that we were given. The middle information is distorted by proactive and retroactive interference effects.

66.   **(C)**   Adolescence, a period between infancy and adulthood, is a Western concept that was developed during the last century. In many other cultures, children are given adult responsibilities at puberty. They marry, are apprenticed, or join the military as early as 10 years of age. Allowing young people the luxury of a few years to develop before assuming the responsibilities of adults is a Western concept. Some psychologists believe that these freedoms can be detrimental rather than fostering the development of maturity.

67.   **(C)**   Carl Rogers developed a new form of psychotherapy based on the premise that people constantly strive to fulfill their inherent potential. Client-centered therapy views the therapist as an aide to the client's striv-

ing for self-actualization. Similarly, Rogers conceptualized personality theory as being person-centered.

68. **(D)** People can be motivated to perform slower (social loafing) or faster (social facilitation) depending on the nature of the influencing agent and the response of those people around them.

69. **(C)** The limbic system, which includes the amygdala, has been shown to control emotions. Electrical stimulation of this area produces rage reactions in animals. The sympathetic and parasympathetic systems are located in the spinal cord, not the brain.

70. **(D)** Projection is an ego defense mechanism wherein we blame other people or things for our failures. "The coach had it in for me," "It was in my stars," are two examples. The other four choices are also ego defense mechanisms. Fantasy refers to daydreaming. Rationalization is providing socially acceptable reasons for inappropriate behavior. Denial is a case where we refuse to accept the truth. For example, a neighbor denies that her son has a drinking problem although he frequently comes home drunk. Displacement is taking out our frustrations on substitute objects or people. The boss says "You're an idiot" and you say nothing. When you get home, your spouse asks how your day went. "Can't a person ever find a hot meal waiting when they get home?" is your reply. The spouse turns to the son and says "Why aren't you doing your homework?" The boy kicks the dog on his way to his room.

71. **(B)** People tend to blame environmental factors for their own mistakes, but do not extend this courtesy to others. They hold people totally responsible for their behavior. Attributing behavior solely to dispositional factors and discounting environmental influences is the fundamental attribution error.

72. **(B)** The James-Lange theory states that environmental stimuli trigger physiological changes, i.e., hormone and glandular activity. When these changes register in the brain, we feel an emotion. Hence, when threatened we may begin running and then sense the fear afterwards.

73. **(C)** According to Carroll Izard, the eight basic emotions an infant is capable of include joy, anger, surprise, distress, interest, disgust, sadness, and fear. Feelings of envy, revenge, and guilt require cognitive abilities beyond the infant's capabilities.

74. **(B)** Skinner developed an apparatus consisting of a small enclosure with a lever device and a food receptacle. A hungry rat was placed in the box and in time usually pressed the lever by chance and automatically received food (a reward). After some time, most of the rats learned to make this response (lever-pressing) as soon as they entered the box. This learning was termed operant conditioning because the animal had to perform an operation to get a reward.

75. **(C)** In the fixed-interval schedule, reinforcement is given after a fixed period of time no matter how much work is done. This schedule has the lowest yield in terms of performance. However, just before the reinforcement is given, activity increases.

76. **(A)** Extinction occurs when the conditioned stimulus is repeatedly presented without the unconditioned stimulus. The strength of the response elicited by the CS and its ability to elicit the CR at all gradually decreases as the CS continues to be presented alone. The CR strength eventually declines to at least the level present before conditioning began.

77. **(D)** Social reinforcement occurs when the reinforcer consists of feedback from individuals in one's environment. Approval from a boss is clearly an example of positive social reinforcement. Other examples of positive social reinforcement would be attention and affection, while examples of negative social reinforcement would be indifference or enmity.

78. **(C)** Extinction of conditioned respondent behavior occurs when the CS is presented without the UCS a number of times. The magnitude of the response elicited by the CS and the percentage of presentations of the CS that elicits responses gradually decreases as the CS continues to be presented without the UCS. If CS presentation continues without the UCS, the CR will decline to at least the level present before the classical conditioning was begun.

79. **(B)** Examples of unconditioned responses are salivation to food and adrenal gland responses to fear stimuli.

80. **(D)** In terms of this example, falling off one's bicycle (UCS) reliably elicits fear and anxiety (UCR). The single pairing of the sight of a dead pigeon (CS) with the act of falling (UCS) created a conditioned response (CR) of fear and anxiety elicited upon seeing pigeons in future situations. The UCS of falling off the bicycle was no longer needed to be present to create the CR of fear and anxiety. Although this theory sounds

like a good explanation for the occurrence of phobias, in many cases phobics have never had any early traumatic experiences with the phobic object.

81. **(D)** Adolescents are more likely to act out, be hostile, or be suspicious than a younger student. Adolescents usually band together in groups or gangs, making group therapy less personally threatening to them. Younger students tend to benefit more from individualized treatment. Because they are older, adolescents may have problems (e.g., sex, drugs) that the younger student wouldn't have. They also are not considered children and must, therefore, consent to treatment. People of all ages can benefit positively from counseling.

82. **(B)** Assessment tests should be designed to encompass a two-year period. If test items cover too broad an age range, the easier items may falsely raise the grades of older students while the more difficult items would be beyond the range of the younger students tested.

83. **(B)** The Stanford Binet test has a heavy emphasis on verbal skills while the WISC uses verbal and nonverbal tasks equally. Neither test is appropriate for psychotic students or students with limited command of the English language.

84. **(D)** The Sica Personality Inventory test doesn't exist. All of the other tests are frequently used to assess personality. Other useful tests include the Make-A-Picture-Story, Blacky, and the House-Tree-Person tests.

85. **(C)** The average score on the test is 100. A score below 70 suggests mental retardation. The low IQ may not necessarily be due to visual motor problems. The student would be expected to have problems keeping up in a class appropriate for his or her age.

86. **(E)** Repeated hand-washing is known as an obsessive-compulsive neurosis, although, as in other obsessive-compulsive disorders, the two components need not exist simultaneously. Repeated hand-washing is termed compulsive if the person feels compelled to perform the behavior, thus interfering with more appropriate behavior. As opposed to a compulsion, an obsession is a recurring thought rather than an action that a person cannot control or stop. This disorder is thought to arise as a defense against anxiety. In the case of repeated hand-washing, the act may be associated with a conflict between masturbation and guilt.

87. **(C)**   The resolution of the transference neurosis is one of the most important parts of the cure in classical psychoanalysis. For it to occur successfully, the analyst must be able to maintain the stance of compassionate neutrality. Transference neurosis refers specifically to displaced and usually intense and inappropriate reactions of the patient to the analyst.

88. **(C)**   A conduct disorder is characterized by observed behavior that varies from the norm of acceptable behaviors. An antisocial reaction is a type of conduct disorder. Antisocial reactions are typically characterized by poor judgment, insensitivity, disregard for authority and law, and emotional immaturity. Psychologists generally agree that such a problem is a function of poor development of the conscience aggravated by environmental factors.

89. **(A)**   Although ECT was once used as a treatment for schizophrenia, it has been shown to be ineffective in the treatment of the disorder. In fact, ECT has been shown to be effective only in the treatment of severe depression.

90. **(B)**   A rapid and sudden onset of symptoms is characteristic of reactive schizophrenia. The patient may suffer a pronounced shock, or trauma, just before the outbreak of the schizophrenia. If the patient was moderately well-adjusted before the disturbance, the chances for recovery are fairly good.

PRACTICE
TEST 3

This test is also on CD-ROM in our special interactive CLEP Human Growth & Development TEST*ware*®. It is highly recommended that you first take this exam on computer. You will then have the additional study features and benefits of enforced timed conditions, individual diagnostic analysis, and instant scoring. See page 2 for guidance on how to get the most out of our CLEP Human Growth & Development book and software.

CLEP HUMAN GROWTH AND DEVELOPMENT
Test 3

(Answer sheets appear in the back of this book.)

TIME: 90 Minutes
90 Questions

DIRECTIONS: Each of the questions or incomplete statements below is followed by five possible answers or completions. Select the best choice in each case and fill in the corresponding oval on the answer sheet.

---

1. In Piaget's theory of child development, object permanence occurs at the end of the _____ stage.

   (A) sensorimotor   (D) concrete operational

   (B) preoperational   (E) intuitive preoperational

   (C) formal operational

2. According to Piaget's theory of cognitive development, middle childhood is characterized by

   (A) hypothetical reasoning.   (D) egocentric thinking.

   (B) deductive thinking.   (E) INRC binary grouping.

   (C) concrete operations.

3. If, during a child's development, the amount of frustration and anxiety concerning movement to the next stage becomes too great, development may come to a halt. The individual is said to become

   (A) dependent.   (D) regressive.

   (B) passive.   (E) repressed.

   (C) fixated.

4. According to psychoanalytic theory, when an unpleasant or threatening thought or idea is not permitted into awareness, it is due to

   (A) repression.   (D) reaction formation.

   (B) projection.   (E) compensation.

   (C) displacement.

5. Conscience and morality are conceptually defined within the Freudian theory as the

   (A) conscious.   (D) ego.

   (B) id.   (E) superego.

   (C) preconscious.

6. Jean Piaget gauged intelligence as a matter of

   (A) psychosexual development.

   (B) cognitive development.

   (C) moral development.

   (D) scores on standardized IQ tests.

   (E) All of the above.

7. Profoundly retarded individuals function at which one of Piaget's stages of development?

   (A) Preoperational   (D) Sensorimotor

   (B) Concrete   (E) None of the above.

   (C) Formal

8. The method that makes use of daily living, sensory, academic, and cultural and artistic materials was developed by which of the following?

   (A) Bruner   (D) Montessori

   (B) Maslow   (E) Piaget

   (C) Bereiter

9. Which of the following approaches in psychology provides the majority of the teaching techniques used with the retarded?

   (A) Psychoanalytic   (D) Neurobiological

   (B) Humanistic   (E) Phenomenological

   (C) Behavioral

10. A few extreme scores in a distribution will affect

   (A) the value of the median more than that of the mean.

   (B) the value of the mean more than that of the median.

   (C) the values of the mean and median equally.

   (D) the value of the mode more than that of the median.

   (E) neither the value of the mean nor the median.

11. What is the main disadvantage of cross-cultural tests?

   (A) Reliability problems

   (B) They compare people of different cultures.

   (C) Predictive and diagnostic values are lost.

   (D) None of the above.

   (E) All of the above.

12. As an approach to personality research Gordon Allport favored

   (A) nomothetic studies.   (D) case conference studies.

   (B) nonparametric studies.   (E) cross-cultural studies.

   (C) ideographic studies.

13. The simplest measure of variability is the

   (A) standard deviation.   (D) range.

   (B) Z-score.   (E) chi-square.

   (C) variance.

14. A platykurtic curve is

    (A) flat.   (D) negatively skewed.

    (B) peaked.   (E) hyperbolic.

    (C) positively skewed.

15. Movements that are rapid and automatic after practice are known as

    (A) feedback-guided movements.

    (B) gross movements.

    (C) ballistic movements.

    (D) fine movements.

    (E) involuntary movements.

16. When a man with cerebellar damage is performing the "finger-to-nose" test, his finger reaches a point just in front of his nose and then begins shaking out of control. This supports the fact that

    (A) putting one's finger on one's nose is a purely ballistic movement.

    (B) the cerebellum is responsible for maintaining the steady, non-relaxed positioning of a limb or other body part.

    (C) the person may be developing Parkinson's disease.

    (D) Both B and C.

    (E) Both A and B.

For **QUESTIONS** 17 and 18 below, choose the term that does NOT belong.

17. (A) Bipolar cell   (D) Schwann cell

    (B) Dendrites   (E) Axon

    (C) Myelin sheath

18. (A) Decrease in heartbeat   (D) Increased secretion of saliva

    (B) Digestion of food   (E) Pupil dilation

    (C) Constriction of bronchi

19. A discrete motor task differs from a continuous motor task in

    (A) difficulty.

    (B) length.

    (C) enjoyment of task.

    (D) the dexterity needed to perform the task.

    (E) the type of movements performed.

20. The sympathetic and parasympathic nervous systems constitute the

    (A) autonomic nervous system.

    (B) central nervous system.

    (C) peripheral nervous system.

    (D) somatic nervous system.

    (E) antagonistic nervous system.

21. The "white matter" of the central nervous system is actually

    (A) nerve fiber pathways.   (D) cortical tissue.

    (B) cell bodies.   (E) cerebral tissue.

    (C) cell centers.

22. Which of the following is present in the synaptic vesicles?

    (A) Action potential   (D) Synaptic inhibitors

    (B) Neurotransmitters   (E) K^+

    (C) Na^+

23. Which of the following has direct control over the function of the pituitary gland?

    (A) Pons   (D) Midbrain

    (B) Cerebral cortex   (E) Cerebellum

    (C) Hypothalamus

24. The wavelength of green is

    (A) greater than yellow but less than blue.

    (B) greater than either yellow or blue.

    (C) the same wavelength as yellow.

    (D) greater than blue but less than yellow.

    (E) greater than red.

25. Physical sounds from our environment are translated into electrical messages in the

    (A) spiral geniculate.   (D) spiral ganglion.

    (B) trapezoid body.   (E) eustachian tube.

    (C) cochlea.

26. ECHOIC CODE : AUDITORY SYSTEM :: ICONIC CODE:

    (A) tactile experience   (D) olfactory system

    (B) visual system   (E) None of the above.

    (C) sensory system

27. When we say that our visual system is 50 percent crossed, we mean that

    (A) half of the information from the right visual field is perceived by the left retina.

    (B) half of the fibers from the optic nerve cross over to the opposite side of the brain.

    (C) half of the visual image strikes the left side of the retina and the other half strikes the right side of the retina.

    (D) half of the visual image is inverted in the retina.

    (E) None of the above.

28. The opponent-process theory of color perception was proposed by

    (A) E. Hering.   (D) E. Land.

    (B) H. Helmholtz.   (E) D. Premack.

    (C) C. L. Franklin.

29. The sensitivity of the eye to light varies with

  (A) wavelength.

  (B) the eye's state of adaptation.

  (C) the region of the retina.

  (D) the contraction or dilation of the iris.

  (E) All of the above.

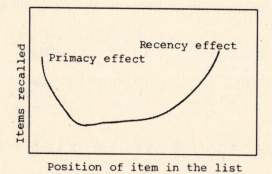

30. The above diagram depicts which of the following choices?

  (A) Learning curve   (D) Memory curve

  (B) Threshold effect   (E) None of the above.

  (C) Serial position curve

QUESTIONS 31 and 32 refer to the following passage:

In a learning experiment, subjects were presented with a list of words paired with cues. Some words were paired with strong cues and others with weak cues. After presentation, they were given a cued recall test in which some of the cues were the same as before but others did not match the original cues. The results, of course, were best for those words presented with a strong cue and retrieved with the same strong cue. Recall was found to be superior for words rehearsed and retrieved with the same weak cue rather than when rehearsed with a weak cue and retrieved with a strong cue.

31. The results of this experiment demonstrate the principle of

   (A) paired-associate learning.

   (B) parallel processing.

   (C) encoding specificity.

   (D) reconstructive memory.

   (E) nonspecific transfer.

32. This principle implies that

   (A) items are stored in memory the way they are first perceived.

   (B) memory is context dependent.

   (C) the uniqueness of the link between retrieval cues and the information to be recalled is a major factor in recall ability.

   (D) Both A and B.

   (E) All of the above.

QUESTION 33 refers to the following passage:

An early experiment by Kohler (1926), investigating the mentality of chimpanzees, involved placing a banana outside the cage beyond the ape's reach and giving him several short, hollow sticks that would have to be pushed together in order to reach the banana. The brightest ape in the experiment tried at first to get the banana with one stick, then he pushed the stick out as far as possible with a second stick without success. Eventually, he saw that the sticks could be connected to form a longer stick, thus perceiving a completely new relationship between the sticks.

33. According to Kohler, problem solving involves

   (A) restructuring the perceptual field.

   (B) insight.

   (C) a long process of trial-and-error.

   (D) Both A and B.

   (E) All of the above.

34. The earliest recorded studies of verbal learning and memory were conducted by

    (A) Thorndike.

    (B) Pavlov.

    (C) Skinner.

    (D) Ebbinghaus.

    (E) Mowrer.

35. The short-term memory can hold how many items at one time?

    (A) Seven items, plus or minus two

    (B) Ten items, plus or minus two

    (C) Ten items, plus or minus five

    (D) Five items

    (E) None of the above.

36. Which of the following is NOT a factor that influences the learning of a list?

    (A) Position of the items

    (B) Frequency of the items

    (C) Similarity of the items

    (D) Concreteness

    (E) All are factors that influence learning.

37. Which is/are the most important factor(s) in rehearsal?

    (A) Individual presentation rate

    (B) Number of trials

    (C) Time spent learning

    (D) Both A and C.

    (E) Both B and C.

38. In which of Piaget's stages of cognitive development will a child realize that when a volume of water is poured from a tall, narrow beaker to a wide beaker, the volume remains the same even though it reaches a lower level?

    (A) Preoperational

    (B) Sensorimotor

    (C) Concrete operational

    (D) Latency

    (E) Formal operations

39. Which group represents the three ways to measure the amount of long-term memory retention?

    (A) Recognition, recall, and rehearsal

    (B) Recall, recognition, and savings

    (C) Recognition, savings, and rate of forgetting

    (D) Savings, recall, and retrieval

    (E) Recognition, recall, and retrieval

40. In studies of attention, shadowing is used to

    (A) mask all information from attention.

    (B) differentially mask irrelevant information.

    (C) be sure the subject's attention is concentrated on a single task.

    (D) mediate the subject's attention between two or more tasks.

    (E) stimulate retroactive inhibition.

41. Criticisms of the claims that chimps can learn to communicate using American Sign Language include which of the following?

    (A) The animals seldom make up statements they weren't specifically taught.

    (B) Word order doesn't seem important to the animals.

    (C) They appear incapable of grasping syntax.

    (D) Trainers have inadvertently cued the animals so they would emit certain signs.

    (E) All of the above.

42. The vocal apparatus for producing speech sounds (vocal cords, muscle control of lips, throat, tongue, and jaw) are useless unless the organism has the _____ in its brain developed in order to coordinate these movements.

    (A) hypothalamus

    (B) thalamus

    (C) Broca's area

    (D) lateral ventricles

    (E) fissure of Rolando

43. In language, grammar refers to

    (A) the morphemes used.

    (B) the phonemes used.

    (C) Both A and B.

    (D) the rules used to connect phrases.

    (E) the morphology of the statement.

44. Morphology refers to the

    (A) relationship between sounds and their meanings.

    (B) origins of words.

    (C) relationship between different languages.

    (D) study of infant babbling.

    (E) non-verbal forms of communication.

45. Psychologists who specialize in the study of language are called

    (A) psychogrammartists.

    (B) psycholinguists.

    (C) psychometricians.

    (D) morphemologists.

    (E) phonemologists.

46. The ability of young children to use two-word sentences is referred to as

    (A) telegraphic speech.   (D) morpheme induction.

    (B) aphasia.   (E) Broca's language.

    (C) babbling.

47. In order to acquire a language, a species must have the following ability:

    (A) latent learning   (D) trial and error learning

    (B) concept formation   (E) All of the above.

    (C) hearing

48. Of the following tests, the most suitable for determining the I.Q. of most 12-year-olds is the

    (A) Raven Progressive Matrices.

    (B) WAIS.

    (C) WISC.

    (D) WPPSI.

    (E) Bayley Scales.

49. Intelligence tests measure

    (A) innate ability.   (D) Both A and B.

    (B) performance.   (E) Both A and C.

    (C) educational level.

50. Which of the following researchers developed the Culture Fair Intelligence Test?

    (A) Spearman   (D) Wechsler

    (B) Raven   (E) Rorschach

    (C) Cattell

51. A man gets a job at a factory. He wants to make a good impression, so he works quickly and efficiently. He notices that some of the other employees are frowning at him, so he slows down his work output. This is an example of

(A) social facilitation.

(D) consolidation.

(B) bystander apathy.

(E) social loafing.

(C) learned helplessness.

52. A three-year-old obeys rules in order to gain rewards and avoid punishment. This child is at Kohlberg's _____ stage of moral development.

(A) preconventional

(D) level six

(B) societal

(E) altruistic

(C) conventional

53. The fact that under certain circumstances many people immerse themselves totally into a group and behave as the group dictates is called

(A) deindividuation.

(D) groupthink.

(B) mob control.

(E) dictatorial herding.

(C) a fugue state.

54. The experiences a person has while being brainwashed by a cult are

(A) torture, fear, and threat.

(B) deprivation, terror, reeducations.

(C) loneliness, religion, fanaticism.

(D) rejection, dominance, and acceptance.

(E) compliance, identification, and internalization.

55. According to Kohlberg's theory of moral development, people who make up their own minds about sex, drugs, and other issues are functioning at

    (A) level six.

    (B) autonomy.

    (C) concrete operations.

    (D) level three.

    (E) the primary stage.

56. Erikson proposed that trust or mistrust develops during the

    (A) muscular-anal stage.

    (B) locomotor-genital stage.

    (C) latency stage.

    (D) oral-sensory stage.

    (E) maturity stage.

57. The approach in which it is believed that aggression is an inborn tendency has been most supported by the work of

    (A) Sigmund Freud.

    (B) Konrad Lorenz.

    (C) Carl Rogers.

    (D) Albert Bandura.

    (E) B.F. Skinner.

58. During the premoral stage described by Kohlberg's moral development theory, children

    (A) think bad behavior is punished and good behavior is not punished.

    (B) have no conception of good or bad behavior.

    (C) are amoral.

    (D) are uncooperative.

    (E) conform to authority figures.

59. The fundamental attribution error is a tendency in humans to

    (A) blame people for situationally induced behavior.

    (B) engage in sexist stereotypes.

    (C) emphasize dispositional factors in determining people's behavior.

    (D) accept placebo effects.

    (E) emphasize I.Q. and race when forming opinions.

60. Parents who beat their children severely and frequently

    (A) believe the bible mandates it.

    (B) are honestly trying to teach their children good discipline.

    (C) were seldom disciplined themselves as children.

    (D) are following modern theories of child rearing.

    (E) were probably victims of the battered child syndrome themselves.

61. Who of the following was particularly interested in the effect of birth order on personality?

    (A) Rogers   (D) Sullivan

    (B) Adler   (E) Sheldon

    (C) Fromm

62. When two people are introduced for the first time, an initial impression is formed. Which factor most powerfully affects this first impression?

    (A) Method of handshake

    (B) Physical appearance

    (C) Nonverbal communication

    (D) External locus of control

    (E) Speech mannerisms

63. Suppose you meet a person at a party. Which theory assumes you calculate the costs and benefits of developing a relationship with the person?

    (A) Social exchange   (D) Altruism

    (B) Attribution   (E) Social judgment

    (C) Two factor

64. Suppose that a father believes his first-born daughter will be more intelligent than his second-born. This belief then influences how he behaves toward his daughter, giving more time and attention to his first-born. What does this illustrate?

(A) Prejudice

(D) Self-fulfilling prophecy

(B) Social schema

(E) Primacy effect

(C) Social reality

65. According to the fundamental attribution error, how would you explain the behavior of a stranger who gives a $100 bill to a Salvation Army collector outside a department store?

(A) Presume the person is kind and generous

(B) Presume the person is trying to impress others

(C) Presume the person's employer requires such contributions

(D) Presume the person used to receive support from the Salvation Army

(E) Presume the person was ordered to do so by a court as part of a criminal sentence

66. In Harry Harlow's experiments with surrogate mothers, he found that baby monkeys

(A) preferred proximity to cloth mothers over eating.

(B) preferred eating over interacting with peers.

(C) preferred interaction with peers over surrogate mothers.

(D) preferred proximity to wire mothers over interacting with peers.

(E) preferred playing alone over interacting with surrogate mothers.

67. Rotter's Locus of Control scale attempts to measure

(A) independence-dependence.

(B) internality-externality.

(C) rationality-irrationality.

(D) masculine-feminine characteristics.

(E) Both B and C.

68. Based on his study of work performance, Vroom states that an individual's motivation to work is a function of

(A) job incentives.

(B) expectation and valence of goal.

(C) employee status.

(D) meaningfulness of job.

(E) managerial style.

69. An "index of centrality" refers to

(A) a measure of work equality.

(B) a measure of the extent to which a given individual interacts with others.

(C) a measure of the extent to which individuals are excluded from interaction with others.

(D) a measure of management potential.

(E) the coherence of employee organization in a business.

70. All secondary sources of drive are

(A) homeostatic.　　　　　(D) self-propelling.

(B) physiogenic.　　　　　(E) learned.

(C) goal-seeking.

71. Any behavior that can be engaged in without much concentration and effort is called

(A) autonomic behavior.　　(D) automatic behavior.

(B) learned behavior.　　　(E) conscious process.

(C) overlearned behavior.

72. According to Fromm, a truly healthy person manifests a (an)

(A) receptive orientation.　(D) marketing orientation.

(B) exploitative orientation.　(E) hoarding orientation.

(C) productive orientation.

73. According to Clark Hull, Drive × Habit =

    (A) Performance.

    (B) Achievement.

    (C) Need for Achievement.

    (D) Goal.

    (E) Activation-Arousal.

74. Prior to training in the classical conditioning paradigm, which of the following is true?

    (A) CS → UCR

    (B) CS → UCS

    (C) CS → CR

    (D) UCS → UCR

    (E) UCS → CR

75. Which of the following types of learning CANNOT be directly observed?

    (A) Operant conditioning

    (B) Response learning

    (C) Verbal learning

    (D) Perceptual learning

    (E) Classical conditioning

76. Avoidance conditioning can produce

    (A) active avoidance.

    (B) extinction.

    (C) passive avoidance.

    (D) suppression.

    (E) Both A and C.

77. Suppose a pigeon is trained to peck a key when a red light is presented on the key. Then the key color is changed to pink. If the pigeon pecks the pink key, what principle is illustrated?

    (A) Stimulus generalization

    (B) Response generalization

    (C) Primary reinforcement

    (D) Secondary reinforcement

    (E) Partial reinforcement

78. Which operant conditioning procedure increases the rate of a response by terminating an aversive stimulus?

    (A) Positive reinforcement

    (B) Negative reinforcement

    (C) Punishment

    (D) Omission training

    (E) Shaping

79. In classical conditioning, the conditioned response occurs after the presentation of the

   (A) unconditioned response.   (D) conditioned response.

   (B) primary reinforcer.   (E) conditioned stimulus.

   (C) unconditioned stimulus.

80. In Pavlov's classic experiment, a dog hears the sound of a bell and then is given food powder. After a few trials, the dog salivates to both the bell and the food powder. The conditioned response is _____ while the unconditioned response is _____.

   (A) the bell, salivation   (D) salivation, the bell

   (B) salivation, also salivation   (E) the dog, the bell

   (C) the bell, the food

81. The longest running philosophical trend in the education of children with behavioral problems has been the _____ approach.

   (A) structured school   (D) gestalt

   (B) behavioral   (E) permissive-sentimental

   (C) conservative

82. One primary difference in the way a school psychologist would administer I.Q. tests to second-grade and tenth-grade students is in the

   (A) size of the groups.

   (B) type of tasks.

   (C) number of proctors necessary.

   (D) time limits.

   (E) All of the above are differences.

83. All of the following are cognitive behavior modification techniques recommended by guidance counselors EXCEPT

   (A) modeling.

   (B) discussions of ego-defense mechanisms.

   (C) thought stopping.

(D) behavior rehearsal.

(E) self-management.

84. In addition to the Wechsler Intelligence Scale for Children (Revised), the test that is frequently used to diagnose mental retardation or learning disabilities is the

(A) Wide Range Achievement Test.

(B) Stanford-Binet Intelligence Scale.

(C) Thematic Apperception Test.

(D) Slosson Intelligence Test.

(E) Department of Mental Health Assessment Battery for Children.

85. For classroom management, a teacher places an uncooperative, disruptive student in a small room by himself for five minutes. The technique that the instructor is using is called

(A) punishment.   (D) overcorrection.

(B) extinction.   (E) timeout.

(C) negative reinforcement.

86. Which of the following concepts are most closely related?

(A) Thought disorder — schizophrenia

(B) Multiple personality — schizophrenia

(C) Hallucinations — depression

(D) Amnesia — catatonia

(E) Drug abuse — autism

87. About two-thirds of all mental hospital admissions are for

(A) mania.   (D) obsessive-compulsive disorder.

(B) depression.   (E) hypochondria.

(C) schizophrenia.

88. What is the best treatment for bipolar disorder?

    (A) Electroconvulsive therapy (D) Chlorpromazine

    (B) Psychosurgery   (E) Iproniazid

    (C) Lithium chloride

89. Which of the following is no longer classified as a mental disorder?

    (A) Mental retardation   (D) Aphasia

    (B) Alzheimer's disease   (E) All of the above.

    (C) Homosexuality

90. According to Freud, paranoia is caused by

    (A) a fixation at the anal stage.

    (B) an unresolved Oedipal Complex.

    (C) destruction of the superego.

    (D) unacceptable homosexual impulses.

    (E) sublimation of feelings of guilt.

CLEP HUMAN GROWTH
AND DEVELOPMENT
TEST 3

1.	(A)	23.	(C)	46.	(A)	69.	(B)
2.	(C)	24.	(D)	47.	(B)	70.	(E)
3.	(C)	25.	(C)	48.	(C)	71.	(D)
4.	(A)	26.	(B)	49.	(B)	72.	(C)
5.	(E)	27.	(B)	50.	(C)	73.	(A)
7.	(D)	28.	(A)	51.	(E)	74.	(D)
8.	(D)	29.	(E)	52.	(A)	75.	(D)
6.	(B)	30.	(C)	53.	(A)	76.	(E)
9.	(C)	31.	(C)	54.	(E)	77.	(A)
10.	(B)	32.	(E)	55.	(A)	78.	(B)
11.	(C)	33.	(D)	56.	(D)	79.	(E)
12.	(C)	34.	(D)	57.	(B)	80.	(B)
13.	(D)	35.	(A)	58.	(A)	81.	(E)
14.	(A)	36.	(E)	59.	(A)	82.	(E)
15.	(C)	37.	(C)	60.	(E)	83.	(B)
16.	(B)	38.	(C)	61.	(B)	84.	(A)
17.	(A)	39.	(B)	62.	(B)	85.	(E)
18.	(E)	40.	(C)	63.	(A)	86.	(A)
19.	(E)	41.	(E)	64.	(D)	87.	(B)
20.	(A)	42.	(C)	65.	(A)	88.	(C)
21.	(A)	43.	(D)	66.	(A)	89.	(C)
22.	(B)	44.	(A)	67.	(B)	90.	(D)
		45.	(B)	68.	(B)		

DETAILED EXPLANATIONS
OF ANSWERS

TEST 3

1. **(A)**   In the Piagetian theory of child development, object perma-nence occurs at the end of the sensorimotor stage. This is a critical achievement of this early period of life. Object permanence is the aware-ness that objects exist outside of the child's own sensory experiences and motor manipulations and that they endure even when the child neither sees them nor moves them around.

2. **(C)**   In Piaget's theory, an operation is a thought. Thought refers to the mental representation of something that is not immediately perceived. During this period of concrete operations, the child is capable of invoking a mental representation or image of an object or event. This representation is linked to a mental image of the "concrete" perceptual experience. It must exist in the physical sense and not be hypothetical.

3. **(C)**   According to Freud, fixation is the result of abnormal person-ality development. In his scheme of personality development, consisting of progressive stages, Freud stated that there is a certain amount of frustra-tion and anxiety as the person passes from one stage to the next. If the amount of frustration and anxiety over the next stage is too great, develop-ment will halt and the person becomes fixated at one stage. A very depen-dent child is an example of an early fixation preventing him or her from becoming independent.

4. **(A)**   Repression is a major defense mechanism in psychoanalytic theory. Repression describes the mechanism whereby an unpleasant or threatening thought or idea is not permitted into awareness. Repression occurs when an individual experiences a painful event and tries to forget it. He or she represses the experience by burying it in the unconscious. The unconscious mind is replete with repressed feelings toward painful experiences.

5. **(E)** Morality and conscience are conceptually defined as the superego functions. The superego represents the taboos and mores, or rules, of the society in which the child lives. It may encompass religious rules as well. The process by which the child learns cultural norms and identifies with them is called socialization. Hence, the development of the superego represents the socialization functions in the child.

6. **(B)** Piaget's life work explored the cognitive development of humans. His research demonstrated that humans had to be a minimum age in order to grasp certain concepts and reason abstractly. Psychosexual and moral development represent the views of Freud and Kohlberg, respectively.

7. **(D)** Humans develop different cognitive abilities as a function of maturity and brain development. A profoundly retarded human would function at the lowest level of cognitive development—the sensorimotor stage, where their abilities are comparable to a two-year-old.

8. **(D)** The question describes best Marie Montessori's materials. Bruner is noted for his theory of the structure of the discipline. Maslow states that there is a hierarchy of needs, with the basic needs of food and shelter at the bottom and self-actualization at the top. Bereiter, with others, developed an academic program for early childhood education; this academic program (DISTAR) is frequently used with disadvantaged children. Piaget is best known for his work in identifying developmental stages of young children.

9. **(C)** The behavioral approach, with its emphasis on the influence of environment on behavior, provides the bulk of the training techniques used with the retarded. Because of their limited cognitive abilities, the psychoanalytic (Freudian) and humanistic (phenomenological) approaches have limited application to the training of the retarded.

10. **(B)** Since the median is the single middle score in a distribution, it is not affected by a few extreme scores, unless it is one of those extreme scores. Then it would not be a representative median. In contrast, the mean is an average of all the scores in a distribution; therefore, it would always be affected by extreme scores.

11. **(C)** The disadvantage of cross-cultural tests is that the predictive and diagnostic value of the intelligence test is lost. There is little gained by administering culture-fair tests if they do not provide useful information

concerning the culturally relevant knowledge and abilities of a student. Cross-cultural tests often miss this relevant information and, therefore, have little meaningful predictive value.

12. **(C)**   Ideographic study involves selecting methods of study that will not blur or conceal the uniqueness of the individual subject. The ideographic approach emphasizes the importance of individual traits in determining behavior, and thus recommends study of the individual as the most effective approach to understanding behavior. Since Allport did not believe in the validity of general principles of behavior, he preferred to use the ideographic method. Allport was the first psychologist to stress the ideographic approach.

13. **(D)**   The range is the simplest measure of variation since it gives the limits within which all the elements of a distribution are confined. The range of a set of scores is the difference between the highest and lowest score in a set of scores. For example, if you have the scores 18, 12, 23, 30, and 34, then 12 is the lowest score and 34 is the highest score. The difference between the highest and lowest score is 22. Hence, the range is 22.

14. **(A)**   A platykurtic curve is marked by flatness, indicating a wide dispersion of measurements. It is possible for this kind of curve to be positively or negatively skewed, but skewness in itself does not determine a platykurtic curve. A curve that is peaked is called leptokurtic.

15. **(C)**   Rapid movements that are automatic after practice are known as ballistic movements. In a ballistic movement, a sequence of movements is carried out as an organized whole, in proper order and with proper timing. Sensory feedback kicks in only after a group of movements and not between each separate movement.

16. **(B)**   The cerebellar nuclei are important for maintaining body parts in a steady, nonrelaxed position. In the diagnosis of cerebellar damage, the "finger-to-nose" movement is often tested. A normal person creates this movement in three steps. The finger moves ballistically to a point just in front of the nose, where it is then held for a moment. Then, the finger again begins to move toward the nose, slowly and under the control of the basal ganglia.

17. **(A)**   Bipolar cells are involved in vision. The other four choices are components of neurons. Dendrites receive information from the axons of other neurons, while axons send information to neurons, glands, or muscles. The myelin sheath surrounds the axon.

18. **(E)** Pupil dilation is controlled by the sympathetic branch of the nervous system, whereas the parasympathetic branch controls heartbeat, constriction of bronchi, digestion, and secretion of saliva.

19. **(E)** A discrete motor task differs from a continuous motor task because it involves a series of movements that are separate from each other. Typing is an example of a discrete task. Continuous tasks are made up of a series of smooth movements that merge together. An example of a continuous movement is steering the driving wheel in an automobile. In general, discrete skills are more easily forgotten than continuous skills.

20. **(A)** The autonomic nervous system is divided into two parts, both structurally and functionally. One part is called the sympathetic nervous system and the other is known as the parasympathetic nervous system. These two branches act antagonistically to each other. If one system stimulates an effector, the other would inhibit its action. The basis for homeostatic regulation by the autonomic system lies in the fact that the sympathetic and parasympathetic systems each send a branch to the same organ, causing double innervation.

21. **(A)** The "white matter" of the central nervous system is actually the nerve fiber pathways. The white matter consists mainly of axons. The axons are surrounded by a fatty, white covering called the myelin sheath, hence the nickname, white matter.

22. **(B)** Synaptic vesicles are small, sac-like structures located at the axon of the neuron. They contain neurotransmitters, which are chemicals that permit unidirectional transmission of an action potential from one neuron to another. Acetylcholine and noradrenaline are two types of neurotransmitters.

23. **(C)** The hypothalamus, located under the thalamus, is a collection of nuclei concerned with many important homeostatic regulations. Electrical stimulation of certain cells in the hypothalamus produces sensations of hunger, thirst, pain, pleasure, or sexual drive. The hypothalamus is also important for its influence on the pituitary gland, which is functionally under its control. Cells of the hypothalamus synthesize chemical factors that modulate the release of hormones produced and stored in the pituitary.

24. **(D)** Within the color spectrum, blue is perceived at 470–475 nanometers wavelength, green at 495–535 nanometers, yellow at 575–580 nanometers, and red is perceived at 595–770 nanometers wavelength. Hence, the wavelength of green is greater than blue but less than yellow or red.

25.   **(C)**   Physical sounds from the environment in the form of waves are translated into electrical messages in the cochlea. The cochlea contains special hair cells that are bent as part of a chain reaction due to the vibrations of the ossicles, namely the stapes, which push against the oval window on the cochlea. As these hairs are bent, an electrical event called a generator potential occurs. This potential stimulates nearby nerve cells. The activated nerve cells then carry an electrical message about the original sound wave vibrations along to the brain.

26.   **(B)**   Iconic coding represents a fleeting, visual experience that is of great importance in the study of information processing. In the visual realm, the iconic image is that which occurs during a single glance. Usually lasting about one-fifteenth of a second, iconic storage consists of a series of successive glances each representing a small section of a larger object.

27.   **(B)**   The retina sends visual information it receives from the environment through various nerve fibers to the brain. These fibers are known collectively as the optic nerve. There is a right and left optic nerve, one from each eye. These join in a region called the optic chiasm. At this point, half of the fibers of each optic nerve cross over to the opposite side of the brain. This is what we mean when we say our visual system is 50 percent crossed.

28.   **(A)**   Ewald Hering (1878), a German physiologist, proposed that there were three different receptor types, each composed of a pair of opponent processes. He thought there was a white-black receptor, a red-green receptor, and a blue-yellow receptor. If one member of the opponent pairs was stimulated more than the other, that color was seen. If red was stimulated more than green, red was the color observed.

29.   **(E)**   Several factors influence the sensitivity of the eye to light. The eyes are affected by the nature of light, which itself is a function of wavelength, intensity, and composition. The eye's state of adaptation varies with the surrounding stimuli and is subject to great variability. The region of the retina is directly associated with light sensitivity because it contains the rod and cone photoreceptor cells. The iris regulates the amount of light entering through the pupil.

30.   **(C)**   The diagram depicts a serial position curve, which always has this characteristic shape. Psychologists suggest that the curve is due to a primacy-recency effect. A primacy effect occurs when the items at the

beginning of the list are the most easily remembered. A recency effect occurs when items near the end of the list are remembered well. When both effects occur, it is called a primacy-recency effect. It is believed that the accuracy of recalling the last few items in a list is a result of the short-term memory store and that recall of early items that subjects had been able to rehearse reflects the contribution of long-term memory.

31. **(C)** The encoding specificity principle states that recall is highly dependent on the congruity between encoding and retrieval cues. Thus, even though a strong cue is better than a weak cue by itself, it is not effective at retrieval if the word was encoded with a weak cue. The uniqueness of the encoding leads to better recall.

32. **(E)** According to the encoding specificity principle, items are stored in memory the way they are first perceived. Uniqueness of the connection made between the word and the cue is very important, as is the context in which the item was presented.

33. **(D)** As a Gestalt theorist, Kohler held that problem solving involves restructuring the perceptual field. This can only be accomplished when the subject can view the task as a whole. He believed that true problem solving requires insight and realistic thinking.

34. **(D)** The German philosopher Hermann Ebbinghaus was the first to examine learning and memory scientifically. His experiments in the late 1800s attempted to provide an empirical basis for the study of human learning, memory, and association theory.

35. **(A)** Short-term memory (STM) is very limited in its capacity. It can only hold about seven items (plus or minus two items) of information at a time. This brief memory span requires deliberate rehearsal to prevent a specific memory from decaying over time.

36. **(E)** Characteristics of verbal materials that influence how effectively they are learned include position in the list, similarity in appearance, meaning or category, frequency, and concreteness. The type and amount of past learning a person has done also affects his rate of acquisition of new material.

37. **(C)** The time spent learning is the important factor in rehearsal. The individual presentation rate and the number of trials are not as important.

38.   **(C)**   In Piaget's concrete operational period, which lasts from age 7 to 11 years, the child consistently conserves such qualities as length, quantity, weight, and volume. The child also classifies concrete objects by category and begins to understand the relations among categories.

39.   **(B)**   There are three ways by which to measure the amount of retention in long-term memory. The recall method requires that the subject reproduce something previously learned with a minimum of cues. The smallest amount of retention is measured with this method. In recognition, the subject must recognize whether or not he has seen the information before. This method is used in multiple-choice exams. In the savings method, the subject learns something that he has already learned before to see if the amount of trials it takes has decreased.

40.   **(C)**   "Shadowing" is the name given to the popular technique for being sure that a subject's attention is concentrated on a single task. This is done to study the limits of attention capacity. In a shadowing task, a series of words is read to the subject and the subject is asked to repeat everything he or she hears out loud.

41.   **(E)**   Several reports have questioned the original claims made concerning the ability of apes and chimps to acquire and use symbolic language. All four of the criticisms listed have been made.

42.   **(C)**   Broca's area, located in the left frontal lobe of the brain, coordinates speech. Damage to this area produces expressive aphasia, i.e., difficulty in making statements. Paul Broca discovered the function of this part of the brain in 1861.

43.   **(D)**   Grammar, which includes syntax, refers to the rules used to connect meaningful phases.

44.   **(A)**   Morphology is the study of how particular sounds are related to the meanings that they convey.

45.   **(B)**   The branch of psychology concerned with language development and use is psycholinguistics. How we speak is indicative of how we think. To study language is to explore brain logic and function.

46. **(A)**   The ability of young children to use two-word sentences is referred to as telegraphic speech. Inclusion of articles, i.e., "the," "a," comes later. Aphasia refers to a speech disorder. Choices (D) and (E) do not exist.

47. **(B)**   Concept formation refers to the ability to learn to classify objects by common properties and to generalize to novel instances of the concept. Concepts are a symbolic precursor to the acquisition of language.

48. **(C)**   The Wechsler Intelligence Scale for Children (WISC) would be the most appropriate choice for the majority of 12-year-olds. The WISC is normally administered to children from the ages of $6\frac{1}{2}$–$16\frac{1}{2}$. There are subscales that measure mathematical ability, vocabulary, problem solving, and digit span problems.

49. **(B)**   All intelligence tests, and psychological tests in general, measure the performance or behavior of the subject. From the measure of performance we infer the knowledge and ability, as well as predict future performance, of the subject. It is important to consider that factors such as motivation can affect the performance on tests by either enhancing it or deterring it.

50. **(C)**   R.B. Cattell developed the Culture Fair Intelligence Test, a paper-and-pencil test available on three levels, each having a varying number of subtests. Unfortunately, Cattell's test does not completely compensate for cultural disadvantages. In cultures different from the one in which the test was designed, performance was considerably lower than the original norms.

51. **(E)**   People have a need for acceptance and approval from their peers. Social loafing refers to the fact that people will regulate their performance to coincide with the group mean performance.

52. **(A)**   Kohlberg's theory of moral development states that human morality evolves in a certain order. During the preconventional phase, children accept and obey rules not because they believe in them but because of the different consequences associated with obeying or disobeying them. He considered the ability to resist natural impulses to explore and manipulate the environment (playing with the dials on a TV for example) in order to conform to rules, as the first step in moral development.

53. **(A)** Many of the people in a lynch mob, as well as looters, have never engaged in criminal behavior before. They report that they were caught up in the moment. A group often takes on a personality very different from the members that make it up.

54. **(E)** Most cults do not use aversive methods to indoctrinate new members. Novices pay lip service to the cult leader (compliance) in order to be accepted by the other members. Over time, the novice begins to identify with the group and comes to internalize the beliefs of the cult.

55. **(A)** Level six is the highest stage of moral development a human can attain. At this level, we have our own philosophy and practice it even if it makes us unpopular with our peers.

56. **(D)** The oral-sensory stage is the first stage in Erikson's developmental theory. During the oral-sensory stage, the basic crisis centers on the development of either trust or mistrust. If these needs are consistently satisfied and if the infant receives love, he will develop a sense of trust, not only in others, but in himself and his ability to handle his needs. If these needs are not met and the infant lacks love, attention, and stimulation, he will develop a sense of mistrust. Erikson believes that the development of a healthy personality is contingent upon the formation of trust at this early stage.

57. **(B)** The belief that aggression is an inborn tendency in all animals, including man, has been most supported by the work of Konrad Lorenz.

58. **(A)** According to Kohlberg, the premoral stage is the first level of moral behavior. During the early stage of this level, children have a good-bad conception of behavior. For the early premoral child, moral behavior is based on the subjective consequences.

59. **(A)** We tend to take credit for our successes. We blame others or situational variables for our errors and mistakes. However, we don't extend that consideration to others. When people make mistakes, we hold them totally responsible and discount any situational variables that may have influenced them.

60. **(E)** Research indicates that, more often than not, people who use excessive levels of corporal punishment were themselves beaten as children. The lessons that our parents taught us as children via modeling were learned by us, whether or not we disliked their behavior. Excessive use of

physical punishment is not recommended by psychologists because the side effects include aggression, distrust, rebelliousness, and blunted initiative in children exposed to it.

61. **(B)** Of the theorists in the neo-Freudian movement, it was Adler who placed the emphasis on the relationship between personality and birth order. He believed that the oldest, middle, and youngest children have very different social experiences resulting in different personality formations. The eldest child is believed to feel "dethroned" upon the birth of a sibling. This leads to lifelong feelings of insecurity and hostility. The middle child is believed to be very ambitious and have a tendency for jealousy. The youngest child is most likely to be spoiled and to have a lifelong behavior problem.

62. **(B)** Research in social psychology indicates that physical appearance is the most important determinant of first impressions. It is also relevant in social attraction and effectiveness in persuading others to change their beliefs.

63. **(A)** Social exchange theory views human interactions in economic terms. When two people meet, they each calculate the costs and benefits of developing a relationship. If the benefits outweigh the costs, then the two people will be attracted to each other. Attribution theory concerns judgments about the factors responsible for our own and others' behavior.

64. **(D)** Self-fulfilling prophecy refers to behaving in a way that is consistent with a belief or hypothesis, which then results in the hypothesis coming true. Prejudice is strong hatred or dislike for members of a group. Social schemata are mental structures that represent our social beliefs. They construct our sense of social reality.

65. **(A)** The fundamental attribution error refers to the tendency to assume that another person's personality or beliefs cause his or her behavior. We underestimate the power of external factors in controlling behavior and overestimate the power of internal factors. Here, attributing the gift of $100 to the trait of kindness is likely. The other attributions listed are related to various external pressures.

66. **(A)** Harlow removed infant monkeys from their mothers and provided them with nonliving surrogate mothers. One type was made of wire and the other was wire with a soft terrycloth covering. He found that the monkeys spent the most time with the cloth mother, regardless of which

one provided milk. Thus, the need for contact comfort was as important as the need for food.

67. **(B)** "Locus of Control" as a determinant of behavior is predicated on the notion that an important determinant of an individual's action is the degree to which an individual perceives that a reward follows from his own behavior (internality) or is controlled by forces outside himself (externality). According to Rotter's Locus of Control Scale, a person with an internal orientation tends to take responsibility for what happens to him, while a person with an external orientation sees the events of life as due to chance and beyond his control.

68. **(B)** Vroom states that an individual's motivation is a function of two factors: (1) the "expectation" that a particular behavior will lead to a desired goal and (2) the "valence" or desirability of the goal. This is called Expectancy Theory. This proposal is not directly related to motivation in the work place, but has received attention by Human Resource Development departments in companies.

69. **(B)** The "index of centrality" is a mathematical measure developed by H. Leavitt. It provides a measure of the extent to which a given individual interacts with others. The higher a person scores on this index, the more that person participates in the communications that occur. High scores on this index of centrality are always associated with those in leadership positions. Leavitt also created the "index of peripherality," which measures the extent to which individuals are excluded from interaction with others.

70. **(E)** All secondary sources of drive are learned. These are acquired drive responses that have been acquired in a particular environmental situation. These sources of drive include such learned drives as success, money, power, appearance, and security. These responses have motivational consequences similar to the primary sources of motivation in that they influence and direct behavior.

71. **(D)** This choice is correct by definition. The term automatic behavior refers to any behavior that can be engaged in without much concentration and effort. For example, activities such as riding a bicycle are performed automatically. Motor responses in such activities are automatic because the person does not need to think about them to perform them. When riding a bicycle, the person is conscious of such responses as steering, pedaling, and braking, but he does not think about them—they are automatic.

72. **(C)**   Fromm believed that a healthy individual manifests the productive orientation in which he achieves goals and, thereby, realizes and actualizes his full potential in life. The essential component of a productive orientation is making a creative contribution to one's family life, career, and to the betterment of society. The other choices are pathological orientations developed by Fromm to characterize neurotic styles of coping with insecurity and isolation.

73. **(A)**   Hull's theory accounted for the appetitive drives of hunger, thirst, and sex, and for the aversive drive of pain avoidance. A physiological need was believed to produce a drive that sought to initiate a behavior that would reduce the drive and satisfy the need. The behavior employed depended on the degree of success with which the behavior had reduced drive in the past. This learned association between the drive and the behavior that reduces it is called a "habit." This theoretical relationship was expressed as Performance = Drive × Habit.

74. **(D)**   Prior to training the animal in the classical conditioning paradigm, only the unconditioned stimulus (UCS) can elicit the unconditioned response (UCR). Conditioned stimuli (CS) are not yet effective because training in the CS + UCS pairing has not yet taken place. For the same reason, a conditioned response (CR) cannot be elicited, as this is defined as the response elicited by the presentation of the CS.

75. **(D)**   Perceptual learning involves the formation of relationships between stimuli. The formation of relationships is an internal process. As such, it cannot be directly observed. In order to determine if perceptual learning has occurred, *indirect* methods of study are required.

76. **(E)**   Avoidance conditioning can produce active avoidance in which the organism must demonstrate a certain response—for instance, jumping over a bar or pressing a lever to avoid shock. It can also produce passive avoidance in which the organism must not respond—not press a lever or step on a section of the box, in order to avoid the aversive stimulus.

77. **(A)**   Stimulus generalization refers to the degree to which an organism responds to stimuli that are similar to the original training stimulus. Primary reinforcers refer to natural reinforcers that require no conditioning, e.g., food or water. Secondary reinforcers refer to stimuli that the organism is taught are rewards, e.g., medals, trophies, or certificates. Partial reinforcement refers to a reinforcement schedule that does not reinforce every response.

78. **(B)** Negative reinforcement involves terminating an aversive stimulus (escape), or postponing its occurrence (avoidance) of a particular response. This increases the likelihood of the response. Negative reinforcement is often confused with punishment in which an aversive stimulus is introduced to decrease the rate of a response.

79. **(E)** During acquisition in classical conditioning, a conditioned stimulus (tone) is presented just before an unconditioned stimulus (food) and an unconditioned response (salivating) occurs automatically. After learning, presentation of the conditioned stimulus (tone) alone elicits the conditioned response (salivating).

80. **(B)** The unconditioned (unlearned) response to food is salivation. The dog learns to salivate to the bell that signals that food is about to be presented. The other choices are incorrect because each contains at least one stimulus (the bell, the food) and the question is asking for you to identify two responses.

81. **(E)** This approach dates back to the late nineteenth century. G. Stanley Hall, a pioneer in education, was very influenced by Freud's psychoanalytic approach. Children were expected to have to drain off hostilities, act out aggressive and sexual themes as a means of maturing. Hence, unrestricted permissive environments were recommended.

82. **(E)** All four variables would differ depending on the age of the students. Younger students take tests with more pictorial tasks. Group testing of young students should be limited to 10 or less due to their tendency to get distracted or attempt to innocently help friends. Because of the differences in tasks, verbal content, ages of the students, the number of proctors, and test duration will vary.

83. **(B)** Ego-defense mechanisms are found in the Freudian approach to personality. The other four choices are behavioral in nature because they stress the influence of environment on behavior.

84. **(A)** The Wide Range Achievement Test developed by J. Jastak and S. Jastak in 1978 is used frequently as a diagnostic tool. It enables the user to gauge frustration tolerance, performance anxiety, achievement motivation, and impulse control.

85. **(E)** Timeout is a technique wherein a student is momentarily deprived of privileges, in this case, social contact. Punishment requires the

presentation of an aversive stimulus, not the removal of positive reinforcer conditions.

86. **(A)** The defining feature of schizophrenia is thought disorder. Multiple personality, a form of dissociative disorder in the general class of anxiety disorders, is often confused with schizophrenia. Although delusions may occur in severe depression, hallucinations are symptoms of psychosis and not affective disorders.

87. **(B)** Depression has been called the common cold of mental illness, accounting for two-thirds of all psychiatric hospital admissions. Schizophrenia, in contrast, affects only about 1 percent of the population. Mania, obsessive-compulsive disorders, and hypochondria are also relatively uncommon.

88. **(C)** Lithium is the drug used most often to control this disorder. It is by far the most effective treatment available. Unfortunately, lithium does not cure manic-depression, it only controls the symptoms that usually reappear. Electroconvulsive Therapy (ECT) is sometimes used to bring a patient out of the severe depressive side of the disorder, but this treatment is not nearly as effective in controlling the entire disorder.

89. **(C)** All of the other disorders are still listed in the APA manual. Homosexuality is no longer considered a sexual deviation or a mental disorder. In fact, most findings indicate that homosexuals have no more personality maladjustment problems than their heterosexual peers.

90. **(D)** Freud stated that paranoia was a mixture of two defense mechanisms created by the ego to deal with unacceptable homosexual impulses. "I love him" is rejected and transformed into "I hate him" by the process of reaction formation. The cognition "I hate him" is then rejected because of its aggressive, anti-social content. By the process of projection, this is changed into "He hates me and is persecuting me" and, thus, paranoia is created.

ANSWER SHEETS

CLEP HUMAN GROWTH AND DEVELOPMENT – TEST 1

1. Ⓐ Ⓑ Ⓒ Ⓓ Ⓔ
2. Ⓐ Ⓑ Ⓒ Ⓓ Ⓔ
3. Ⓐ Ⓑ Ⓒ Ⓓ Ⓔ
4. Ⓐ Ⓑ Ⓒ Ⓓ Ⓔ
5. Ⓐ Ⓑ Ⓒ Ⓓ Ⓔ
6. Ⓐ Ⓑ Ⓒ Ⓓ Ⓔ
7. Ⓐ Ⓑ Ⓒ Ⓓ Ⓔ
8. Ⓐ Ⓑ Ⓒ Ⓓ Ⓔ
9. Ⓐ Ⓑ Ⓒ Ⓓ Ⓔ
10. Ⓐ Ⓑ Ⓒ Ⓓ Ⓔ
11. Ⓐ Ⓑ Ⓒ Ⓓ Ⓔ
12. Ⓐ Ⓑ Ⓒ Ⓓ Ⓔ
13. Ⓐ Ⓑ Ⓒ Ⓓ Ⓔ
14. Ⓐ Ⓑ Ⓒ Ⓓ Ⓔ
15. Ⓐ Ⓑ Ⓒ Ⓓ Ⓔ
16. Ⓐ Ⓑ Ⓒ Ⓓ Ⓔ
17. Ⓐ Ⓑ Ⓒ Ⓓ Ⓔ
18. Ⓐ Ⓑ Ⓒ Ⓓ Ⓔ
19. Ⓐ Ⓑ Ⓒ Ⓓ Ⓔ
20. Ⓐ Ⓑ Ⓒ Ⓓ Ⓔ
21. Ⓐ Ⓑ Ⓒ Ⓓ Ⓔ
22. Ⓐ Ⓑ Ⓒ Ⓓ Ⓔ
23. Ⓐ Ⓑ Ⓒ Ⓓ Ⓔ
24. Ⓐ Ⓑ Ⓒ Ⓓ Ⓔ
25. Ⓐ Ⓑ Ⓒ Ⓓ Ⓔ
26. Ⓐ Ⓑ Ⓒ Ⓓ Ⓔ
27. Ⓐ Ⓑ Ⓒ Ⓓ Ⓔ
28. Ⓐ Ⓑ Ⓒ Ⓓ Ⓔ
29. Ⓐ Ⓑ Ⓒ Ⓓ Ⓔ
30. Ⓐ Ⓑ Ⓒ Ⓓ Ⓔ

31. Ⓐ Ⓑ Ⓒ Ⓓ Ⓔ
32. Ⓐ Ⓑ Ⓒ Ⓓ Ⓔ
33. Ⓐ Ⓑ Ⓒ Ⓓ Ⓔ
34. Ⓐ Ⓑ Ⓒ Ⓓ Ⓔ
35. Ⓐ Ⓑ Ⓒ Ⓓ Ⓔ
36. Ⓐ Ⓑ Ⓒ Ⓓ Ⓔ
37. Ⓐ Ⓑ Ⓒ Ⓓ Ⓔ
38. Ⓐ Ⓑ Ⓒ Ⓓ Ⓔ
39. Ⓐ Ⓑ Ⓒ Ⓓ Ⓔ
40. Ⓐ Ⓑ Ⓒ Ⓓ Ⓔ
41. Ⓐ Ⓑ Ⓒ Ⓓ Ⓔ
42. Ⓐ Ⓑ Ⓒ Ⓓ Ⓔ
43. Ⓐ Ⓑ Ⓒ Ⓓ Ⓔ
44. Ⓐ Ⓑ Ⓒ Ⓓ Ⓔ
45. Ⓐ Ⓑ Ⓒ Ⓓ Ⓔ
46. Ⓐ Ⓑ Ⓒ Ⓓ Ⓔ
47. Ⓐ Ⓑ Ⓒ Ⓓ Ⓔ
48. Ⓐ Ⓑ Ⓒ Ⓓ Ⓔ
49. Ⓐ Ⓑ Ⓒ Ⓓ Ⓔ
50. Ⓐ Ⓑ Ⓒ Ⓓ Ⓔ
51. Ⓐ Ⓑ Ⓒ Ⓓ Ⓔ
52. Ⓐ Ⓑ Ⓒ Ⓓ Ⓔ
53. Ⓐ Ⓑ Ⓒ Ⓓ Ⓔ
54. Ⓐ Ⓑ Ⓒ Ⓓ Ⓔ
55. Ⓐ Ⓑ Ⓒ Ⓓ Ⓔ
56. Ⓐ Ⓑ Ⓒ Ⓓ Ⓔ
57. Ⓐ Ⓑ Ⓒ Ⓓ Ⓔ
58. Ⓐ Ⓑ Ⓒ Ⓓ Ⓔ
59. Ⓐ Ⓑ Ⓒ Ⓓ Ⓔ
60. Ⓐ Ⓑ Ⓒ Ⓓ Ⓔ

61. Ⓐ Ⓑ Ⓒ Ⓓ Ⓔ
62. Ⓐ Ⓑ Ⓒ Ⓓ Ⓔ
63. Ⓐ Ⓑ Ⓒ Ⓓ Ⓔ
64. Ⓐ Ⓑ Ⓒ Ⓓ Ⓔ
65. Ⓐ Ⓑ Ⓒ Ⓓ Ⓔ
66. Ⓐ Ⓑ Ⓒ Ⓓ Ⓔ
67. Ⓐ Ⓑ Ⓒ Ⓓ Ⓔ
68. Ⓐ Ⓑ Ⓒ Ⓓ Ⓔ
69. Ⓐ Ⓑ Ⓒ Ⓓ Ⓔ
70. Ⓐ Ⓑ Ⓒ Ⓓ Ⓔ
71. Ⓐ Ⓑ Ⓒ Ⓓ Ⓔ
72. Ⓐ Ⓑ Ⓒ Ⓓ Ⓔ
73. Ⓐ Ⓑ Ⓒ Ⓓ Ⓔ
74. Ⓐ Ⓑ Ⓒ Ⓓ Ⓔ
75. Ⓐ Ⓑ Ⓒ Ⓓ Ⓔ
76. Ⓐ Ⓑ Ⓒ Ⓓ Ⓔ
77. Ⓐ Ⓑ Ⓒ Ⓓ Ⓔ
78. Ⓐ Ⓑ Ⓒ Ⓓ Ⓔ
79. Ⓐ Ⓑ Ⓒ Ⓓ Ⓔ
80. Ⓐ Ⓑ Ⓒ Ⓓ Ⓔ
81. Ⓐ Ⓑ Ⓒ Ⓓ Ⓔ
82. Ⓐ Ⓑ Ⓒ Ⓓ Ⓔ
83. Ⓐ Ⓑ Ⓒ Ⓓ Ⓔ
84. Ⓐ Ⓑ Ⓒ Ⓓ Ⓔ
85. Ⓐ Ⓑ Ⓒ Ⓓ Ⓔ
86. Ⓐ Ⓑ Ⓒ Ⓓ Ⓔ
87. Ⓐ Ⓑ Ⓒ Ⓓ Ⓔ
88. Ⓐ Ⓑ Ⓒ Ⓓ Ⓔ
89. Ⓐ Ⓑ Ⓒ Ⓓ Ⓔ
90. Ⓐ Ⓑ Ⓒ Ⓓ Ⓔ

CLEP HUMAN GROWTH AND DEVELOPMENT – TEST 2

1. Ⓐ Ⓑ Ⓒ Ⓓ Ⓔ	31. Ⓐ Ⓑ Ⓒ Ⓓ Ⓔ	61. Ⓐ Ⓑ Ⓒ Ⓓ Ⓔ
2. Ⓐ Ⓑ Ⓒ Ⓓ Ⓔ	32. Ⓐ Ⓑ Ⓒ Ⓓ Ⓔ	62. Ⓐ Ⓑ Ⓒ Ⓓ Ⓔ
3. Ⓐ Ⓑ Ⓒ Ⓓ Ⓔ	33. Ⓐ Ⓑ Ⓒ Ⓓ Ⓔ	63. Ⓐ Ⓑ Ⓒ Ⓓ Ⓔ
4. Ⓐ Ⓑ Ⓒ Ⓓ Ⓔ	34. Ⓐ Ⓑ Ⓒ Ⓓ Ⓔ	64. Ⓐ Ⓑ Ⓒ Ⓓ Ⓔ
5. Ⓐ Ⓑ Ⓒ Ⓓ Ⓔ	35. Ⓐ Ⓑ Ⓒ Ⓓ Ⓔ	65. Ⓐ Ⓑ Ⓒ Ⓓ Ⓔ
6. Ⓐ Ⓑ Ⓒ Ⓓ Ⓔ	36. Ⓐ Ⓑ Ⓒ Ⓓ Ⓔ	66. Ⓐ Ⓑ Ⓒ Ⓓ Ⓔ
7. Ⓐ Ⓑ Ⓒ Ⓓ Ⓔ	37. Ⓐ Ⓑ Ⓒ Ⓓ Ⓔ	67. Ⓐ Ⓑ Ⓒ Ⓓ Ⓔ
8. Ⓐ Ⓑ Ⓒ Ⓓ Ⓔ	38. Ⓐ Ⓑ Ⓒ Ⓓ Ⓔ	68. Ⓐ Ⓑ Ⓒ Ⓓ Ⓔ
9. Ⓐ Ⓑ Ⓒ Ⓓ Ⓔ	39. Ⓐ Ⓑ Ⓒ Ⓓ Ⓔ	69. Ⓐ Ⓑ Ⓒ Ⓓ Ⓔ
10. Ⓐ Ⓑ Ⓒ Ⓓ Ⓔ	40. Ⓐ Ⓑ Ⓒ Ⓓ Ⓔ	70. Ⓐ Ⓑ Ⓒ Ⓓ Ⓔ
11. Ⓐ Ⓑ Ⓒ Ⓓ Ⓔ	41. Ⓐ Ⓑ Ⓒ Ⓓ Ⓔ	71. Ⓐ Ⓑ Ⓒ Ⓓ Ⓔ
12. Ⓐ Ⓑ Ⓒ Ⓓ Ⓔ	42. Ⓐ Ⓑ Ⓒ Ⓓ Ⓔ	72. Ⓐ Ⓑ Ⓒ Ⓓ Ⓔ
13. Ⓐ Ⓑ Ⓒ Ⓓ Ⓔ	43. Ⓐ Ⓑ Ⓒ Ⓓ Ⓔ	73. Ⓐ Ⓑ Ⓒ Ⓓ Ⓔ
14. Ⓐ Ⓑ Ⓒ Ⓓ Ⓔ	44. Ⓐ Ⓑ Ⓒ Ⓓ Ⓔ	74. Ⓐ Ⓑ Ⓒ Ⓓ Ⓔ
15. Ⓐ Ⓑ Ⓒ Ⓓ Ⓔ	45. Ⓐ Ⓑ Ⓒ Ⓓ Ⓔ	75. Ⓐ Ⓑ Ⓒ Ⓓ Ⓔ
16. Ⓐ Ⓑ Ⓒ Ⓓ Ⓔ	46. Ⓐ Ⓑ Ⓒ Ⓓ Ⓔ	76. Ⓐ Ⓑ Ⓒ Ⓓ Ⓔ
17. Ⓐ Ⓑ Ⓒ Ⓓ Ⓔ	47. Ⓐ Ⓑ Ⓒ Ⓓ Ⓔ	77. Ⓐ Ⓑ Ⓒ Ⓓ Ⓔ
18. Ⓐ Ⓑ Ⓒ Ⓓ Ⓔ	48. Ⓐ Ⓑ Ⓒ Ⓓ Ⓔ	78. Ⓐ Ⓑ Ⓒ Ⓓ Ⓔ
19. Ⓐ Ⓑ Ⓒ Ⓓ Ⓔ	49. Ⓐ Ⓑ Ⓒ Ⓓ Ⓔ	79. Ⓐ Ⓑ Ⓒ Ⓓ Ⓔ
20. Ⓐ Ⓑ Ⓒ Ⓓ Ⓔ	50. Ⓐ Ⓑ Ⓒ Ⓓ Ⓔ	80. Ⓐ Ⓑ Ⓒ Ⓓ Ⓔ
21. Ⓐ Ⓑ Ⓒ Ⓓ Ⓔ	51. Ⓐ Ⓑ Ⓒ Ⓓ Ⓔ	81. Ⓐ Ⓑ Ⓒ Ⓓ Ⓔ
22. Ⓐ Ⓑ Ⓒ Ⓓ Ⓔ	52. Ⓐ Ⓑ Ⓒ Ⓓ Ⓔ	82. Ⓐ Ⓑ Ⓒ Ⓓ Ⓔ
23. Ⓐ Ⓑ Ⓒ Ⓓ Ⓔ	53. Ⓐ Ⓑ Ⓒ Ⓓ Ⓔ	83. Ⓐ Ⓑ Ⓒ Ⓓ Ⓔ
24. Ⓐ Ⓑ Ⓒ Ⓓ Ⓔ	54. Ⓐ Ⓑ Ⓒ Ⓓ Ⓔ	84. Ⓐ Ⓑ Ⓒ Ⓓ Ⓔ
25. Ⓐ Ⓑ Ⓒ Ⓓ Ⓔ	55. Ⓐ Ⓑ Ⓒ Ⓓ Ⓔ	85. Ⓐ Ⓑ Ⓒ Ⓓ Ⓔ
26. Ⓐ Ⓑ Ⓒ Ⓓ Ⓔ	56. Ⓐ Ⓑ Ⓒ Ⓓ Ⓔ	86. Ⓐ Ⓑ Ⓒ Ⓓ Ⓔ
27. Ⓐ Ⓑ Ⓒ Ⓓ Ⓔ	57. Ⓐ Ⓑ Ⓒ Ⓓ Ⓔ	87. Ⓐ Ⓑ Ⓒ Ⓓ Ⓔ
28. Ⓐ Ⓑ Ⓒ Ⓓ Ⓔ	58. Ⓐ Ⓑ Ⓒ Ⓓ Ⓔ	88. Ⓐ Ⓑ Ⓒ Ⓓ Ⓔ
29. Ⓐ Ⓑ Ⓒ Ⓓ Ⓔ	59. Ⓐ Ⓑ Ⓒ Ⓓ Ⓔ	89. Ⓐ Ⓑ Ⓒ Ⓓ Ⓔ
30. Ⓐ Ⓑ Ⓒ Ⓓ Ⓔ	60. Ⓐ Ⓑ Ⓒ Ⓓ Ⓔ	90. Ⓐ Ⓑ Ⓒ Ⓓ Ⓔ

CLEP HUMAN GROWTH AND DEVELOPMENT – TEST 3

1. Ⓐ Ⓑ Ⓒ Ⓓ Ⓔ
2. Ⓐ Ⓑ Ⓒ Ⓓ Ⓔ
3. Ⓐ Ⓑ Ⓒ Ⓓ Ⓔ
4. Ⓐ Ⓑ Ⓒ Ⓓ Ⓔ
5. Ⓐ Ⓑ Ⓒ Ⓓ Ⓔ
6. Ⓐ Ⓑ Ⓒ Ⓓ Ⓔ
7. Ⓐ Ⓑ Ⓒ Ⓓ Ⓔ
8. Ⓐ Ⓑ Ⓒ Ⓓ Ⓔ
9. Ⓐ Ⓑ Ⓒ Ⓓ Ⓔ
10. Ⓐ Ⓑ Ⓒ Ⓓ Ⓔ
11. Ⓐ Ⓑ Ⓒ Ⓓ Ⓔ
12. Ⓐ Ⓑ Ⓒ Ⓓ Ⓔ
13. Ⓐ Ⓑ Ⓒ Ⓓ Ⓔ
14. Ⓐ Ⓑ Ⓒ Ⓓ Ⓔ
15. Ⓐ Ⓑ Ⓒ Ⓓ Ⓔ
16. Ⓐ Ⓑ Ⓒ Ⓓ Ⓔ
17. Ⓐ Ⓑ Ⓒ Ⓓ Ⓔ
18. Ⓐ Ⓑ Ⓒ Ⓓ Ⓔ
19. Ⓐ Ⓑ Ⓒ Ⓓ Ⓔ
20. Ⓐ Ⓑ Ⓒ Ⓓ Ⓔ
21. Ⓐ Ⓑ Ⓒ Ⓓ Ⓔ
22. Ⓐ Ⓑ Ⓒ Ⓓ Ⓔ
23. Ⓐ Ⓑ Ⓒ Ⓓ Ⓔ
24. Ⓐ Ⓑ Ⓒ Ⓓ Ⓔ
25. Ⓐ Ⓑ Ⓒ Ⓓ Ⓔ
26. Ⓐ Ⓑ Ⓒ Ⓓ Ⓔ
27. Ⓐ Ⓑ Ⓒ Ⓓ Ⓔ
28. Ⓐ Ⓑ Ⓒ Ⓓ Ⓔ
29. Ⓐ Ⓑ Ⓒ Ⓓ Ⓔ
30. Ⓐ Ⓑ Ⓒ Ⓓ Ⓔ

31. Ⓐ Ⓑ Ⓒ Ⓓ Ⓔ
32. Ⓐ Ⓑ Ⓒ Ⓓ Ⓔ
33. Ⓐ Ⓑ Ⓒ Ⓓ Ⓔ
34. Ⓐ Ⓑ Ⓒ Ⓓ Ⓔ
35. Ⓐ Ⓑ Ⓒ Ⓓ Ⓔ
36. Ⓐ Ⓑ Ⓒ Ⓓ Ⓔ
37. Ⓐ Ⓑ Ⓒ Ⓓ Ⓔ
38. Ⓐ Ⓑ Ⓒ Ⓓ Ⓔ
39. Ⓐ Ⓑ Ⓒ Ⓓ Ⓔ
40. Ⓐ Ⓑ Ⓒ Ⓓ Ⓔ
41. Ⓐ Ⓑ Ⓒ Ⓓ Ⓔ
42. Ⓐ Ⓑ Ⓒ Ⓓ Ⓔ
43. Ⓐ Ⓑ Ⓒ Ⓓ Ⓔ
44. Ⓐ Ⓑ Ⓒ Ⓓ Ⓔ
45. Ⓐ Ⓑ Ⓒ Ⓓ Ⓔ
46. Ⓐ Ⓑ Ⓒ Ⓓ Ⓔ
47. Ⓐ Ⓑ Ⓒ Ⓓ Ⓔ
48. Ⓐ Ⓑ Ⓒ Ⓓ Ⓔ
49. Ⓐ Ⓑ Ⓒ Ⓓ Ⓔ
50. Ⓐ Ⓑ Ⓒ Ⓓ Ⓔ
51. Ⓐ Ⓑ Ⓒ Ⓓ Ⓔ
52. Ⓐ Ⓑ Ⓒ Ⓓ Ⓔ
53. Ⓐ Ⓑ Ⓒ Ⓓ Ⓔ
54. Ⓐ Ⓑ Ⓒ Ⓓ Ⓔ
55. Ⓐ Ⓑ Ⓒ Ⓓ Ⓔ
56. Ⓐ Ⓑ Ⓒ Ⓓ Ⓔ
57. Ⓐ Ⓑ Ⓒ Ⓓ Ⓔ
58. Ⓐ Ⓑ Ⓒ Ⓓ Ⓔ
59. Ⓐ Ⓑ Ⓒ Ⓓ Ⓔ
60. Ⓐ Ⓑ Ⓒ Ⓓ Ⓔ

61. Ⓐ Ⓑ Ⓒ Ⓓ Ⓔ
62. Ⓐ Ⓑ Ⓒ Ⓓ Ⓔ
63. Ⓐ Ⓑ Ⓒ Ⓓ Ⓔ
64. Ⓐ Ⓑ Ⓒ Ⓓ Ⓔ
65. Ⓐ Ⓑ Ⓒ Ⓓ Ⓔ
66. Ⓐ Ⓑ Ⓒ Ⓓ Ⓔ
67. Ⓐ Ⓑ Ⓒ Ⓓ Ⓔ
68. Ⓐ Ⓑ Ⓒ Ⓓ Ⓔ
69. Ⓐ Ⓑ Ⓒ Ⓓ Ⓔ
70. Ⓐ Ⓑ Ⓒ Ⓓ Ⓔ
71. Ⓐ Ⓑ Ⓒ Ⓓ Ⓔ
72. Ⓐ Ⓑ Ⓒ Ⓓ Ⓔ
73. Ⓐ Ⓑ Ⓒ Ⓓ Ⓔ
74. Ⓐ Ⓑ Ⓒ Ⓓ Ⓔ
75. Ⓐ Ⓑ Ⓒ Ⓓ Ⓔ
76. Ⓐ Ⓑ Ⓒ Ⓓ Ⓔ
77. Ⓐ Ⓑ Ⓒ Ⓓ Ⓔ
78. Ⓐ Ⓑ Ⓒ Ⓓ Ⓔ
79. Ⓐ Ⓑ Ⓒ Ⓓ Ⓔ
80. Ⓐ Ⓑ Ⓒ Ⓓ Ⓔ
81. Ⓐ Ⓑ Ⓒ Ⓓ Ⓔ
82. Ⓐ Ⓑ Ⓒ Ⓓ Ⓔ
83. Ⓐ Ⓑ Ⓒ Ⓓ Ⓔ
84. Ⓐ Ⓑ Ⓒ Ⓓ Ⓔ
85. Ⓐ Ⓑ Ⓒ Ⓓ Ⓔ
86. Ⓐ Ⓑ Ⓒ Ⓓ Ⓔ
87. Ⓐ Ⓑ Ⓒ Ⓓ Ⓔ
88. Ⓐ Ⓑ Ⓒ Ⓓ Ⓔ
89. Ⓐ Ⓑ Ⓒ Ⓓ Ⓔ
90. Ⓐ Ⓑ Ⓒ Ⓓ Ⓔ

CLEP HUMAN GROWTH AND DEVELOPMENT – TEST __

1. Ⓐ Ⓑ Ⓒ Ⓓ Ⓔ	31. Ⓐ Ⓑ Ⓒ Ⓓ Ⓔ	61. Ⓐ Ⓑ Ⓒ Ⓓ Ⓔ
2. Ⓐ Ⓑ Ⓒ Ⓓ Ⓔ	32. Ⓐ Ⓑ Ⓒ Ⓓ Ⓔ	62. Ⓐ Ⓑ Ⓒ Ⓓ Ⓔ
3. Ⓐ Ⓑ Ⓒ Ⓓ Ⓔ	33. Ⓐ Ⓑ Ⓒ Ⓓ Ⓔ	63. Ⓐ Ⓑ Ⓒ Ⓓ Ⓔ
4. Ⓐ Ⓑ Ⓒ Ⓓ Ⓔ	34. Ⓐ Ⓑ Ⓒ Ⓓ Ⓔ	64. Ⓐ Ⓑ Ⓒ Ⓓ Ⓔ
5. Ⓐ Ⓑ Ⓒ Ⓓ Ⓔ	35. Ⓐ Ⓑ Ⓒ Ⓓ Ⓔ	65. Ⓐ Ⓑ Ⓒ Ⓓ Ⓔ
6. Ⓐ Ⓑ Ⓒ Ⓓ Ⓔ	36. Ⓐ Ⓑ Ⓒ Ⓓ Ⓔ	66. Ⓐ Ⓑ Ⓒ Ⓓ Ⓔ
7. Ⓐ Ⓑ Ⓒ Ⓓ Ⓔ	37. Ⓐ Ⓑ Ⓒ Ⓓ Ⓔ	67. Ⓐ Ⓑ Ⓒ Ⓓ Ⓔ
8. Ⓐ Ⓑ Ⓒ Ⓓ Ⓔ	38. Ⓐ Ⓑ Ⓒ Ⓓ Ⓔ	68. Ⓐ Ⓑ Ⓒ Ⓓ Ⓔ
9. Ⓐ Ⓑ Ⓒ Ⓓ Ⓔ	39. Ⓐ Ⓑ Ⓒ Ⓓ Ⓔ	69. Ⓐ Ⓑ Ⓒ Ⓓ Ⓔ
10. Ⓐ Ⓑ Ⓒ Ⓓ Ⓔ	40. Ⓐ Ⓑ Ⓒ Ⓓ Ⓔ	70. Ⓐ Ⓑ Ⓒ Ⓓ Ⓔ
11. Ⓐ Ⓑ Ⓒ Ⓓ Ⓔ	41. Ⓐ Ⓑ Ⓒ Ⓓ Ⓔ	71. Ⓐ Ⓑ Ⓒ Ⓓ Ⓔ
12. Ⓐ Ⓑ Ⓒ Ⓓ Ⓔ	42. Ⓐ Ⓑ Ⓒ Ⓓ Ⓔ	72. Ⓐ Ⓑ Ⓒ Ⓓ Ⓔ
13. Ⓐ Ⓑ Ⓒ Ⓓ Ⓔ	43. Ⓐ Ⓑ Ⓒ Ⓓ Ⓔ	73. Ⓐ Ⓑ Ⓒ Ⓓ Ⓔ
14. Ⓐ Ⓑ Ⓒ Ⓓ Ⓔ	44. Ⓐ Ⓑ Ⓒ Ⓓ Ⓔ	74. Ⓐ Ⓑ Ⓒ Ⓓ Ⓔ
15. Ⓐ Ⓑ Ⓒ Ⓓ Ⓔ	45. Ⓐ Ⓑ Ⓒ Ⓓ Ⓔ	75. Ⓐ Ⓑ Ⓒ Ⓓ Ⓔ
16. Ⓐ Ⓑ Ⓒ Ⓓ Ⓔ	46. Ⓐ Ⓑ Ⓒ Ⓓ Ⓔ	76. Ⓐ Ⓑ Ⓒ Ⓓ Ⓔ
17. Ⓐ Ⓑ Ⓒ Ⓓ Ⓔ	47. Ⓐ Ⓑ Ⓒ Ⓓ Ⓔ	77. Ⓐ Ⓑ Ⓒ Ⓓ Ⓔ
18. Ⓐ Ⓑ Ⓒ Ⓓ Ⓔ	48. Ⓐ Ⓑ Ⓒ Ⓓ Ⓔ	78. Ⓐ Ⓑ Ⓒ Ⓓ Ⓔ
19. Ⓐ Ⓑ Ⓒ Ⓓ Ⓔ	49. Ⓐ Ⓑ Ⓒ Ⓓ Ⓔ	79. Ⓐ Ⓑ Ⓒ Ⓓ Ⓔ
20. Ⓐ Ⓑ Ⓒ Ⓓ Ⓔ	50. Ⓐ Ⓑ Ⓒ Ⓓ Ⓔ	80. Ⓐ Ⓑ Ⓒ Ⓓ Ⓔ
21. Ⓐ Ⓑ Ⓒ Ⓓ Ⓔ	51. Ⓐ Ⓑ Ⓒ Ⓓ Ⓔ	81. Ⓐ Ⓑ Ⓒ Ⓓ Ⓔ
22. Ⓐ Ⓑ Ⓒ Ⓓ Ⓔ	52. Ⓐ Ⓑ Ⓒ Ⓓ Ⓔ	82. Ⓐ Ⓑ Ⓒ Ⓓ Ⓔ
23. Ⓐ Ⓑ Ⓒ Ⓓ Ⓔ	53. Ⓐ Ⓑ Ⓒ Ⓓ Ⓔ	83. Ⓐ Ⓑ Ⓒ Ⓓ Ⓔ
24. Ⓐ Ⓑ Ⓒ Ⓓ Ⓔ	54. Ⓐ Ⓑ Ⓒ Ⓓ Ⓔ	84. Ⓐ Ⓑ Ⓒ Ⓓ Ⓔ
25. Ⓐ Ⓑ Ⓒ Ⓓ Ⓔ	55. Ⓐ Ⓑ Ⓒ Ⓓ Ⓔ	85. Ⓐ Ⓑ Ⓒ Ⓓ Ⓔ
26. Ⓐ Ⓑ Ⓒ Ⓓ Ⓔ	56. Ⓐ Ⓑ Ⓒ Ⓓ Ⓔ	86. Ⓐ Ⓑ Ⓒ Ⓓ Ⓔ
27. Ⓐ Ⓑ Ⓒ Ⓓ Ⓔ	57. Ⓐ Ⓑ Ⓒ Ⓓ Ⓔ	87. Ⓐ Ⓑ Ⓒ Ⓓ Ⓔ
28. Ⓐ Ⓑ Ⓒ Ⓓ Ⓔ	58. Ⓐ Ⓑ Ⓒ Ⓓ Ⓔ	88. Ⓐ Ⓑ Ⓒ Ⓓ Ⓔ
29. Ⓐ Ⓑ Ⓒ Ⓓ Ⓔ	59. Ⓐ Ⓑ Ⓒ Ⓓ Ⓔ	89. Ⓐ Ⓑ Ⓒ Ⓓ Ⓔ
30. Ⓐ Ⓑ Ⓒ Ⓓ Ⓔ	60. Ⓐ Ⓑ Ⓒ Ⓓ Ⓔ	90. Ⓐ Ⓑ Ⓒ Ⓓ Ⓔ

CLEP HUMAN GROWTH AND DEVELOPMENT – TEST __

1. Ⓐ Ⓑ Ⓒ Ⓓ Ⓔ	31. Ⓐ Ⓑ Ⓒ Ⓓ Ⓔ	61. Ⓐ Ⓑ Ⓒ Ⓓ Ⓔ
2. Ⓐ Ⓑ Ⓒ Ⓓ Ⓔ	32. Ⓐ Ⓑ Ⓒ Ⓓ Ⓔ	62. Ⓐ Ⓑ Ⓒ Ⓓ Ⓔ
3. Ⓐ Ⓑ Ⓒ Ⓓ Ⓔ	33. Ⓐ Ⓑ Ⓒ Ⓓ Ⓔ	63. Ⓐ Ⓑ Ⓒ Ⓓ Ⓔ
4. Ⓐ Ⓑ Ⓒ Ⓓ Ⓔ	34. Ⓐ Ⓑ Ⓒ Ⓓ Ⓔ	64. Ⓐ Ⓑ Ⓒ Ⓓ Ⓔ
5. Ⓐ Ⓑ Ⓒ Ⓓ Ⓔ	35. Ⓐ Ⓑ Ⓒ Ⓓ Ⓔ	65. Ⓐ Ⓑ Ⓒ Ⓓ Ⓔ
6. Ⓐ Ⓑ Ⓒ Ⓓ Ⓔ	36. Ⓐ Ⓑ Ⓒ Ⓓ Ⓔ	66. Ⓐ Ⓑ Ⓒ Ⓓ Ⓔ
7. Ⓐ Ⓑ Ⓒ Ⓓ Ⓔ	37. Ⓐ Ⓑ Ⓒ Ⓓ Ⓔ	67. Ⓐ Ⓑ Ⓒ Ⓓ Ⓔ
8. Ⓐ Ⓑ Ⓒ Ⓓ Ⓔ	38. Ⓐ Ⓑ Ⓒ Ⓓ Ⓔ	68. Ⓐ Ⓑ Ⓒ Ⓓ Ⓔ
9. Ⓐ Ⓑ Ⓒ Ⓓ Ⓔ	39. Ⓐ Ⓑ Ⓒ Ⓓ Ⓔ	69. Ⓐ Ⓑ Ⓒ Ⓓ Ⓔ
10. Ⓐ Ⓑ Ⓒ Ⓓ Ⓔ	40. Ⓐ Ⓑ Ⓒ Ⓓ Ⓔ	70. Ⓐ Ⓑ Ⓒ Ⓓ Ⓔ
11. Ⓐ Ⓑ Ⓒ Ⓓ Ⓔ	41. Ⓐ Ⓑ Ⓒ Ⓓ Ⓔ	71. Ⓐ Ⓑ Ⓒ Ⓓ Ⓔ
12. Ⓐ Ⓑ Ⓒ Ⓓ Ⓔ	42. Ⓐ Ⓑ Ⓒ Ⓓ Ⓔ	72. Ⓐ Ⓑ Ⓒ Ⓓ Ⓔ
13. Ⓐ Ⓑ Ⓒ Ⓓ Ⓔ	43. Ⓐ Ⓑ Ⓒ Ⓓ Ⓔ	73. Ⓐ Ⓑ Ⓒ Ⓓ Ⓔ
14. Ⓐ Ⓑ Ⓒ Ⓓ Ⓔ	44. Ⓐ Ⓑ Ⓒ Ⓓ Ⓔ	74. Ⓐ Ⓑ Ⓒ Ⓓ Ⓔ
15. Ⓐ Ⓑ Ⓒ Ⓓ Ⓔ	45. Ⓐ Ⓑ Ⓒ Ⓓ Ⓔ	75. Ⓐ Ⓑ Ⓒ Ⓓ Ⓔ
16. Ⓐ Ⓑ Ⓒ Ⓓ Ⓔ	46. Ⓐ Ⓑ Ⓒ Ⓓ Ⓔ	76. Ⓐ Ⓑ Ⓒ Ⓓ Ⓔ
17. Ⓐ Ⓑ Ⓒ Ⓓ Ⓔ	47. Ⓐ Ⓑ Ⓒ Ⓓ Ⓔ	77. Ⓐ Ⓑ Ⓒ Ⓓ Ⓔ
18. Ⓐ Ⓑ Ⓒ Ⓓ Ⓔ	48. Ⓐ Ⓑ Ⓒ Ⓓ Ⓔ	78. Ⓐ Ⓑ Ⓒ Ⓓ Ⓔ
19. Ⓐ Ⓑ Ⓒ Ⓓ Ⓔ	49. Ⓐ Ⓑ Ⓒ Ⓓ Ⓔ	79. Ⓐ Ⓑ Ⓒ Ⓓ Ⓔ
20. Ⓐ Ⓑ Ⓒ Ⓓ Ⓔ	50. Ⓐ Ⓑ Ⓒ Ⓓ Ⓔ	80. Ⓐ Ⓑ Ⓒ Ⓓ Ⓔ
21. Ⓐ Ⓑ Ⓒ Ⓓ Ⓔ	51. Ⓐ Ⓑ Ⓒ Ⓓ Ⓔ	81. Ⓐ Ⓑ Ⓒ Ⓓ Ⓔ
22. Ⓐ Ⓑ Ⓒ Ⓓ Ⓔ	52. Ⓐ Ⓑ Ⓒ Ⓓ Ⓔ	82. Ⓐ Ⓑ Ⓒ Ⓓ Ⓔ
23. Ⓐ Ⓑ Ⓒ Ⓓ Ⓔ	53. Ⓐ Ⓑ Ⓒ Ⓓ Ⓔ	83. Ⓐ Ⓑ Ⓒ Ⓓ Ⓔ
24. Ⓐ Ⓑ Ⓒ Ⓓ Ⓔ	54. Ⓐ Ⓑ Ⓒ Ⓓ Ⓔ	84. Ⓐ Ⓑ Ⓒ Ⓓ Ⓔ
25. Ⓐ Ⓑ Ⓒ Ⓓ Ⓔ	55. Ⓐ Ⓑ Ⓒ Ⓓ Ⓔ	85. Ⓐ Ⓑ Ⓒ Ⓓ Ⓔ
26. Ⓐ Ⓑ Ⓒ Ⓓ Ⓔ	56. Ⓐ Ⓑ Ⓒ Ⓓ Ⓔ	86. Ⓐ Ⓑ Ⓒ Ⓓ Ⓔ
27. Ⓐ Ⓑ Ⓒ Ⓓ Ⓔ	57. Ⓐ Ⓑ Ⓒ Ⓓ Ⓔ	87. Ⓐ Ⓑ Ⓒ Ⓓ Ⓔ
28. Ⓐ Ⓑ Ⓒ Ⓓ Ⓔ	58. Ⓐ Ⓑ Ⓒ Ⓓ Ⓔ	88. Ⓐ Ⓑ Ⓒ Ⓓ Ⓔ
29. Ⓐ Ⓑ Ⓒ Ⓓ Ⓔ	59. Ⓐ Ⓑ Ⓒ Ⓓ Ⓔ	89. Ⓐ Ⓑ Ⓒ Ⓓ Ⓔ
30. Ⓐ Ⓑ Ⓒ Ⓓ Ⓔ	60. Ⓐ Ⓑ Ⓒ Ⓓ Ⓔ	90. Ⓐ Ⓑ Ⓒ Ⓓ Ⓔ

CLEP HUMAN GROWTH AND DEVELOPMENT – TEST __

1. Ⓐ Ⓑ Ⓒ Ⓓ Ⓔ	31. Ⓐ Ⓑ Ⓒ Ⓓ Ⓔ	61. Ⓐ Ⓑ Ⓒ Ⓓ Ⓔ
2. Ⓐ Ⓑ Ⓒ Ⓓ Ⓔ	32. Ⓐ Ⓑ Ⓒ Ⓓ Ⓔ	62. Ⓐ Ⓑ Ⓒ Ⓓ Ⓔ
3. Ⓐ Ⓑ Ⓒ Ⓓ Ⓔ	33. Ⓐ Ⓑ Ⓒ Ⓓ Ⓔ	63. Ⓐ Ⓑ Ⓒ Ⓓ Ⓔ
4. Ⓐ Ⓑ Ⓒ Ⓓ Ⓔ	34. Ⓐ Ⓑ Ⓒ Ⓓ Ⓔ	64. Ⓐ Ⓑ Ⓒ Ⓓ Ⓔ
5. Ⓐ Ⓑ Ⓒ Ⓓ Ⓔ	35. Ⓐ Ⓑ Ⓒ Ⓓ Ⓔ	65. Ⓐ Ⓑ Ⓒ Ⓓ Ⓔ
6. Ⓐ Ⓑ Ⓒ Ⓓ Ⓔ	36. Ⓐ Ⓑ Ⓒ Ⓓ Ⓔ	66. Ⓐ Ⓑ Ⓒ Ⓓ Ⓔ
7. Ⓐ Ⓑ Ⓒ Ⓓ Ⓔ	37. Ⓐ Ⓑ Ⓒ Ⓓ Ⓔ	67. Ⓐ Ⓑ Ⓒ Ⓓ Ⓔ
8. Ⓐ Ⓑ Ⓒ Ⓓ Ⓔ	38. Ⓐ Ⓑ Ⓒ Ⓓ Ⓔ	68. Ⓐ Ⓑ Ⓒ Ⓓ Ⓔ
9. Ⓐ Ⓑ Ⓒ Ⓓ Ⓔ	39. Ⓐ Ⓑ Ⓒ Ⓓ Ⓔ	69. Ⓐ Ⓑ Ⓒ Ⓓ Ⓔ
10. Ⓐ Ⓑ Ⓒ Ⓓ Ⓔ	40. Ⓐ Ⓑ Ⓒ Ⓓ Ⓔ	70. Ⓐ Ⓑ Ⓒ Ⓓ Ⓔ
11. Ⓐ Ⓑ Ⓒ Ⓓ Ⓔ	41. Ⓐ Ⓑ Ⓒ Ⓓ Ⓔ	71. Ⓐ Ⓑ Ⓒ Ⓓ Ⓔ
12. Ⓐ Ⓑ Ⓒ Ⓓ Ⓔ	42. Ⓐ Ⓑ Ⓒ Ⓓ Ⓔ	72. Ⓐ Ⓑ Ⓒ Ⓓ Ⓔ
13. Ⓐ Ⓑ Ⓒ Ⓓ Ⓔ	43. Ⓐ Ⓑ Ⓒ Ⓓ Ⓔ	73. Ⓐ Ⓑ Ⓒ Ⓓ Ⓔ
14. Ⓐ Ⓑ Ⓒ Ⓓ Ⓔ	44. Ⓐ Ⓑ Ⓒ Ⓓ Ⓔ	74. Ⓐ Ⓑ Ⓒ Ⓓ Ⓔ
15. Ⓐ Ⓑ Ⓒ Ⓓ Ⓔ	45. Ⓐ Ⓑ Ⓒ Ⓓ Ⓔ	75. Ⓐ Ⓑ Ⓒ Ⓓ Ⓔ
16. Ⓐ Ⓑ Ⓒ Ⓓ Ⓔ	46. Ⓐ Ⓑ Ⓒ Ⓓ Ⓔ	76. Ⓐ Ⓑ Ⓒ Ⓓ Ⓔ
17. Ⓐ Ⓑ Ⓒ Ⓓ Ⓔ	47. Ⓐ Ⓑ Ⓒ Ⓓ Ⓔ	77. Ⓐ Ⓑ Ⓒ Ⓓ Ⓔ
18. Ⓐ Ⓑ Ⓒ Ⓓ Ⓔ	48. Ⓐ Ⓑ Ⓒ Ⓓ Ⓔ	78. Ⓐ Ⓑ Ⓒ Ⓓ Ⓔ
19. Ⓐ Ⓑ Ⓒ Ⓓ Ⓔ	49. Ⓐ Ⓑ Ⓒ Ⓓ Ⓔ	79. Ⓐ Ⓑ Ⓒ Ⓓ Ⓔ
20. Ⓐ Ⓑ Ⓒ Ⓓ Ⓔ	50. Ⓐ Ⓑ Ⓒ Ⓓ Ⓔ	80. Ⓐ Ⓑ Ⓒ Ⓓ Ⓔ
21. Ⓐ Ⓑ Ⓒ Ⓓ Ⓔ	51. Ⓐ Ⓑ Ⓒ Ⓓ Ⓔ	81. Ⓐ Ⓑ Ⓒ Ⓓ Ⓔ
22. Ⓐ Ⓑ Ⓒ Ⓓ Ⓔ	52. Ⓐ Ⓑ Ⓒ Ⓓ Ⓔ	82. Ⓐ Ⓑ Ⓒ Ⓓ Ⓔ
23. Ⓐ Ⓑ Ⓒ Ⓓ Ⓔ	53. Ⓐ Ⓑ Ⓒ Ⓓ Ⓔ	83. Ⓐ Ⓑ Ⓒ Ⓓ Ⓔ
24. Ⓐ Ⓑ Ⓒ Ⓓ Ⓔ	54. Ⓐ Ⓑ Ⓒ Ⓓ Ⓔ	84. Ⓐ Ⓑ Ⓒ Ⓓ Ⓔ
25. Ⓐ Ⓑ Ⓒ Ⓓ Ⓔ	55. Ⓐ Ⓑ Ⓒ Ⓓ Ⓔ	85. Ⓐ Ⓑ Ⓒ Ⓓ Ⓔ
26. Ⓐ Ⓑ Ⓒ Ⓓ Ⓔ	56. Ⓐ Ⓑ Ⓒ Ⓓ Ⓔ	86. Ⓐ Ⓑ Ⓒ Ⓓ Ⓔ
27. Ⓐ Ⓑ Ⓒ Ⓓ Ⓔ	57. Ⓐ Ⓑ Ⓒ Ⓓ Ⓔ	87. Ⓐ Ⓑ Ⓒ Ⓓ Ⓔ
28. Ⓐ Ⓑ Ⓒ Ⓓ Ⓔ	58. Ⓐ Ⓑ Ⓒ Ⓓ Ⓔ	88. Ⓐ Ⓑ Ⓒ Ⓓ Ⓔ
29. Ⓐ Ⓑ Ⓒ Ⓓ Ⓔ	59. Ⓐ Ⓑ Ⓒ Ⓓ Ⓔ	89. Ⓐ Ⓑ Ⓒ Ⓓ Ⓔ
30. Ⓐ Ⓑ Ⓒ Ⓓ Ⓔ	60. Ⓐ Ⓑ Ⓒ Ⓓ Ⓔ	90. Ⓐ Ⓑ Ⓒ Ⓓ Ⓔ

INSTALLING REA's TEST*ware*®

SYSTEM REQUIREMENTS

Pentium 75 MHz (300 MHz recommended), or a higher or compatible processor; Microsoft Windows 95, 98, NT 4 (SP6), ME, 2000, or XP; 64 MB Available RAM; Internet Explorer 5.5 or higher (Internet Explorer 5.5 is included on the CD); minimum 60 MB available hard-disk space; VGA or higher-resolution monitor, 800x600 resolution setting; Microsoft Mouse, Microsoft Intellimouse, or compatible pointing device.

INSTALLATION

1. Insert the CLEP Human Growth & Development TEST*ware*® CD-ROM into the CD-ROM drive.
2. If the installation doesn't begin automatically, from the Start Menu, choose the RUN command. When the RUN dialog box appears, type d:\setup (where D is the letter of your CD-ROM drive) at the prompt and click OK.
3. The installation process will begin. A dialog box proposing the directory "Program Files\REA\CLEP_HGD" will appear. If the name and location are suitable, click OK. If you wish to specify a different name or location, type it in and click OK.
4. Start the CLEP Human Growth & Development TEST*ware*® application by double-clicking on the icon.

REA's CLEP Human Growth & Development TEST*ware*® is **EASY** to **LEARN AND USE**. To achieve maximum benefits, we recommend that you take a few minutes to go through the on-screen tutorial on your computer. The "screen buttons" are also explained here to familiarize you with the program.

TECHNICAL SUPPORT

REA's TEST*ware*® is backed by customer and technical support. For questions about **installation or operation of your software**, contact us at:

Research & Education Association
Phone: (732) 819-8880 (9 a.m. to 5 p.m. ET, Monday–Friday)
Fax: (732) 819-8808
Website: http://www.rea.com
E-mail: info@rea.com

Note to Windows XP Users: In order for the TEST*ware* to function properly, please install and run the application under the same computer-administrator level user account. Installing the TEST*ware* as one user and running it as another could cause file access path conflicts.

USING YOUR INTERACTIVE TEST*ware*®

Exam Directions

The **Exam Directions** button allows you to review the specific exam directions during any part of the test.

Stop Test

At any time during the test or when you are finished taking the test, click on the **Stop** button. The program will advance you to the following screen.

> **REA's TESTware** ✕
>
> **?** Are you sure that you would like to end this exam?
>
> [Yes]   [No]

This screen allows you to quit the entire test, or return to the last question viewed prior to clicking the **Stop** button.

Back / Next Buttons

These two buttons allow you to move successfully between questions. The **Next** button moves you to the next question, while the **Back** button allows you to view the previous question.

Mark/Q's List

If you are unsure about an answer to a particular question, the program allows you to mark it for later review. Flag the question by clicking on the **Mark** button. The **Q's List** button allows you to navigate through the questions and explanations. This is particularly useful if you want to view marked questions in Explanations Mode.

View Scores

Three score reports are available: Chart, Summary and Detail (shown below). All are accessed by clicking on the **View Scores** button from the Main Menu.

Section #	Question Number	Correct Answer	Your Answer	Result
Section - 1	1	B	B	Correct
Section - 1	2	B	B	Correct
Section - 1	3	D	D	Correct
Section - 1	4	A	A	Correct
Section - 1	5	B	D	Incorrect
Section - 1	6	D	D	Correct
Section - 1	7	C	C	Correct
Section - 1	8	A	A	Correct
Section - 1	9	B	D	Incorrect
Section - 1	10	B	B	Correct
Section - 1	11	C	C	Correct
Section - 1	12	B	B	Correct
Section - 1	13	B	B	Correct
Section - 1	14	D	B	Incorrect
Section - 1	15	A	A	Correct
Section - 1	16	D	D	Correct
Section - 1	17	B	B	Correct
Section - 1	18	A	A	Correct
Section - 1	19	B	B	Correct
Section - 1	20	C	C	Correct
Section - 1	21	D	D	Correct
Section - 1	22	B	B	Correct
Section - 1	23	B	C	Incorrect
Section - 1	24	C	D	Incorrect

Explanations

In Explanations mode, click on the **Q & A Explanations** button to display a detailed explanation to any question. The split window shown below can be resized for easier reading.

Questions 13 and 14 refer to the following passage:

A classical experiment in conformity research done by Muzafer Sherif involved the effects of group judgments on "the autokinetic phenomenon." A light projected on the wall appears to move although this movement is actually due to the movement of the subject's eyes. It was found that individuals' judgments of the rate of movement of the light were influenced very much by the opinions of others. Even when the group was no longer present, the individual estimates were still in agreement with previous group opinions.

The fact that the subjects still agreed with the confederate group although they were no longer present shows that

(A) compliance took place.

(B) private acceptance took place.

(C) internalization has occurred.

(D) Both A and B.

(E) All of the above.

Congratulations!

By studying the reviews in this book, taking the written and computerized practice exams, and reviewing your correct and incorrect answers, you'll be well prepared for the CLEP Human Growth & Development exam. Best of luck from everyone at REA.